THE BIG

BOOK OF

DRESSAGE
EXERCISES

CREATED BY HOW TO DRESSAGE

HowToDressage.com

CONTENTS

FLOORPLANS WITH POLES **495**

CREATE YOUR OWN FLOORPLANS

FREE STUFF!

FINAL WORD

THE TRUTH ABOUT THIS BOOK...

When it comes to creating dressage floorplans, there's actually not that much you can do.

Think about it; a dressage floorplan is no more than a series of straight lines and circles.

That's it!

The level of difficulty is increased by riding these straight lines and circles in different places, including transitions, and riding lateral exercises. But ultimately, when it comes to navigating your 20x40 or 20x60 arena, you will either be following a straight line or riding around a circle.

Even when riding lateral exercises such as half-pass and leg-yield, you're still following a straight line. The only difference is that you are following the line in two or three tracks, rather than on one track only.

So technically, we lied to you a little bit! This guide isn't a book of dressage exercises. It's really a book of dressage floorplans.

BUT each floorplan can be modified to included different combinations of paces, transitions, and lateral work, giving you an almost infinite amount of dressage exercise combinations.

We've created some of the exercises for you (over 190!), but there's also space for you to modify them and create your own.

After working through this book, you'll never look at straight lines and circles in the same way again!

<u>HOW TO USE THIS BOOK</u>

We have created 41 floorplans that can all be modified to create different exercises that meet you and your horse's level of training.

That means you can use EVERY floorplan in this book!

If you are working on specific movements, for example, leg-yield or trot-canter transitions, we'll show you how the floorplan can include those movements.

THE DIFFERENCE BETWEEN A FLOORPLAN AND AN EXERCISE

- **Floorplan** – Effectively, a floorplan is where you are going in the arena. For example, down the center line from A-C.

- **Exercise** – The exercise is what you do while following that floorplan. For example, you could come down the center line from A-C in trot and ride a trot-walk-trot transition over X. Or you could come down the center line in collected canter and ride a canter-walk transition at D.

FLOORPLAN NAMES

Yes, you may notice that we've given nicknames to all of our floorplans. Please note that these are not industry names so please don't go around saying you've ridden a 'Ying & Yang' (page 339) because nobody will have the slightest clue what you're talking about!

ARENA SIZE

All of our floorplans are accompanied by handy diagrams for both a 20 x 40 and a 20 x 60 arena.

Use these diagrams to help you position your horse correctly and ensure that you are riding your straight lines and circles accurately and in the right places.

SPACE FOR NOTES

You'll find a blank section at the end of every exercise where you can make notes. We've included a notes section because we want you to do more than just read this book, we want you to USE IT!

After every training session, take the time to write down the date, how the exercises went, what was good, what was bad, and what could be better.

Not only does this allow you to remember what exercises you have done, but it also helps you track your progress.

CREATE YOUR OWN EXERCISES

We've included three blank spaces for every floorplan, which allows you to create your individual exercises for that floorplan.

If you are practicing specific movements, such as simple changes or leg-yielding, you can use this space to modify the exercises to include these movements.

USE IT!

... and we mean physically use it!

Take the exercise book to the yard, keep it in your tack locker or outside your stable.

Look at which floorplans and exercises you want to practice, and then fill it out once you've finished.

This book is no good if it's kept clean and pristine. After a few weeks, it should be dog-eared, maybe a bit dirty, covered in scribbles and well-worn in!

HOW TO SET UP YOUR ARENA

To enable you to practice these exercises accurately, you'll need to set up your home arena correctly.

Fortunately, that's not as tricky as it sounds, and you won't need lots of expensive equipment to do it.

WHAT YOU'LL NEED:

Before you begin setting up your arena, you'll need to have the following items on hand:

- Four stakes
- Arena fencing or boards (plastic guttering works well for this)
- Arena letters
- Two 60-meter or 40-meter measuring tape (depending on the length of the arena you require)
- Two 20-meter measuring tapes
- Arena diagrams (see pages 5 and 6)
- A willing helper! (optional, but beneficial)

[Instructions continue on page 7]

20X40 ARENA DIMENSIONS

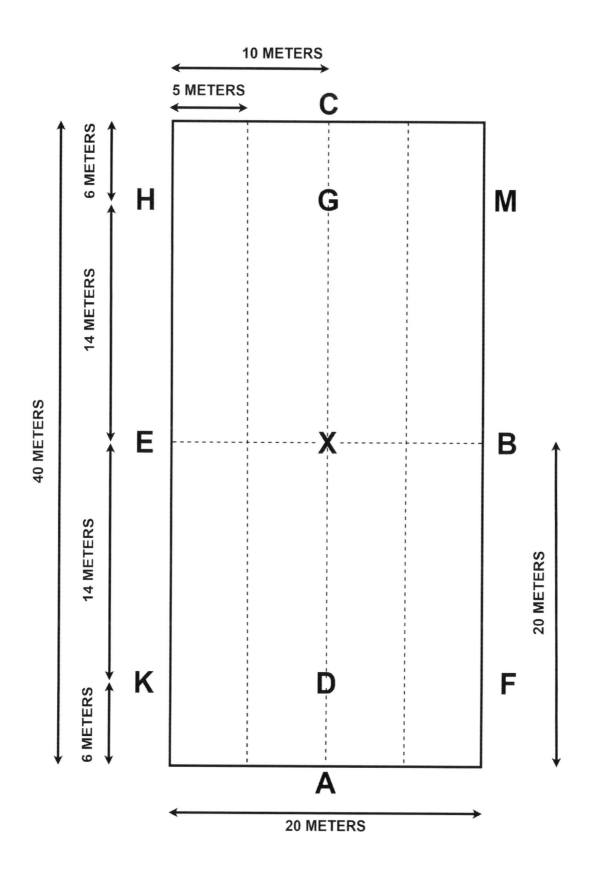

20X60 ARENA DIMENSIONS

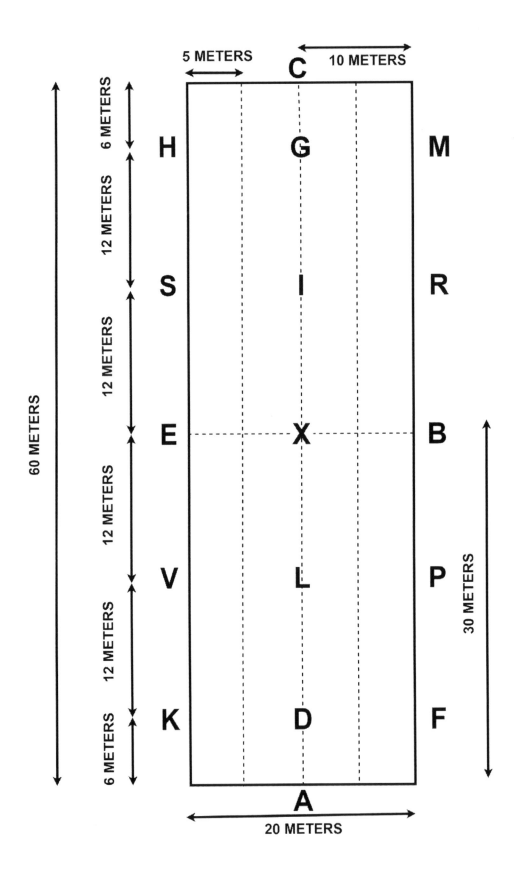

HOW TO DO IT:

Step 1 – Choose a location for the arena

Choose a suitable space for the size of the arena you require.

If you are building your arena on grass, ensure the ground is flat and even. Walk the area you've chosen to make sure that there are no holes or other obstructions such as hidden rocks. Try to find a patch that doesn't get waterlogged during wet weather.

Checking the area is vital for safety and also ensures that you won't need to move the arena once you've set it up.

Step 2 – Set up the first two corners

Use your **first stake** to set up your first corner (between "C" and "M").

Establish a 90-degree angle in the corner. You can use a square piece of card or a set square to measure it and ensure that the corner is accurate.

Measure 15-meters of the first long side (where "M" will be), using one of your 60-meter/40-meter measuring tapes. Mark the end of the 15-meter line with a **Temporary Stake**.

Now, take a 20-meter measuring tape and mark out the short side of the arena, where "C" will be located. The short side should measure 20 meters. Mark the end of the short side with your **2nd stake**.

You'll know when the 90-degree angle is accurate when you can connect these points with a hypotenuse of 25-meters. Check that the first and second measurements are still 15 and 20 meters, respectively.

The **2nd stake** marks your first 20-meter short side and should be left in place because this now indicates the second corner of the arena's short side.

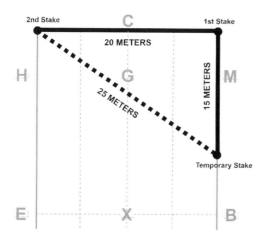
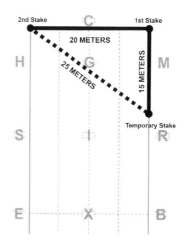

Step 3 – Set up the final two corners

Now you're going to mark out the first full long side of your arena, where "M" and "F" will be.

From the **first stake**, (the "C"/"M" corner) measure 60 or 40 meters to the other corner on the same long side. The length will depend on whether you want a short or long arena.
When the tape is taut, you have an approximate location for your corner. Check that your measurements are correct by measuring the distance from the new corner to the second corner (where your second stake is).

You'll know when your measurement is correct when you get the following:

- Large arena diagonal length: 63.25 meters
- Small arena diagonal length: 44.72 meters

Now, move the **temporary stake** to the end of this long side. That then becomes the **third stake** and marks the third corner (between "A" and "F").

Lastly, measure 20-meters from your third corner (where "C" will be) and measure 60 Or 40 meters from your second corner. The final corner is situated where these two measuring tapes meet.

When you've located this point, mark the final corner (between "A" and "K") with your **4th stake**. Now, you have the outline of your arena with accurate short and long sides and four exact square corners.

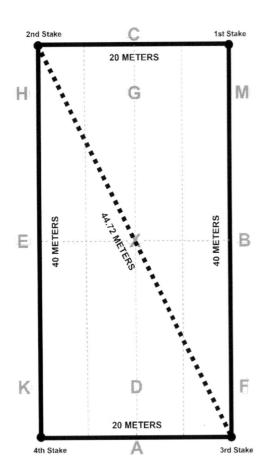
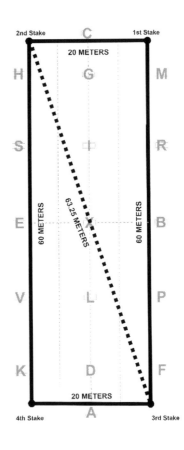

Step 4 – Set up the boards and letters

With your measuring tapes still in place between the stakes, place your boards to connect the stakes, beginning with the corners. Remember to leave an opening in the center of the short side at the "A" end of the arena to allow horses to enter down the center line.

As you set out the boards, keep checking that the distance between the long sides of the arena is consistently 20 meters and that the length of the arena is consistently 40 or 60 meters.

When you have all your boards set up, measure the diagonal lines again to confirm that they are still 63.25 meters for a long arena or 44.72 meters for a short arena.

Finally, set out your arena letters. Use the arena diagrams above to make sure that the letters are set out in the correct place. You should leave six meters from the short sides to "H," "M," "F," and "K." The other letters should have 12 or 14 meters between them, depending on whether you're setting out a long or short arena.

Finish off by marking the precise location of each letter on your boards. That will help competitors and judges to determine their position with more accuracy.

HOW TO STRUCTURE YOUR TRAINING SESSIONS

Every training session should include a warm-up, a training phase, and a cool-down phase.

THE WARM-UP PHASE

The idea of the warm-up phase is to allow your horse to stretch his muscles and loosen his body in preparation for the training section of his workout.

Begin with an energetic walk on a long rein and some basic work, including large circles, transitions in and out of the working paces, and some center lines.

All your trot work should be done rising so that the horse can use his back freely.

Gradually, the warm-up will include your horse's confirmed level of work, enabling you to find out what he finds comfortable and what he sees as a more significant challenge, both physically and attitudinally.

So, the greater your horse's repertoire, the more time it will take to warm him up.

The warm-up is a good way of evaluating and identifying where your horse is at in his training and allows you to determine the focus of the training phase of your schooling plan.

Also, the warm-up allows you to know how long it takes for your horse to be "in the zone" and ready to perform a test. So, when you go to a competition, you will know exactly how long your working-in period should be.

THE TRAINING PHASE

Once your horse is warm and mentally focused on the aids, you can begin the training phase of your schooling session.

Ideally, your horse should be working forward from behind through his back and into an elastic contact. However, in practice, and depending on the level at which your horse is working, you may need to begin the training phase when you get an acceptable reaction to your basic aids.

The training phase must always be based around the "Scales of Training" (see page 18)
i.e., rhythm, suppleness (through the back), contact, impulsion, straightness, and collection (or balance in novice horses.)

The training scale tells you how to challenge your horse, and it also reminds you when you've pushed him too far.

For example, if the rhythm starts to suffer or there's resistance to the contact, you know you are asking too much of the horse, and you should take a step back.

Find out what's caused the problem: perhaps take a walk break, lighten your hand or seat, or try giving your horse a sympathetic pat, and then begin work again.

The inclusion of frequent walk breaks in the training phase is a useful tactic.

Firstly, the horse learns that walking doesn't mean that work is over for the day! That's important when it comes to riding a dressage test; you don't want your horse to think he's finished as soon as you get to the walk exercises!

Walking also allows the horse to get his breath back between bouts of more strenuous work, gradually increases his stamina and strength, and allows tired muscles to recover.

THE COOL-DOWN PHASE

All professional athletes include a cool-down phase, both in their training sessions and in competition. And your horse is no different!

Cooling down helps to prevent injury and muscle stiffness, and it's crucial to your horse's wellbeing.

When you've finished the training phase of your workout, finish off each schooling session with a few simple exercises in rising trot that allow the horse to stretch his muscles and loosen his back, followed by a period of walking on a long rein.

The cooling-off walk allows the horse's heart rate to slow down, lets his circulation return to normal, and prevents the horse's muscles from stiffening-up when he is at rest.

HOW TO USE POLES

Polework can be a great way of improving your horse's general way of going, as well as adding variety and fun to his usual work routine.

Although poles are not a substitute for correct and systematic schooling, they do make a handy addition to your training armoury.

Eleven out of the 41 floorplans we've devised for you include poles.

Here's are some top tips on how to use poles to enhance your horse's dressage schooling routine.

SETTING THE CORRECT DISTANCE

The distance between the poles is extremely important.

In pole exercises, your horse needs to be able to comfortably move over the poles without changing his rhythm or tempo. Therefore, you'll need to take into consideration your horse's natural rhythm and the length of his stride in all the paces.

Smaller ponies, or horses with shorter stride lengths, will need the poles placed closer together. Conversely, larger horses and those with bigger stride lengths will need poles further apart.

Here is a guide to help you place the poles at the correct distance apart:
- Trotting poles: 3.5ft-4.5ft (1-1.5 of your strides)
- Canter poles: 9ft-12ft (3-4 of your strides)

If you would like to use the poles to help encourage your horse to increase or decrease his stride length, then you can adjust the distance between them accordingly.

Make the poles further apart to encourage your horse to take longer strides, and place the poles closer together to encourage your horse to take shorter, more collected strides.

SET YOURSELF UP FOR SUCCESS

If you and your horse are new to pole work, it's a good idea to start with just a single pole before building up to a whole series.

Poles require your horse (and you!) to think extra hard about where he puts his feet. If you use too many poles the first time you use them, you could cause your horse to back off, make mistakes, and possibly frighten himself.

Introduce your horse to exercises with multiple poles only when he is confidently going over a single pole. Take things one step at a time.

RAISED POLES

Once you and your horse have mastered moving over poles on the ground, you can increase the difficulty by raising the poles using cavaletti.

Raise the cavaletti slightly at one end or both ends.

Riding your horse over poles in this way can help to increase activity and engagement. That's because, as the horse lifts his feet over the poles, he will be flexing his leg joints.

POLES ON A CIRCLE

If you want to teach your horse to shorten and lengthen his stride length without having to set up a new line of poles each time, try arranging the poles on a circle.

Set the poles out like the spokes on a wheel so that they are spaced wider apart on the outside of the wheel and closer together on the inside. (See floorplan #36 on page 565)

Lunge your horse around the circle, moving him in and out to encourage him to lengthen or shorten his stride.

HAVE A HELPER AT HAND

Whenever you're using poles or jumps, always do so with an assistant on hand.

Horses can trip over poles, potentially falling, and so always put safety first, and never ride over poles or jumps when you're alone.

Also, if your horse knocks a pole out of formation, it's helpful to have a helper on the ground who can put them back up again when required.

<u>HOW TO SET RIDER GOALS</u>

What are your dressage riding goals? And do you have a plan in place to help you achieve your goals?

Without a clear idea of what you hope to achieve from your riding, you run the risk of never progressing.

That's why having a set of goals is so crucial for your dressage career.

In this section, we look at how to set rider goals and how you can take positive steps towards achieving them.

THE ANATOMY OF A GOAL

Every goal can be divided into several key parts. This is crucial if you are to be successful in achieving your goals in the long run.

S.M.A.R.T goals are:

Specific
Your goals must be specific. If your aspirations are vague, you won't have a clear direction, and you run the risk of losing sight of what you want to achieve.

Measurable
Your goals must be measurable so that you can assess your progress towards achieving them. However, be wary of using your dressage scores to evaluate your progress, as they can be subjective. And you will by now have noticed that some dressage judges mark more kindly than others!

Attainable
If you set goals that are unrealistic and beyond your reach, you will end up feeling demoralized. A useful tip when setting your riding goals is to discuss them with your trainer. An expert will quickly tell you whether a target is attainable or not.

Relevant
Your goal must be relevant to what you hope to accomplish. Trainers are especially important here too, as an expert eye can help you to determine what goals are pertinent to your progress.

Time-bound
Applying a timeframe to your goals is essential because it will increase your motivation. However, the element of time should not be used to force a result. A timeline helps you to keep moving forward, rather than making you feel stressed about having something done by a particular date.

Now, let's look at a few important considerations when setting rider goals.

PUT YOUR GOALS INTO PERSPECTIVE

Many people set themselves unrealistic goals. There's nothing wrong with having ambition, but you need to be careful that you don't end up craving a big goal that's unachievable. That road leads to disappointment and demotivation!

Each day, write down two things:

- A riding goal that you've achieved in the last year.
- A goal you achieved that morning (not necessarily riding-related)

For example, perhaps you finally taught your horse to halt square, and that morning, you made it into work on time for a change! These are both achievements, albeit small ones in the scheme of things.

However, a reliable square halt now earns you a mark of eight in your dressage tests, so your scores have improved. And improving your timekeeping at work could lead to a more substantial pay rise.

The point of this exercise is to demonstrate that the biggest goals are usually achieved through successfully meeting the smaller ones.

DON'T BE TOO CRITIAL

Unfortunately, it's human nature to be hypercritical. So, when you encounter a setback in your horse's training, you dismiss all the things you *have* achieved, and that makes your goals seem even further away.

Be kind to yourself, and don't lose sight of what you have achieved.

BE POSITIVE!

When you set a goal, use positive language. For example, if you want to improve your contact with the horse's mouth, state your goal as, "I would like to keep my hands more still." Don't say, "I don't want my fidgeting hands to disturb the contact."

Positive phraseology is crucial because it helps to focus your brain on the right idea. So, if someone tells you, "Don't think about a blue crocodile," you'll immediately imagine a blue crocodile!

Keep your focus firmly on what you want, rather than on what you don't want.

MAKE YOUR FIRST STEP AN EASY ONE

Be careful that you don't make the first step towards your goal a difficult one. If you struggle to achieve the very first part of your plan, it's unlikely that you'll succeed in the longer term.

For example, having your horse stand still while you mount is a significant accomplishment, because if you can't even get on board, you won't achieve anything else!

GOALS DO NOT EXIST IN ISOLATION

Remember that your goals are your end game, but to achieve them you'll need positivity, resources, good instruction, and support from your friends and family.

YOUR GOALS ARE A STEERING WHEEL!

Think of your goals as a steering wheel, channeling your energy and providing you with direction.

GOALS ARE MULTI-DIMENSIONAL

Your goals can exist in several ways.

A goal can be implicit, perhaps just an idea that you have in your mind. A goal can be explicit, i.e., something that you've written down on paper.

Goals can be driven internally or externally, and they can be short-term or long-term.

For example, dressage test scores are an outcome goal, as is winning a red rosette. Goals like these are inspiring, fun, and meaningful, but you don't have control over outcome goals.

It's more helpful to have most of your goals as process goals, which involves focusing on gradual, progressive improvement through the training and education of you and your horse.

RIDING IS COMPLICATED, SO BREAK IT DOWN

Riding is a very complicated endeavor.

Think about what's happening when you school your horse. There are emotional facets, cognitive demands, physiological elements, and then you add the horse to the equation!

So, when you're setting goals, it's extremely helpful to think of them in terms of multiple elements.

You will have an overarching final destination, but you'll need to break the journey down into small segments to complete it successfully.

USE MIND-MAPPING

Mind mapping is a method of visually organizing and breaking down your goals into the steps you'll need to take to attain them.

This technique can stop you from becoming overwhelmed when you're dealing with something as complex as riding goals.

LEARN TO WORK ON "HORSE TIME"

As every horse owner knows, horses are horses, and unfortunately, that means you will inevitably experience setbacks that may prevent you from achieving your goals.

Learn to work on "horse time" not "people time" by accepting that you need to be flexible.

Build some slippage time into your goal schedule to allow for the unexpected such as lameness, a frozen arena, etc.

IN SUMMARY

Setting some goals is essential if you are to progress in your dressage adventure.

Keep your goals realistic and achievable, divide goals into smaller sub-achievements, use mind mapping to help visualize your journey, and expect a few setbacks along the way.

To help you with your riding and competition goals, check out our range of equestrian training diaries available on Amazon.

THINGS TO REMEMBER

When riding through these exercises, there are a few things that you need to remember.

THE SCALES OF TRAINING

The six Scales of Training are what the riders in one of the world's most successful dressage nations are taught throughout their early years of riding.

The Scales are designed, through systematic training, to create an equine athlete who works in a perfect balance and makes the most of the movement they naturally possess.

The Scales of Training are:

1. **Rhythm**: Rhythm is the most important of the Scales.

   Each of the horse's gaits must reflect the correct rhythm for the pace, and it must be regular. For example, the trot is two-time, canter is three- time, and walk is four-time. A pacing or lateral walk will be severely penalized in competition for lack of regularity because the sequence has become corrupted.

2. **Suppleness**: Suppleness refers to the looseness of the horse's muscles along his back and neck. If the horse is to be able to swing through his back and neck, giving his natural paces elasticity and carriage, his back must be relaxed and supple.

3. **Contact**: The contact into which the horse works must be elastic and soft. If the horse is against the rider's hand, his back will become hollow and not supple, making it impossible for the rider to engage the horse's hocks and develop impulsion.

4. **Impulsion**: The horse should work forwards with a lively impulsion, using his quarters to propel him forwards with active hocks that are placed well underneath his body.

5. **Straightness**: When moving on a straight line, the horse must move on one track only. The same rule applies when the horse is negotiating curves and circles. Only when working through lateral exercises is it acceptable for the horse to move on two or more tracks.

6. **Collection:** Collection refers to the ability of the horse to take more weight onto his hindquarters and elevating the forehand.
   True collection is the result of working the horse correctly through the other Scales. At the lower levels, "collection" refers to the horse's balance. Advanced horses can be collected to such an extent that they can perform canter pirouettes, piaffe, and passage.

The Training Scales are meant to be approached in this order, although there are occasions when one can be skipped over so that you can work on improving another, BUT there are no shortcuts!

For your horse to achieve his maximum potential, it's crucial that you work methodically through the Scales, making steady progress.

YOU ARE NOT DOING A DRESSAGE TEST

In a dressage test, if you feel you horse tip a little bit onto the forehand or lose his balance you still have to ride the test as directed.

However, you are not doing a dressage test; you are training!

Therefore, take the opportunity to correct your horse and rebalance him before continuing.

You can rebalance your horse by taking up a circle, riding a few half-halts, making a transition, or a combination of all three.

Don't feel as though you have to plow on regardless and complete the exercise.

SET YOURSELF UP FOR SUCCESS

No one likes to be thrown in at the deep end, and that especially goes for your horse.

Just because a floorplan can include four flying changes, two canter pirouettes, and an extended trot, doesn't mean that you should throw them in all at once!

Take your time and increase the difficulty of each routine slowly so that you give your horse every opportunity to get the questions correct that are being asked of him.

TAKE FREQUENT BREAKS

Help keep your horse loose, relaxed, and enjoying his work.

You don't need to drill him through the exercises from beginning to end. Allow yourself and your horse time to have a quick break and a breather. Let your horse stretch his muscles and let go of any tension.

That's a great time to practice your free walk on a long rein and for you to assess how the last exercise went, along with planning the moves for your next exercise.

VARY YOUR HORSE'S TRAINING

Dressage training can be pretty full-on, especially if that is your passion and the only discipline you compete in.

However, it's essential to give your horse variety in his life. After all, just imagine how bored you'd get if all you ever did were the same job day after day!

Vary your horse's routine by giving him a day off each week, allowing him some time out in the field every day, taking him out hacking with friends for a change of scenery, and maybe including some jumping and pole work.

HAVE FUN!

I think we are all aware that dressage can get a little bit stressful at times.

Try to remember that (for most people reading this) dressage is your hobby and it's meant to be fun!

As soon as schooling stops being enjoyable, simply stop. Take your horse out for a hack and start schooling afresh tomorrow.

You spend far too much money on your horse not to enjoy your training sessions together. And if you're not enjoying it, it's highly likely that your horse isn't enjoying it either.

DRESSAGE MOVEMENTS

All our floorplans can be modified to suit the level that you and your horse are working at.

So that you don't get stuck or end up including the same movements over and over again. Here's a list of all the dressage exercises that you can incorporate into any floorplan.

If you are stuck on how to ride a particular movement or you want to know what the judge is looking for when marking the exercise, head over to our website where you'll find an article explaining how to ride the movement correctly. And if we can't find the information you need, give us a nudge, and we'll write an article, especially for you!

PACES

	We're learning it	We're good at it	We've nailed it!
Halt			
Medium Walk			
Free Walk on a Long Rein			
Working Trot			
Working Canter			
Medium Trot			
Medium Canter			
Collected Walk			
Collected Trot			
Collected Canter			
Extended Walk			
Extended Trot			
Extended Canter			
Counter Canter			
Give and retake of reins in trot			
Give and retake of reins in canter			
Rein-back			
Passage			
Piaffe			

TRANSITIONS

	We're learning it	We're good at it	We've nailed it!
Halt-Walk			
Halt- Trot			
Walk-Halt			
Walk-Trot			
Trot-Walk			
Trot-Walk-Trot			
Trot-Canter			
Canter-Trot			
Walk-Canter			
Canter-Walk			
Change of Lead Through Trot			
Simple Change			
Flying Change			

LATERAL WORK

	We're learning it	We're good at it	We've nailed it!
Leg-yield in Walk			
Leg-yield in Trot			
Shoulder-in in Walk			
Shoulder-in in Trot			
Shoulder-in in Canter			
Travers in Walk			
Travers in Trot			
Travers in Canter			
Renvers in Walk			
Renvers in Trot			
Renvers in Canter			
Half-Pass in Walk			
Half-Pass in Trot			

...hopefully we didn't miss any!

EXERCISE LAYOUT

1. Exercise Instructions

2. Exercise Difficulty

EXERCISE 2A

4. Floorplan Diagrams

3. Tips & Directives

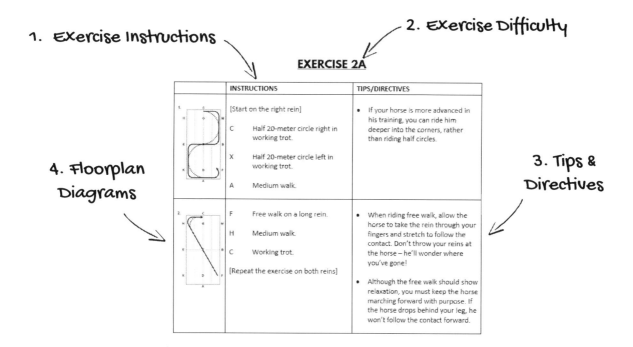

	INSTRUCTIONS	TIPS/DIRECTIVES
	[Start on the right rein]	• If your horse is more advanced in his training, you can ride him deeper into the corners, rather than riding half circles.
	C Half 20-meter circle right in working trot.	
	X Half 20-meter circle left in working trot.	
	A Medium walk.	
	F Free walk on a long rein.	• When riding free walk, allow the horse to take the rein through your fingers and stretch to follow the contact. Don't throw your reins at the horse – he'll wonder where you've gone!
	H Medium walk.	
	C Working trot.	
	[Repeat the exercise on both reins]	• Although the free walk should show relaxation, you must keep the horse marching forward with purpose. If the horse drops behind your leg, he won't follow the contact forward.

1. EXERCISE INSTRUCTIONS

The instructions for our exercises are laid out in a similar style as the standard dressage test with a letter marker, followed by an instruction.

B	A single letter on its own means that you should ride the movement at that marker. In this instance, you will ride the movement at 'B'
A/K	A forward slash between two letters means that you should ride the movement between the markers. In this instance, you will ride the movement between 'A' and 'K'
E-H	A dash between two letters means that you should ride the movement from one marker to the next. In this instance, you will ride the movement from 'E' to 'H'

2. EXERCISE DIFFICULTY

We've tried to demonstrate how a simple floorplan can be made easy or difficult, depending on the movements included and their placement.

For example, Floorplan #12 will have the following exercises: Exercise 12A, Exercise 12B, Exercise 12C, Exercise 12D, and Exercise 12E, with each exercise getting progressively more difficult.

Therefore, the 'A' exercises are more straightforward than the 'B' exercises. The 'B' exercises are simpler than the 'C' exercises, and so on.

3. TIPS & DIRECTIVES

The Tips/Directives column contains extra information to help you to get the most benefit from riding the exercise.

We've highlighted the movements where most mistakes are made to help you to avoid common errors.

4. DIAGRAMS

Each of our floorplans have 20x40 and 20x60 diagrams which are illustrated in a large format before the exercises.

Within the exercise tables, we have included small images of the 20x40 diagrams as a reminder of where you are going.

Please note that although we have made our best effort to make these diagrams as accurate as possible, they are not to exact scale.

FLOORPLANS & EXERCISES

Let the training begin!

FLOORPLAN #1

'The Danger Zone'

PRACTICE LOG – Note the dates when you last practiced this floorplan.

#1 'THE DANGER ZONE' – 20X40 DIAGRAM

1.

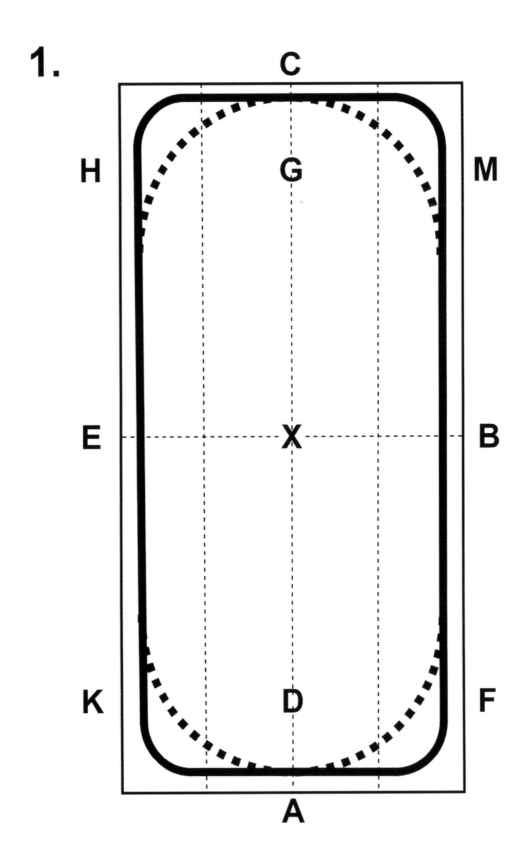

#1 'THE DANGER ZONE' – 20X60 DIAGRAM

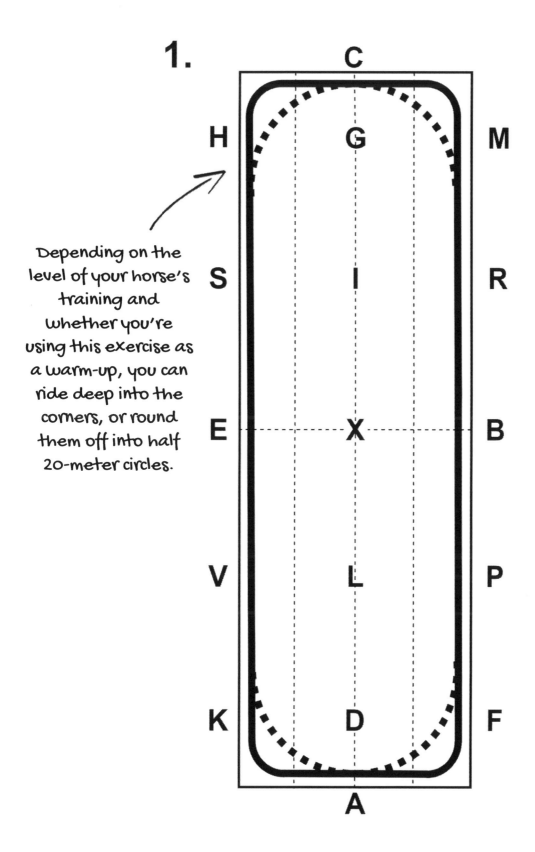

1.

C

H   G   M

Depending on the level of your horse's training and whether you're using this exercise as a warm-up, you can ride deep into the corners, or round them off into half 20-meter circles.

S   I   R

E   X   B

V   L   P

K   D   F

A

EXERCISE 1A

	INSTRUCTIONS	TIPS/DIRECTIVES
1.	[Start on the right rein] C Working trot. B Medium walk. F Working trot. E Halt. Immobility 4 seconds. Procced in working trot. [Repeat the exercise on both reins]	• Keep your horse reactive to your aids through the transitions. • Upward transitions should be sharp and crisp. Downward transitions should be balanced and obedient. • In a good halt, the horse should be straight and square. Each leg should bear the same weight evenly so that the horse has 'a leg at each corner'.

NOTES:

....

....

....

....

....

....

....

....

....

....

....

....

....

....

....

....

....

EXERCISE 1B

	INSTRUCTIONS	TIPS/DIRECTIVES
1.	[Start on the right rein] C Working trot. M Medium trot. F Working trot. E Halt. Immobility 4 seconds. Rein-back one horse's length. Proceed in working trot. [Repeat the exercise on both reins]	• Medium trot is a pace of moderate lengthening. Whilst maintaining a round frame and working over his back to the contact, the horse should clearly lengthen his stride to cover more ground. • If your horse is working at a novice level, ask for a gradual increase in stride length, rather than demanding medium trot from marker to marker. • During the halt, the horse should remain still and relaxed but attentive whilst waiting for his rider's next instruction. • When riding the rein-back, it's important that the halt is square. If the horse is trailing a hind leg at the start, he won't be able to keep his balance or step back clearly in diagonal pairs.

NOTES:

....

....

....

....

....

....

....

....

....

....

....

EXERCISE 1C

	INSTRUCTIONS	TIPS/DIRECTIVES
1.	[Start on the right rein] C/M Walk to working canter right. F Collected canter. K Working canter. H/C Medium walk. [Repeat the exercise on both reins]	• Use half-halts to adjust the horse's balance before the transitions and within the canter. • The collected canter should have shorter and higher steps due to the horse carrying more of the weight towards its haunches, not because you've kept the handbrake on. • Keep the horse balanced and straight through the canter-walk transition. Take up a slight shoulder-fore position to prevent the quarters from coming in.

NOTES:

....

....

....

....

....

....

....

....

....

....

....

....

....

....

....

....

EXERCISE 1D

	INSTRUCTIONS	TIPS/DIRECTIVES
1.	[Start on the right rein] C Working trot. M Shoulder-in right. B Working trot. F Medium walk. A Halt. Immobility 4 seconds. Rein-back one horse's length. Proceed in working trot. K Medium trot. H Working trot. [Repeat the exercise on both reins]	• Make sure that the horse doesn't lose impulsion during the shoulder-in. • Don't ask for too much angle or neck bend in shoulder-in, as this could cause the horse to fall out through his shoulder. • Aim for accurate, obedient, and balanced transitions. • A square halt will only happen if the horse is straight and engaged. If the horse is moving crooked, it's virtually impossible to arrive at a square halt. • The horse should stay relaxed and calm during the rein-back. There should be no resistance to the contact, and he shouldn't rush backwards or lose his rhythm. • During the medium trot the horse's frame should lengthen so that he carries his head slightly in front of the vertical.

NOTES:

....

....

....

....

....

....

....

....

....

EXERCISE 1E

	INSTRUCTIONS	TIPS/DIRECTIVES
1.	[Start on the right rein] C Walk to working canter right. M Medium canter. F Collected canter. K Working trot. E Travers right. H Medium walk. [Repeat the exercise on both reins]	• The horse should be reactive to the upward transition to canter. • Although the medium canter should cover more ground than a working canter, it should also clearly demonstrate an uphill tendency. • When riding medium to collected canter, use a slight shoulder-fore position to keep the horse straight and prevent the quarters from coming in. • The collection in the canter should be thought of as a rebalancing of the weight carriage towards the haunches, and not as a shortening of the stride. • Don't ask for too much angle in travers, as that can kill the impulsion and fluency of the movement. • If the angle of the travers begins to vary, ride away onto a 10-meter circle to re-establish the horse's balance, and then repeat the exercise.

NOTES:

....

....

....

....

....

....

....

EXERCISE 1F – Make Your Own

	INSTRUCTIONS
1. C H G M E X B K D F A	

NOTES:

....

....

....

....

....

....

....

....

....

....

....

....

EXERCISE 1G – Make Your Own

	INSTRUCTIONS
1. H · C · M G E · X · B K · D · F A	

NOTES:

....
....
....
....
....
....
....
....
....
....
....
....
....

EXERCISE 1H – Make Your Own

	INSTRUCTIONS
1. H C M G E X B K D F A	- 37 -

NOTES:

....

....

....

....

....

....

....

....

....

....

....

....

"You can't put expression on top of tension."

FLOORPLAN #2

'S-Bending Backwards'

PRACTICE LOG – Note the dates when you last practiced this floorplan.

#2 'S-BENDING BACKWARDS' – 20X40 DIAGRAMS

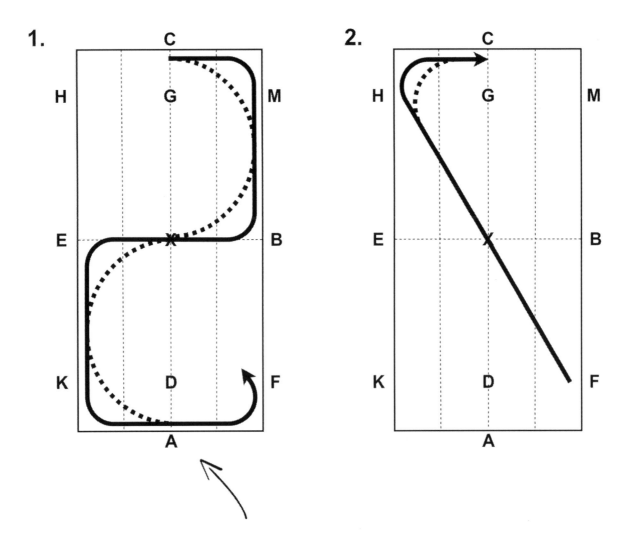

1.

2.

You can ride into the corners OR
ride two half circles.

...It looks like a
backwards 'S'

#2 'S-BENDING BACKWARDS' – 20X60 DIAGRAMS

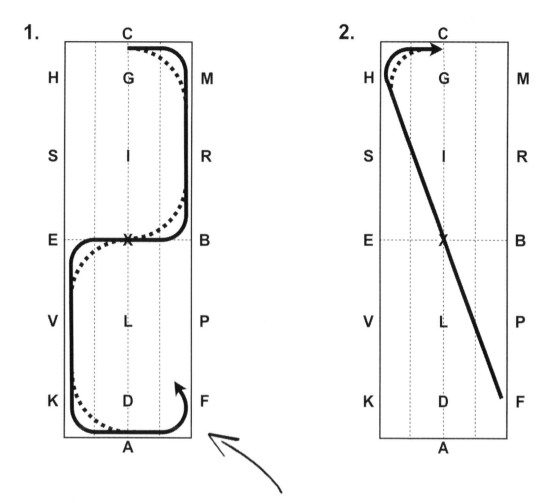

If you are riding in a 20x60 area, notice that you are not able to ride a half 20-meter circle from 'A' to finish at 'X'. Instead, you can round the corners off and ride straight down the long side for a few strides.

EXERCISE 2A

	INSTRUCTIONS	TIPS/DIRECTIVES
1. 	[Start on the right rein] C Half 20-meter circle right in working trot. X Half 20-meter circle left in working trot. A Medium walk.	• The trot has a two-beat rhythm during which the horse's legs move in diagonal pairs. There should be a clear moment of suspension when all the horse's feet are off the floor. It's this moment of suspension that gives the trot its expression and lift. • During the half circles, your horse should continue to work forwards, in a good rhythm, and show a clear uniform bend along his body.
2. 	F Free walk on a long rein. H Medium walk. C Working trot. [Repeat the exercise on both reins]	• When riding free walk, allow the horse to take the rein through your fingers and stretch to follow the contact. Don't throw your reins at the horse – he'll wonder where you've gone! • Although the free walk should show relaxation, you must keep the horse marching forward with purpose. If the horse drops behind your leg, he won't follow the contact forward.

NOTES:

....

....

....

....

....

....

....

....

....

....

EXERCISE 2B

	INSTRUCTIONS	TIPS/DIRECTIVES
1.	[Start on the right rein] C Half 20-meter circle right in working trot. X Halt. Immobility 4 seconds. Proceed in working trot. Half 20-meter circle left.	• When riding the half circles, keep your hips and shoulders parallel with your horse's shoulders, keep your body upright, and look ahead of you around the circle. • Your horse should be straight, square, attentive, relaxed and immobile during the halt, and the move-off should be immediate and obedient.
2.	F Medium trot. H Working trot. [Repeat exercise]	• Medium trot is a pace of moderate lengthening. Whilst maintaining a round frame and working over his back to the contact, the horse should clearly lengthen his stride to cover more ground. • If you have a young, inexperienced horse, ask him to perform a few steps of medium trot first and gradually build up the number of strides you can achieve. If you're riding a horse that's more advanced in his training, aim for clear transitions in and out of medium trot to and from the markers.

NOTES:

....

....

....

....

....

....

....

....

....

EXERCISE 2C

	INSTRUCTIONS	TIPS/DIRECTIVES
1.	[Start on the right rein] C Working trot. B Turn right. Over X transition to medium walk for one horse's stride, then proceed in working trot. E Track left. K/A Working canter left.	• Your goal is to develop a good, rhythmical and active working trot. If you have a young or 'green' horse, always ride rising trot so that he can use his back. • In the trot-walk-trot movement, the rhythm and frame should remain constant and correct throughout the exercise, and the whole thing should appear fluent and effortless. • When riding the trot-canter transition, emphasis should be on the horse pushing from the hind legs rather than launching off the shoulders.
2.	F Working canter. H Working trot. [Repeat the exercise on both reins]	• Your goal during the canter is to develop regularity and lightness of the strides, and an uphill tendency. • Before the downward transition, be sure to keep your leg on and ride a series of small half-halts to keep your horse in a good balance.

NOTES:

....

....

....

....

....

....

....

....

....

EXERCISE 2D

	INSTRUCTIONS	TIPS/DIRECTIVES
1.	[Start on the right rein] C Half 20-meter circle right in working canter right. X Change of lead through trot. Half 20-meter circle left in working canter left.	• Use the bend around the circle to bring the horse's hind leg underneath him for a smooth downward transition to trot. • Help your horse find a balanced and not hurried trot whilst you change the bend ready for the transition back into canter. • When asking for the new canter strike off, make sure that your aids are clear, and your shoulders are turning in the new direction.
2.	F Working canter. X Change of lead through trot. H Working canter. [Repeat the exercise on both reins]	• Changing lead over X is a bit trickier as you must change lead on a straight line. When asking for the upward transition into canter, step a little more firmly into your new inside stirrup (right) and ask for a slight flexion towards the new direction.

NOTES:

....

....

....

....

....

....

....

....

....

....

....

EXERCISE 2E

	INSTRUCTIONS	TIPS/DIRECTIVES

1.	[Start on the right rein]
	
	C Collected canter right.
	
	B Turn right.
	
	X Simple change.
	       Collected canter left.
	
	E Turn left.
	
	A Halt. Immobility 4 seconds.
	       Rein-back one horse's length.
	       Proceed in working trot.
		• Remember that the degree of collection required is only so much as to be able to perform the required movement with ease.
		
		• When riding the simple change, maintain the relaxation and the clarity of the walk steps.
		
		• Make sure the halt is square and maintained before asking for rein-back.
		
		• Use your legs to ask for rein-back, not your hands. If the horse resists, ride forward, straighten him, and then ask for rein-back again.

2.	F Extended trot. H Working trot. C Collected canter right. [Repeat the exercise on both reins]	• In the extended trot, the horse covers the maximum amount of ground he can without hurrying and losing his balance. • Make sure that the transitions in and out of the extended trot are clean and clear.

NOTES:

....

....

....

....

....

....

....

....

....

EXERCISE 2F – Make Your Own

	INSTRUCTIONS
1. C H G M E B K D F A - 47 -	
2. C H G M E B K D F A	

NOTES:

....

....

....

....

....

....

....

....

....

EXERCISE 2G – Make Your Own

	INSTRUCTIONS
1.	
2.	

NOTES:

....

....

....

....

....

....

....

....

....

....

EXERCISE 2H – Make Your Own

	INSTRUCTIONS
1.	
2.	

NOTES:

....

....

....

....

....

....

....

....

....

"Every time you ride,
you're either training or
un-training your horse."

FLOORPLAN #3

'The Skateboard'

PRACTICE LOG – Note the dates when you last practiced this floorplan.

....
....
....
....
....
....
....
....
....
....
....
....
....
....
....
....
....
....
....
....
....

#3 'THE SKATEBOARD' - 20X40 DIAGRAM

1.

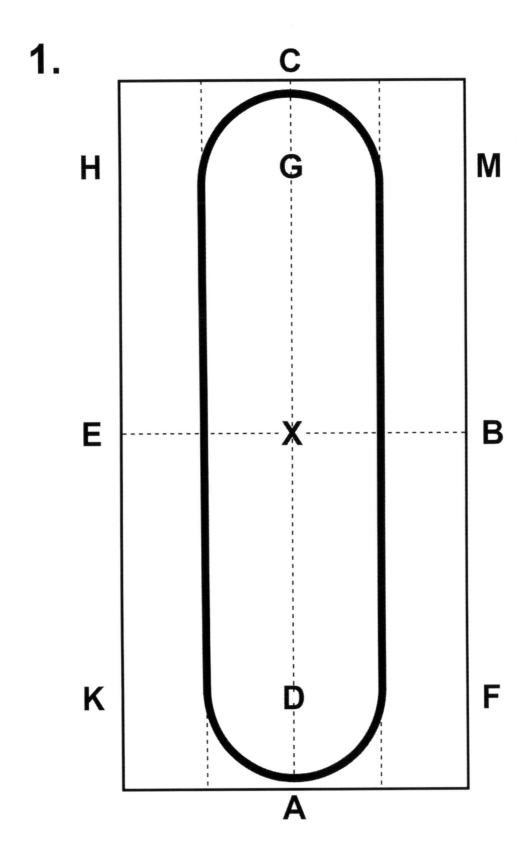

#3 'THE SKATEBOARD' - 20X60 DIAGRAM

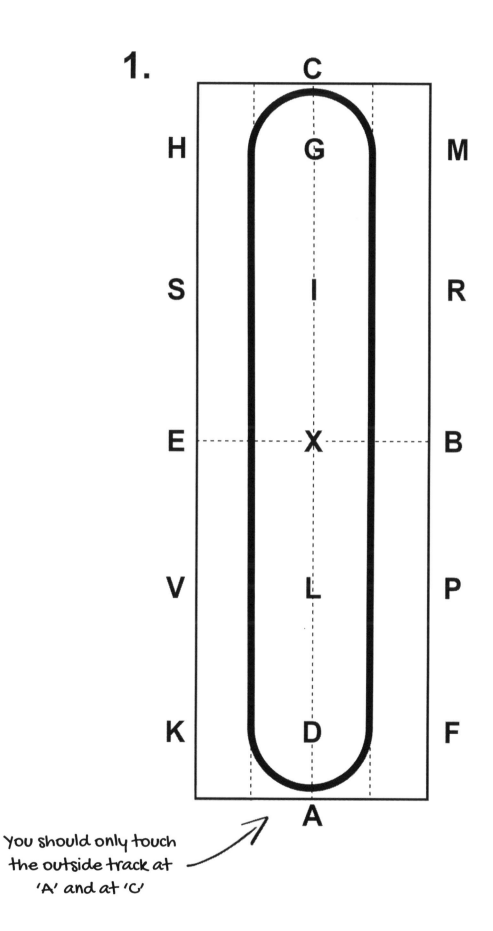

1.

You should only touch
the outside track at
'A' and at 'C'

EXERCISE 3A

	INSTRUCTIONS	TIPS/DIRECTIVES
1.	[Start on the right rein] C Working trot. Turn onto the ¾ line. When approaching the A end of the arena, ride a half 10-meter circle onto the other ¾ line. When approaching the C end of the arena, ride a half 10-meter circle onto the other ¾ line. [Repeat the exercise on both reins]	• Pick a spot at the end of the ¾ line and focus on it as you ride around the turn so that you are accurate. • When riding on the ¾ line, make sure that your horse is working from both your legs into both reins equally. It can be helpful to envisage that your horse is working along a tunnel created by your leg and rein. • Your horse will stay straighter if he is working nicely forward; horses that are dawdling behind their riders' leg are far more likely to wander or drift.

NOTES:

....

....

....

....

....

....

....

....

....

....

....

....

....

....

....

EXERCISE 3B

	INSTRUCTIONS	TIPS/DIRECTIVES
1. *(arena diagram with points C, H, G, M, E, X, B, K, D, F, A)*	[Start on the right rein] C Working trot. Turn onto the ¾ line. When approaching the middle of the arena (between X and B) transition to walk for 3-4 steps then proceed in working trot. When approaching the A end of the arena, ride a half 10-meter circle onto the other ¾ line When approaching the middle of the arena (between E and X) transition to walk for 3-4 steps then proceed in working trot. [Repeat the exercise on both reins]	• Ride forward into the downward transitions so that your horse remains engaged and straight. • The upward transitions should be crisp and reactive to your leg. If the horse is slow to make the transition, back up your leg aid with a flick of your schooling whip. • Look up and round your half 10-meter circles to make sure you don't overshoot your turn onto the ¾ line. • A 10-meter circle is quite a small diameter, so it is your job to choose exactly the right tempo (speed of the rhythm), to enable the horse to manage the rhythm and bend without any disturbances or unevenness to the stride length.

NOTES:

....
....
....
....
....
....
....
....
....
....
....
....

EXERCISE 3C

	INSTRUCTIONS	TIPS/DIRECTIVES

1.
 [arena diagram with points C, H, G, M, E, X, B, K, D, F, A]
	[Start on the right rein]
	
	 C Working trot.
	       Turn onto the ¾ line.
	
	       Medium trot.
	
	       When approaching the A end of the arena, ride a half 10-meter circle in working trot onto the other ¾ line.
	
	       Continue in working trot.
	
	       Between E and X halt.
	       Immobility 4 seconds.
	       Proceed in working trot
	
	 [Repeat the exercise on both reins]
		• The preparation for the medium trot is the most important part of the movement. If your horse is not balanced and engaged, he will fall onto his forehand, break into canter or lose the rhythm as he attempts to lengthen his stride.
		
		 • Use a half-halt to rebalance the horse through the transition back to working trot.
		
		 • If your horse is at an early stage in his training, ride balanced progressive transitions, rather than unbalanced direct ones.
		
		 • A square halt will only happen if the horse was straight and engaged. If the horse is moving crooked, it's virtually impossible to arrive at a square halt.

NOTES:

....

....

....

....

....

....

....

....

....

....

....

....

EXERCISE 3D

	INSTRUCTIONS	TIPS/DIRECTIVES

1.	[Start on the right rein]
	
	C Working trot.
	       Turn onto the ¾ line.
	
	       When approaching the A end of the arena, transition to working canter right.
	       Half 10-meter circle onto the other ¾ line.
	
	       Continue in working canter right.
	
	C Working trot.
	
	[Repeat the exercise on both reins]
		• Use your outside aids to guard the horse's shoulder and quarters to prevent them from drifting out onto the outside track.
		
		• When riding the half circles, keep your hips and shoulders parallel with your horse's shoulders, keep your body upright, and look ahead of you around the circle.
		
		• When riding the trot-canter transition, emphasis should be on the horse pushing from the hind legs that are placed under the body, rather than launching off the shoulders.

NOTES:

....

....

....

....

....

....

....

....

....

....

....

....

....

....

....

....

....

EXERCISE 3E

	INSTRUCTIONS	TIPS/DIRECTIVES
1.	[Start on the right rein] C Working trot. Turn onto the ¾ line. Shoulder-in right until between X and B, then straighten. When approaching the A end of the arena, ride a half 10-meter circle onto the other ¾ line. Travers right until between E and X, then straighten. [Repeat the exercise on both reins]	• These exercises are very useful for teaching obedience and reaction. If your horse tends to lose concentration, this exercise is great for keeping his mind on the job. • You'll need to co-ordinate your aids effectively to maintain the angle and bend consistently in the shoulder-in and travers exercises. • Use the half circles to help position your horse for shoulder-in and travers. • Keep the impulsion and forward movement when riding the lateral exercises.

NOTES:

....

....

....

....

....

....

....

....

....

....

....

....

....

....

....

EXERCISE 3F – Make Your Own

	INSTRUCTIONS
1. C H　G　M E　X　B K　D　F A	- 59 -

NOTES:

....

....

....

....

....

....

....

....

....

....

....

....

....

EXERCISE 3G – Make Your Own

	INSTRUCTIONS
1. H C M G E X B K D F A	

NOTES:

....

....

....

....

....

....

....

....

....

....

....

....

....

EXERCISE 3H – Make Your Own

	INSTRUCTIONS
1. C H G M E X B K D F A	

NOTES:

....
....
....
....
....
....
....
....
....
....
....
....
....

"Sometimes you win,
sometimes you learn."

FLOORPLAN #4

'The Zig Zag'

PRACTICE LOG – Note the dates when you last practiced this floorplan.

#4 'THE ZIG ZAG' - 20X40 DIAGRAM

1.

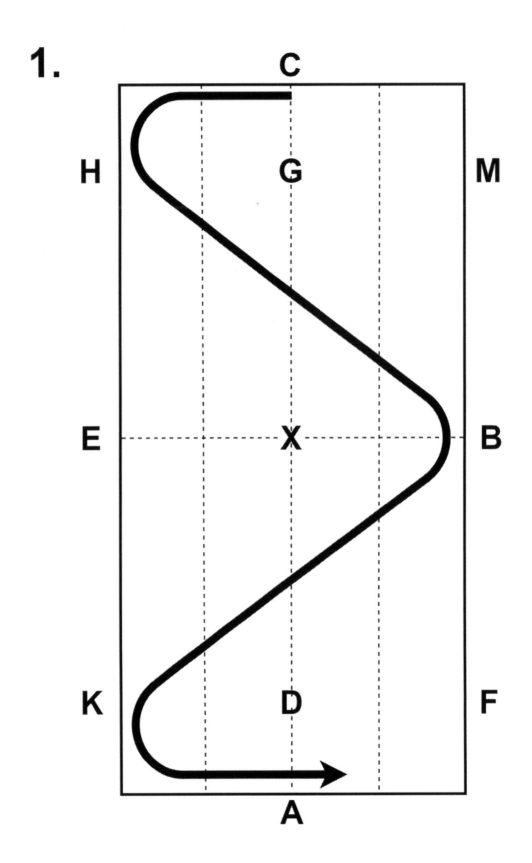

#4 'THE ZIG ZAG' - 20X60 DIAGRAM

1.

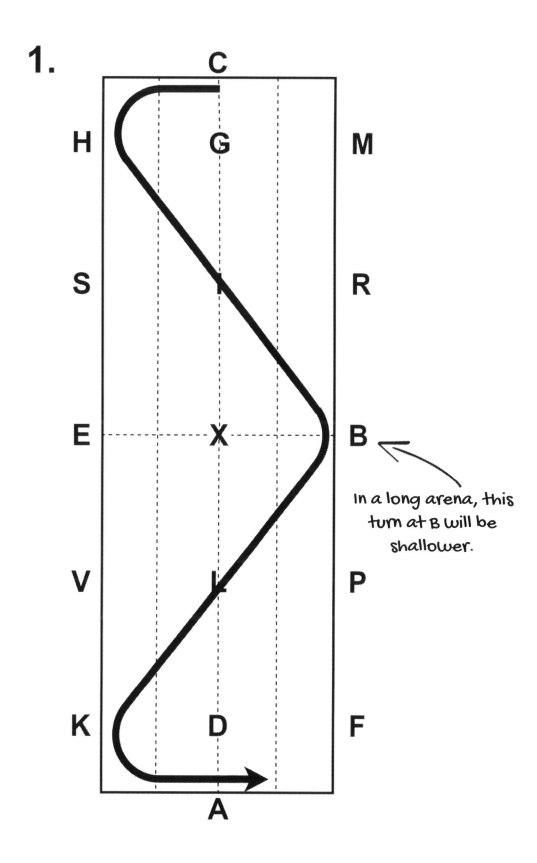

In a long arena, this turn at B will be shallower.

EXERCISE 4A

	INSTRUCTIONS	TIPS/DIRECTIVES
1.	[Start on the left rein] C — Working trot. H-B — Working trot. Medium walk before B. B-K — Free walk on a long rein. K — Medium walk. A — Working trot. [Repeat the exercise on both reins]	• You can use the turns to engage and balance your horse before you head across the diagonal. • The free walk should show the horse in a relaxed state, being allowed freedom to lower and stretch out his head and neck. • When you ride the transition from free walk back to medium walk, don't take your leg off if you think your horse is about to jog. Keep your leg on, maintain an elastic contact, and think about keeping the correct, four-beat rhythm.

NOTES:

....
....
....
....
....
....
....
....
....
....
....
....
....
....
....

EXERCISE 4B

	INSTRUCTIONS	TIPS/DIRECTIVES
1.	[Start on the left rein] C Working trot. H-B Working trot. When crossing the center line transition to medium walk for one horse's length then proceed in working trot. B-K Working trot. K Medium walk. A Halt. Immobility 4 seconds. Proceed in working trot. [Repeat the exercise on both reins]	• These movements all work together to engage your horse through the use of transitions and riding your horse with the correct bend through the corners to bring his hind leg underneath. • In the trot-walk-trot movement, the rhythm and frame should remain constant and correct throughout the movement, and the whole thing should appear fluent and effortless. • Make sure that the halt is square so that your horse can step underneath himself to make a clean, sharp upward transition.

NOTES:

....

....

....

....

....

....

....

....

....

....

....

....

....

....

EXERCISE 4C

	INSTRUCTIONS	TIPS/DIRECTIVES

1.	[Start on the left rein]
	
	C Working canter left.
	
	H-B Working canter left.
	        Working trot before B.
	
	B-K Working trot.
	
	A Halt. Immobility 4 seconds.
	        Rein-back one horse's length.
	        Proceed in working trot.
	
	[Repeat the exercise on both reins]
		• This exercise is all about riding balanced transitions. The transitions come up quickly, so you'll need to keep your horse balanced and engaged through the use of half-halts.
		
		• It's important to 'think forward' when riding into the halt. If you just close the reins and fail to use enough leg, the horse will lose engagement as he halts. The halt will become unbalanced, and he will probably not be square behind.
		
		• It's best not to ask for too many rein-back steps if your horse is just learning. Sometimes, a helper on the ground can be useful in training a youngster to step backward when asked.
		
		• During the rein back, the horse should remain 'on the bit' with the poll as the highest point. He shouldn't drop his head down or curl up behind the bit.

NOTES:

....

....

....

....

....

....

....

....

....

EXERCISE 4D

	INSTRUCTIONS	TIPS/DIRECTIVES
1.	[Start on the left rein] C Working trot. H-B Leg-yield left in working trot. B-K Medium trot. K Working trot. [Repeat the exercise on both reins]	• Ride two straight steps on the long side near H before asking your horse to move away from your leg into leg-yield. Keep the impulsion. • During the leg-yield, keep the horse's neck straight in line with the rest of its spine. You should only be asking for a small amount of flexion at the poll, not for a bend in the horse's neck. • If you have plenty of impulsion in leg-yield, your horse should step right underneath himself as you ride the transition into medium trot. • During the medium trot the horse's frame should lengthen so that he carries his head slightly in front of the vertical.

NOTES:

....

....

....

....

....

....

....

....

....

....

....

....

EXERCISE 4E

	INSTRUCTIONS	TIPS/DIRECTIVES
1.	[Start on the left rein] C Working canter left. H-B Working canter. When crossing the center line simple change to collected canter right. B-K Canter half-pass right. K Working trot. A Working canter left. [Repeat the exercise on both reins]	• This exercise demands a lot of balance and helps to develop engagement and self-carriage. • You'll need to use the half-halt to collect and balance your horse before the simple change and into the half-pass. • Remember that simple changes should always be ridden more from the seat and leg than from the hand. • Establish the correct bend through a wide turn at B so that you can position the horse correctly for the half-pass.

NOTES:

....

....

....

....

....

....

....

....

....

....

....

....

....

....

EXERCISE 4F – Make Your Own

	INSTRUCTIONS
1. C H G M E X B K D F A	

NOTES:

....

....

....

....

....

....

....

....

....

....

....

....

....

EXERCISE 4G – Make Your Own

	INSTRUCTIONS
1. H C G M E X B K D F A	

NOTES:

....

....

....

....

....

....

....

....

....

....

....

....

....

EXERCISE 4H – Make Your Own

	INSTRUCTIONS
1. C H G M E X B K D F A	

NOTES:

....

....

....

....

....

....

....

....

....

....

....

....

....

"Think of your hands being in front of the saddle and always pushing the horse to the bit, not pulling the horse back."

FLOORPLAN #5

'The Diamond'

PRACTICE LOG – Note the dates when you last practiced this floorplan.

....
....
....
....
....
....
....
....
....
....
....
....
....
....
....
....
....
....
....
....

#5 'THE DIAMOND' - 20X40 DIAGRAM

1.

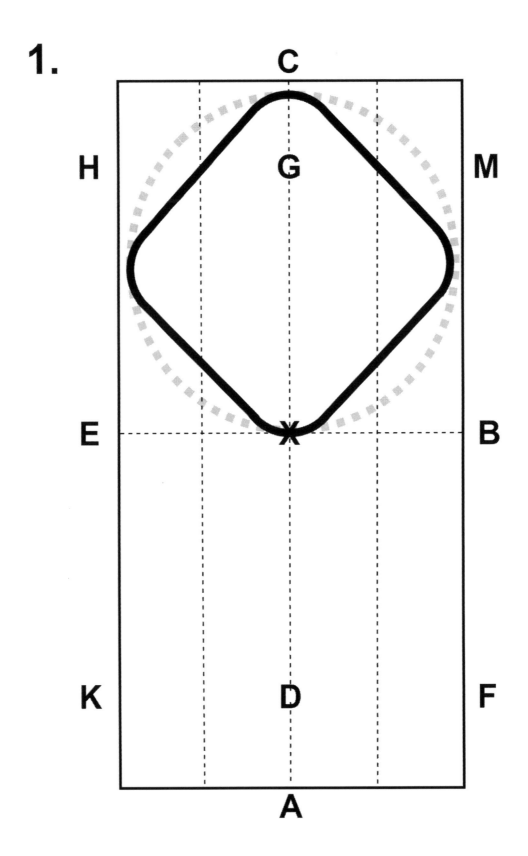

#5 'THE DIAMOND' - 20X60 DIAGRAM

1.

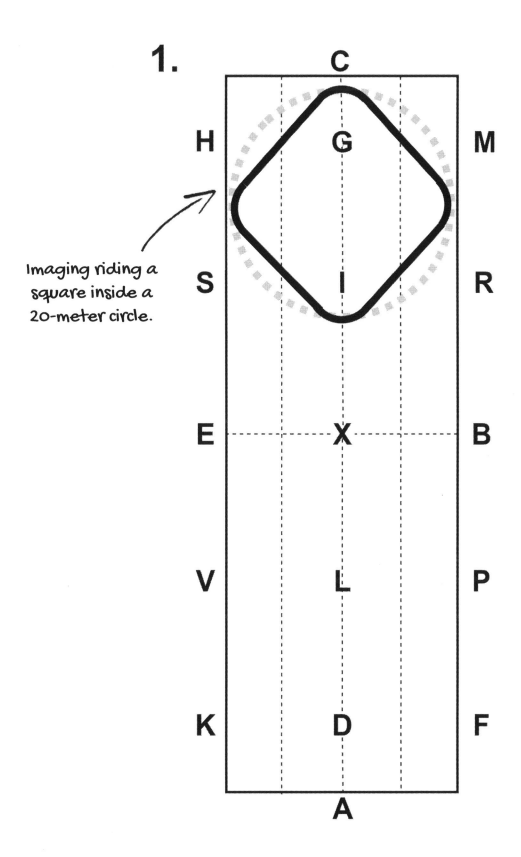

Imaging riding a square inside a 20-meter circle.

EXERCISE 5A

		INSTRUCTIONS	TIPS/DIRECTIVES
1.	C	Complete the diamond in medium walk. [Repeat the exercise on both reins]	• The horse's walk is a four-beat gait without any suspension. Any tension during the walk may disrupt the rhythm and regularity of the steps, so you should prioritize relaxation in the walk. • When riding the 'points' of the diamond, keep your hips and shoulders parallel with your horse's shoulders, keep your body upright, and look ahead of you.

NOTES:

....

....

....

....

....

....

....

....

....

....

....

....

....

....

....

....

....

EXERCISE 5B

	INSTRUCTIONS	TIPS/DIRECTIVES
1.	C Complete the diamond in working trot. [Repeat the exercise on both reins]	• Your goal is to develop a good, rhythmical and active working trot. • Remember to rise on the correct diagonal to help keep your horse balanced as you ride through the 'points' of the diamond. • Guard your horse's shoulders and quarters to with your outside aids to prevent them from drifting out.

NOTES:

....

....

....

....

....

....

....

....

....

....

....

....

....

....

....

....

....

....

....

EXERCISE 5C

	INSTRUCTIONS	TIPS/DIRECTIVES
1. 	C Complete the diamond in working canter. [Repeat the exercise on both reins]	• This is a useful exercise for developing collection and engagement in the canter. • Use a half-halt to set the horse up before each "point" of the diamond. • Your goal during the canter is to develop regularity and lightness of the strides, an uphill tendency, and the natural ability of the horse to carry himself whilst maintaining active well-placed hind legs.

NOTES:

....

....

....

....

....

....

....

....

....

....

....

....

....

....

....

....

....

EXERCISE 5D

	INSTRUCTIONS	TIPS/DIRECTIVES
1.	C Complete the diamond in medium walk and ride a ¼ walk pirouette at each of the corners. [Repeat the exercise on both reins]	• Keep the activity and rhythm as you ride the pirouette. Ensure that a clear 4-beat walk sequence is maintained. • If the horse is lazy or becomes 'stuck' in the pirouettes, use your legs throughout the turn in an alternating fashion, matching each of your legs to his hind legs, so that your left leg asks him to lift his left hind and vice versa. • Use a half-halt to collect the walk before riding the pirouette.

NOTES:

....

....

....

....

....

....

....

....

....

....

....

....

....

....

....

....

....

EXERCISE 5E

	INSTRUCTIONS	TIPS/DIRECTIVES
1. (diagram)	C Complete the diamond in working canter and ride a ¼ canter pirouette at each of the corners [Repeat the exercise on both reins]	• Use half-halts to collect the canter before riding the pirouette. • Keep the impulsion and rhythm as you ride the pirouette. • Ride forwards to maintain jump in the canter steps. • Don't make the pirouette any smaller than in which the horse is able to maintain his balance.

NOTES:

....

....

....

....

....

....

....

....

....

....

....

....

....

....

....

....

....

....

EXERCISE 5F – Make Your Own

	INSTRUCTIONS
1. 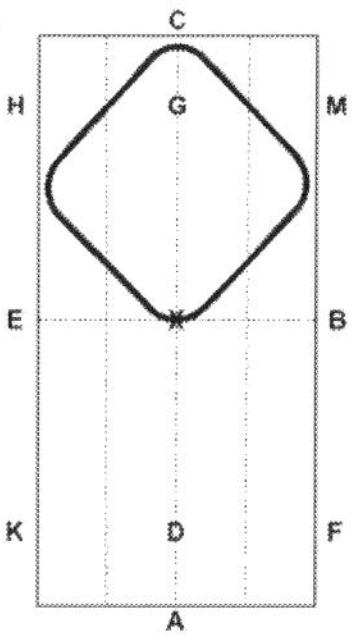 	

NOTES:

EXERCISE 5G – Make Your Own

	INSTRUCTIONS
1.	

NOTES:

....

....

....

....

....

....

....

....

....

....

....

....

....

EXERCISE 5H – Make Your Own

	INSTRUCTIONS
1.	

NOTES:

....

....

....

....

....

....

....

....

....

....

....

....

....

"A loud rider makes
a deaf horse."

FLOORPLAN #6

'Two Swan Necks'

PRACTICE LOG – Note the dates when you last practiced this floorplan.

#6 'TWO SWAN NECKS' - 20X40 DIAGRAMS

1.

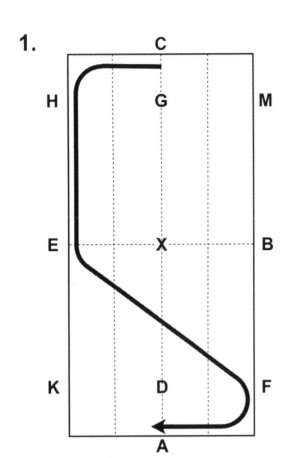

2.

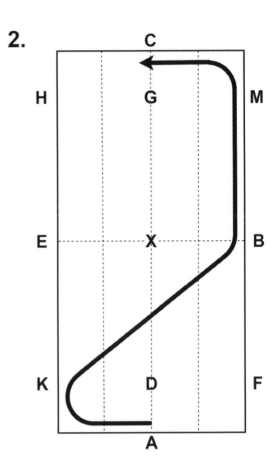

#6 'TWO SWAN NECKS' - 20X60 DIAGRAMS

1.

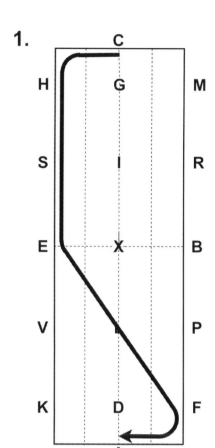

2.

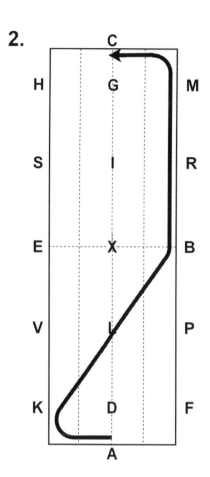

EXERCISE 6A

	INSTRUCTIONS	TIPS/DIRECTIVES
1. 	[Start on the left rein] C Working trot. E-F Working trot. A Medium walk.	• During the trot, the horse's hind feet should step clearly into the prints left by the fore feet. • Through each change of rein, remember to change the bend and your diagonal. • Pay attention to the rhythm and tempo of the trot.
2. 	K-B Free walk on a long rein. B Medium walk. M Halt. Immobility 4 seconds. Proceed in medium walk. C Working trot [Repeat exercise on both reins]	• When riding free walk, don't throw the contact away; he'll wonder where you've suddenly gone! Instead, allow the horse to take the rein from you as he stretches. • Allow a couple of strides at the end of the free walk to shorten your reins, rather than doing so too abruptly. Take deep, slow breaths so that you don't transmit tension to your horse, which could cause him to jog. • Keep the horse straight in halt, guarding the quarters so that they don't swing out.

NOTES:

....

....

....

....

....

....

....

....

EXERCISE 6B

	INSTRUCTIONS	TIPS/DIRECTIVES
1.	[Start on the left rein] C Working canter left. E Working trot. E-F Working trot. A Halt. Immobility 4 seconds. Proceed in working trot.	• Use your outside rein to control the shoulder through the downward transition to trot. • Your aids will need to be well-coordinated here as you will need to balance your horse and turn him too. • A square halt at A will only happen if the horse was straight and engaged. If the horse is moving crooked, it's virtually impossible to arrive at a square halt.
2.	K-B Working trot. B Working canter left. [Repeat exercise on both reins]	• Ask your horse for canter as you are joining the track at B. The bend will help you get the correct strike off and encourage engagement of your horse's hind legs. • The canter is a pace of 3-beat. It should have 'uphill' cadenced strides, followed by a moment of suspension.

NOTES:

....

....

....

....

....

....

....

....

....

....

EXERCISE 6C

	INSTRUCTIONS	TIPS/DIRECTIVES
1.	[Start on the left rein] C Working trot. E-F Medium trot. F Working trot. A Halt. Immobility 4 seconds. Rein-back one horse's length. Proceed in working trot.	• Use the turn at E to engage the horse before asking for medium trot. • Although your horse should be working with good impulsion during the medium trot, he should not hurry or lose rhythm and must remain in a good uphill balance. • When riding the rein-back, it's important that the halt is square. If the horse is trailing a hind leg at the start, he won't be able to keep his balance or step back clearly in diagonal pairs.
2.	K-B Medium trot. B Working trot. M Medium walk. C Working trot. [Repeat the exercise on both reins]	• Keep the impulsion through all the transitions, including the downward ones. That will help to drive the horse's hind legs underneath him, improving his balance and the fluency of the transitions.

NOTES:

....

....

....

....

....

....

....

....

....

....

EXERCISE 6D

	INSTRUCTIONS	TIPS/DIRECTIVES
1.	[Start on the left rein] C Collected trot. H Working trot. E-F Leg-yield left. A Medium walk.	• Although the steps are shorter in the collected trot than in the working trot, the elasticity and cadence are just as pronounced, and the horse should demonstrate greater mobility in the shoulders. • Keep the energy in the collected and working trot. If the trot lacks impulsion, you'll struggle to maintain the position in leg-yield. • Make the horse is straight before asking for leg-yield. You should ask for a small amount of flexion at the poll, not for bend in the horse's neck.
2.	K-B Extended walk. B Working trot. M Collected trot. [Repeat the exercise on both reins]	• When riding extended walk, you should only give enough rein to allow the horse to work over his back to seek the contact and to allow total freedom of the shoulder so he can extend his strides. If you give the horse too much rein, the poll will come too low.

NOTES:

....

....

....

....

....

....

....

....

....

....

EXERCISE 6E

	INSTRUCTIONS	TIPS/DIRECTIVES
1.	[Start on the left rein] C — Working trot. H — Travers left. E-F — Trot half-pass left. F — Working trot. A — Working canter right.	• This exercise tests the horse's obedience and lateral suppleness. • Establish the correct bend for travers by using the C/H corner. Keep the horse's shoulders on the track and allow the quarters to stay on the same line as for the quarter circle. • Keep the impulsion into the half-pass by "thinking" medium trot. If the horse loses impulsion, you'll struggle to keep him engaged and maintain the correct angle.
2.	K-B — Working canter right. B — Counter-canter. M — Working trot. [Repeat the exercise on both reins]	• Don't bend the neck in counter-canter, as you'll risk losing control of the horse's shoulders. You only need to ask for a little flexion over the leading leg, but no more than what would be asked for in true canter.

NOTES:

....
....
....
....
....
....
....
....
....
....

EXERCISE 6F – Make Your Own

	INSTRUCTIONS
1. C H G M E X B K D F A	- 95 -
2. C H G M E X B K D F A	

NOTES:

....
....
....
....
....
....
....
....
....
....

EXERCISE 6G – Make Your Own

	INSTRUCTIONS
1.	
2.	

NOTES:

....

....

....

....

....

....

....

....

....

EXERCISE 6H – Make Your Own

	INSTRUCTIONS
1.	-97-
2.	

NOTES:

....

....

....

....

....

....

....

....

....

....

"Hot horses have to learn to be ridden with your legs on. Lazy horses have to learn to be ridden with your legs off."

FLOORPLAN #7

'The Clothes Hanger'

PRACTICE LOG – Note the dates when you last practiced this floorplan.

#7 'THE CLOTHES HANGER' - 20X40 DIAGRAMS

1.

2.

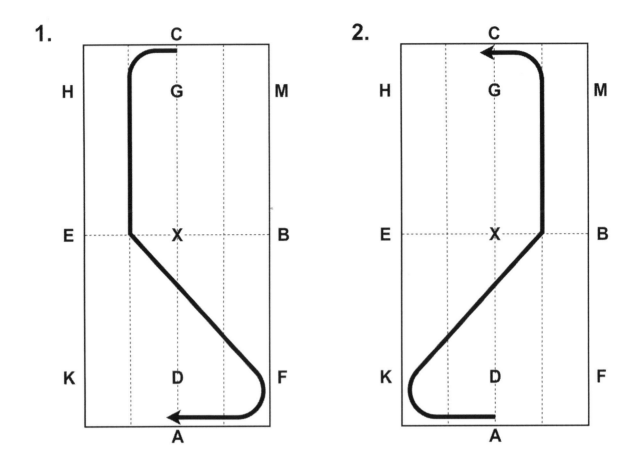

Similar to the previous exercise (page 87) except this
time you are riding straight on the ¾ lines instead of
the outside track.

#7 'THE CLOTHES HANGER' - 20X60 DIAGRAMS

1.

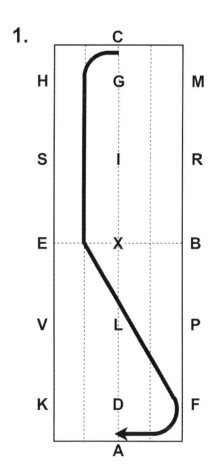

2.

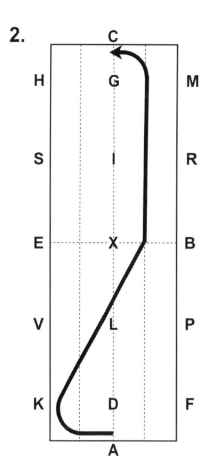

EXERCISE 7A

	INSTRUCTIONS	TIPS/DIRECTIVES

1.
 	
	[Start on the left rein]
	
	 C Medium walk.
	
	          Turn left onto the ¾ line.
	
	          When reaching the center line between E and X, free walk on a long rein towards F.
	
	 F Medium walk.
	
	 A Working trot.
		• When riding the transition back into medium walk, retake your reins gradually and keep your leg on. The rhythm and tempo should remain the same, although the horse's stride will shorten slightly as he makes the transition from free walk to medium walk.
		
		 • The horse's walk is a four-beat gait without any suspension. Any tension during the walk may disrupt the rhythm and regularity of the steps, so you should prioritize relaxation in the walk.

2.
 	
	K Working trot across the short diagonal to the ¾ line.
	
	          Proceed down the ¾ line in working trot towards the C end of the area.
	
	          Track left.
	
	 C Medium walk.
	
	 [Repeat the exercise on both reins]
		• As you reach the ¾ line, be sure to ride straight and use your outside aids to prevent the horse from drifting back towards the fence line.
		
		 • Your horse will stay straighter if he is working nicely forward; horses that are dawdling behind their riders' leg are far more likely to wander.

NOTES:

....

....

....

....

....

....

....

....

....

EXERCISE 7B

	INSTRUCTIONS	TIPS/DIRECTIVES
1.	[Start on the left rein] C Halt. Immobility 4 seconds. Proceed in working trot. Turn left onto the ¾ line. When reaching the center line between E and X, working trot towards F. A Halt. Immobility 4 seconds. Proceed in medium walk.	• Your horse should be straight, square, attentive, relaxed and immobile during the halt, and the move-off should be immediate and obedient. • As you ride the transition from halt into trot, look for your line onto the ¾ line. • Focus on a point at the end of the arena and ride towards it. Imagine riding your horse into a channel between your legs and reins.
2.	K Medium walk across the short diagonal to the ¾ line. Then working trot towards the C end of the arena. Track left [Repeat the exercise on both reins]	• Make the horse straight for a stride or two before asking for the transition into working trot. That will prevent the horse from coming crooked on the ¾ line. • The upward transition to working trot should be smooth and obedient.

NOTES:

....

....

....

....

....

....

....

....

....

....

....

EXERCISE 7C

	INSTRUCTIONS	TIPS/DIRECTIVES

1.	[Start on the left rein]
	
	C Working canter left.
	
	      Turn left onto the ¾ line.
	
	      When reaching the center line between E and X, working canter left towards F.
	
	F Working trot.
	
	A Halt. Immobility 4 seconds. Proceed in working trot.
		• The canter is a pace of 3-beat. It should have 'uphill' cadenced strides, followed by a moment of suspension.
		
		• Use your outside leg and rein to prevent the horse's quarters from escaping as you ride onto the short diagonal.
		
		• If your horse begins to step backwards during the halt, ride forwards immediately. Ride the halt again and ease your hand as you do so. Be positive with your legs and keep thinking forwards.

2.	K Working trot across the short diagonal to the ¾ line.
	
	      Then working trot towards the C end of the arena.
	
	      Track left and transition to working canter left.
	
	[Repeat the exercise on both reins]
		• The trot has a two-beat rhythm during which the horse's legs move in diagonal pairs. There should be a clear moment of suspension when all the horse's feet are off the floor. It's this moment of suspension that gives the trot its expression and lift.
		
		• Your horse will stay straighter if he is working nicely forward; horses that are dawdling behind their riders' leg are far more likely to wander or drift off the ¾ line.

NOTES:

....

....

....

....

....

....

....

EXERCISE 7D

	INSTRUCTIONS	TIPS/DIRECTIVES

1.	[Start on the left rein]
	
	C Working trot.
	
	       Turn left onto the ¾ line.
	
	       When reaching the center line between E and X, leg-yield left in working trot towards F.
	
	F/A Working canter right.
		• During the leg-yield, the horse should move forwards and sideways on two tracks. His body should remain straight, and there should be a slight flexion of his head and neck away from the direction of travel.
		
		• Don't ask for neck bend in leg-yield. That's a common fault that usually leads to the horse falling out through his shoulder and trailing his quarters.

2.	K Working canter right across the short diagonal to the ¾ line. Then transition to working trot and proceed towards the C end of the arena. Track left [Repeat the exercise on both reins]	• Your goal during the canter is to develop regularity and lightness of the strides. • Ride the canter-trot transition before turning onto the ¾ line. That will help to keep the horse balanced. • Remember to focus on a point on the short side at the C end of the arena and ride toward it.

NOTES:

....

....

....

....

....

....

....

....

....

....

EXERCISE 7E

	INSTRUCTIONS	TIPS/DIRECTIVES

1.
 [arena diagram with points C, H, G, M, E, X, B, K, D, F, A]
	[Start on the left rein]
	
	 C Working trot.
	
	        Turn left onto the ¾ line and proceed in travers left.
	
	        When reaching the center line between E and X, half-pass left in working trot towards F.
	
	 F/A Working canter right.
		• Use the turn at C to establish the positioning for travers.
		
		 • Focus on a point at the A end of the arena to help you ride straight.
		
		 • When riding half-pass, always ride forwards (primary) and sideways (secondary).
		
		 • During the travers and half-pass the trot should not change, in terms of energy, elasticity, and suspension, now should the rhythm vary.

2. [arena diagram with points C, H, G, M, E, X, B, K, D, F, A]	K Working canter right across the short diagonal to the ¾ line. Then counter-canter towards the C end of the arena Between G and M, working trot, and then track left. [Repeat the exercise on both reins]	• Take care to maintain a good riding position throughout the counter canter with your weight on the inside (right) seat bone on the side of the horse's leading foreleg. • Just before the trot transition from counter-canter, make the horse's neck straight so that you don't lose the shoulder.

NOTES:

....

....

....

....

....

....

....

....

....

....

EXERCISE 7F – Make Your Own

	INSTRUCTIONS
1.	
2.	

NOTES:

....

....

....

....

....

....

....

....

....

....

EXERCISE 7G – Make Your Own

	INSTRUCTIONS
1.	
2.	

NOTES:

....

....

....

....

....

....

....

....

....

EXERCISE 7H – Make Your Own

	INSTRUCTIONS
1.	
2.	

NOTES:

....

....

....

....

....

....

....

....

....

....

"Every ride that ends in a voluntary dismount is a good ride."

FLOORPLAN #8

'The Middle of Nowhere'

PRACTICE LOG – Note the dates when you last practiced this floorplan.

....
....
....
....
....
....
....
....
....
....
....
....
....
....
....
....
....
....
....
....
....
....
....

1.

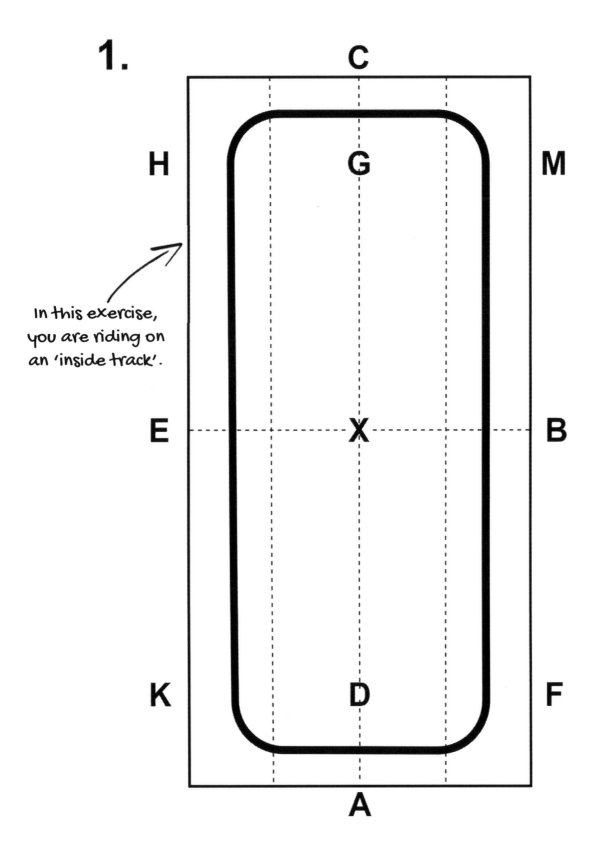

In this exercise, you are riding on an 'inside track'.

#8 'THE MIDDLE OF NOWHERE' - 20X60 DIAGRAM

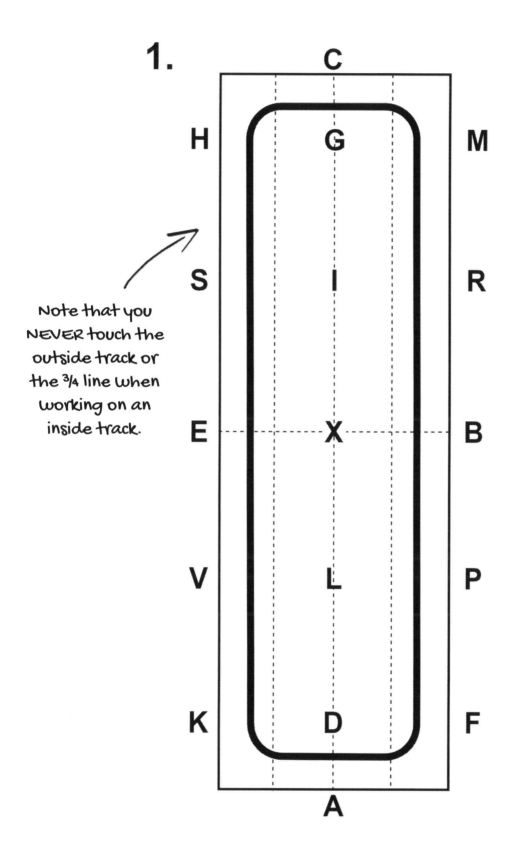

Note that you NEVER touch the outside track or the ¾ line when working on an inside track.

EXERCISE 8A

	INSTRUCTIONS	TIPS/DIRECTIVES
1.	[Start on the left rein on the inside track] C Medium walk. H Working trot. K Medium walk. A Working trot. B Transition to medium walk for one horse's length then proceed in working trot. [Repeat the exercise on both reins]	• Your horse will stay straighter if he is working nicely forward; horses that are dawdling behind their riders' leg are far more likely to wander. • Use your outside rein and outside leg to prevent the horse from drifting onto the outside track. • Be careful not to ask for too much neck bend around the corners as this may lead to your horse falling out through the shoulder. • In the trot-walk-trot movement, the rhythm and frame should remain constant and correct throughout the movement, and the whole thing should appear fluent and effortless.

NOTES:

....

....

....

....

....

....

....

....

....

....

....

....

....

....

EXERCISE 8B

	INSTRUCTIONS	TIPS/DIRECTIVES
1.	[Start on the left rein on the inside track] C Working canter left. K Working trot. B Halt. Immobility 4 seconds. Proceed in working trot. M/C Working canter left. [Repeat the exercise on both reins]	• The horse's natural inclination will be to drift towards the support of the fence. So, you'll need to guard the outside of the horse with your outside hand and leg, especially through the transitions. • A square halt will only happen if the horse was straight and engaged. If the horse is moving crooked, it's virtually impossible to arrive at a square halt. • When riding the trot-canter transition, emphasis should be on the horse pushing from the hind legs that are placed under the body rather than launching off the shoulders.

NOTES:

....
....
....
....
....
....
....
....
....
....
....
....
....
....

EXERCISE 8C

	INSTRUCTIONS	TIPS/DIRECTIVES
1. (arena diagram with markers C, H, G, M, E, X, B, K, D, F, A)	[Start on the left rein on the inside track] C Working trot. H Medium trot. K Working trot. B Transition to medium walk for one horse's length, then proceed in working trot. [Repeat the exercise on both reins]	• Medium trot is a pace of moderate lengthening. Whilst maintaining a round frame and working over his back to the contact, the horse should clearly lengthen his stride to cover more ground. • If you have a young, inexperienced horse, ask him to perform a few steps of medium trot first and gradually build up the number of strides you can achieve. If you're riding a horse that's more advanced in his training, aim for clear transitions in and out of medium trot to and from the markers.

NOTES:

....

....

....

....

....

....

....

....

....

....

....

....

....

....

....

EXERCISE 8D

	INSTRUCTIONS	TIPS/DIRECTIVES
1.	[Start on the left rein on the inside track] C Working canter left. H Medium canter. K Working canter. F Medium walk. B Working trot. M Working canter left. [Repeat exercise on both reins]	• The medium canter is a longer version of the working canter. It covers more ground because the horse's frame and strides lengthen. • When riding the medium canter, maintain the regularity and lightness of the canter strides • Use the corner before F to collect the canter and encourage the horse to take more of his weight behind ready for the downward transition to walk. • The medium walk must show a clear 4-beat walk without any tension or jogging.

NOTES:

....

....

....

....

....

....

....

....

....

....

....

....

....

....

EXERCISE 8E

	INSTRUCTIONS	TIPS/DIRECTIVES
1. *[arena diagram with points C, H, G, M, E, X, B, K, D, F, A]*	[Start on the left rein on the inside track] C Working trot. H-E Shoulder-in left. E-K Travers left. K Working trot. A Working canter left. F Medium canter. M Working canter. C Working trot. [Repeat the exercise on both reins]	• This advanced exercise requires you to have good co-ordination and a very obedient horse. • If your horse is inexperienced, you may find it useful to position your horse for travers by riding a 10-meter circle at E first. • Although the medium canter should cover more ground than a working canter, it should also clearly demonstrate an uphill tendency. • During the medium canter, the horse's hind legs must come further under the body and appear to 'push' the horse forwards, whilst you remain in full control through light and supple seat and rein aids.

NOTES:

....

....

....

....

....

....

....

....

....

....

....

....

....

EXERCISE 8F – Make Your Own

	INSTRUCTIONS
1. C H G M E X B K D F A	

NOTES:

....

....

....

....

....

....

....

....

....

....

....

....

....

EXERCISE 8G – Make Your Own

	INSTRUCTIONS
1. C H G M E X B K D F A	

NOTES:

....

....

....

....

....

....

....

....

....

....

....

....

....

EXERCISE 8H – Make Your Own

	INSTRUCTIONS
1. C H G M E X B K D F A	

NOTES:

....

....

....

....

....

....

....

....

....

....

....

....

....

"The biggest enemy to the partnership of dressage is impatience."

FLOORPLAN #9

'Going Full Circle'

PRACTICE LOG – Note the dates when you last practiced this floorplan.

....
....
....
....
....
....
....
....
....
....
....
....
....
....
....
....
....
....
....
....
....
....
....

#9 'GOING FULL CIRCLE' - 20X40 DIAGRAMS

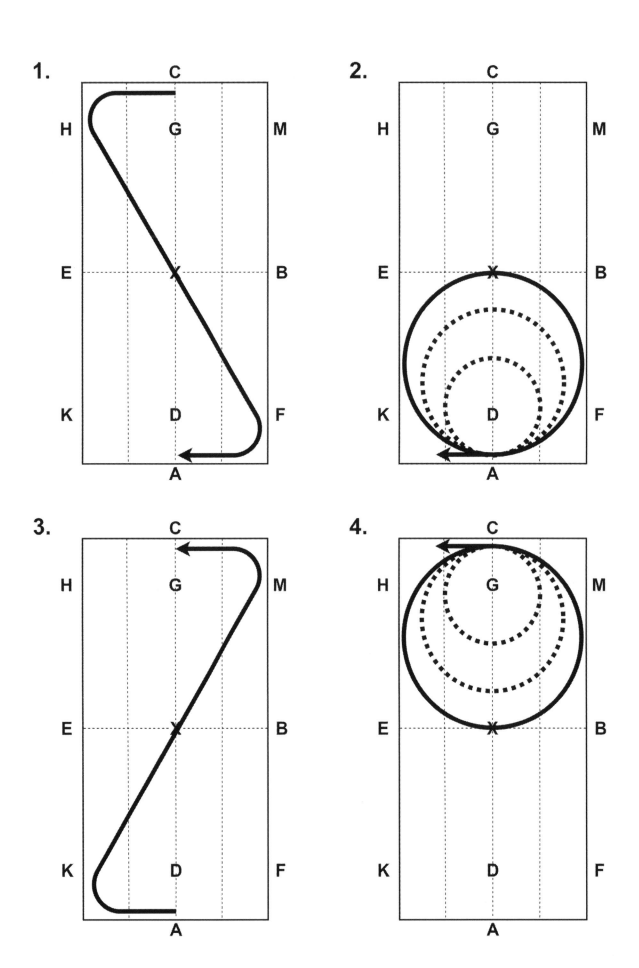

#9 'GOING FULL CIRCLE' - 20X60 DIAGRAMS

1.

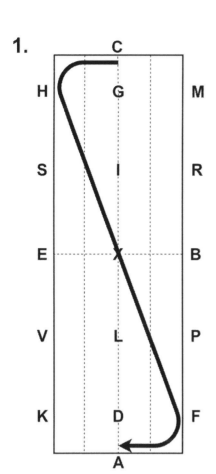

2.

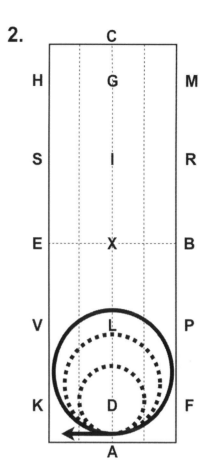

3.

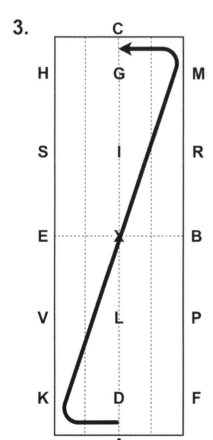

4.

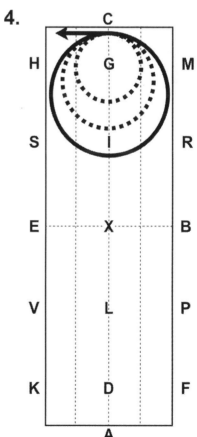

EXERCISE 9A

	INSTRUCTIONS	TIPS/DIRECTIVES
1.	[Start on the left rein] C Medium walk. HXF Free walk on a long rein. F Medium walk. A Working trot.	• The rhythm during the free walk should remain in a clear four beat, with the correct sequence. The horse should clearly over-track, covering maximum ground, and demonstrating complete freedom of his shoulder. • When transitioning back to medium walk, take back the contact over a couple of strides by gradually shortening the reins.
2.	A 20-meter circle in working trot	• Look up and around your circle to ensure that you maintain equal bend and accuracy. • Your goal is to develop a good, rhythmical and active working trot.
3.	KXM Working trot. M Medium Walk. C Halt. Immobility 4 seconds. Proceed in working trot.	• When transitioning to medium walk, ensure that the horse continues to work forwards and doesn't just collapse in a heap! • In a good halt, the horse should be straight and square. Each leg should bear the same weight evenly so that the horse has 'a leg at each corner'.
4.	C 20-meter circle in working trot. C Medium walk. [Repeat the exercise on both reins]	• During the circle you are expected to have even bend (think of an imaginary line) through the horse's body; from the tail, centrally through the hindquarters, through the back and shoulders, through the neck, and finishing at the poll.

NOTES:

EXERCISE 9B

	INSTRUCTIONS	TIPS/DIRECTIVES
1.	[Start on the left rein] C Working trot. HXF Working trot. Over X transition to medium walk for one horse's length, then proceed in working trot.	• Ride forward into the downward transition, keep the walk rhythm, and aim for a sharp, obedient upward transition into trot. • Keep looking up and towards F to help maintain your straightness.
2.	A 20-meter circle in working trot. Over X give and retake the inside rein.	• The purpose of the give and retake is to show that you are not holding the horse into an outline solely with your reins and that you are not supporting his balance or controlling his speed with your hands.
3.	KXM Working trot. M/C Working canter left.	• During the trot, the horse's hind feet should step clearly into the prints left by the fore feet. • Use the corner to establish the correct bend before asking for the canter transition. This will help to bring the horse's hind leg underneath him for a balanced and fluent transition on the correct lead.
4.	C 20-meter circle in working canter. C Working trot. [Repeat the exercise on both reins]	• When riding the circle, remember that your inside leg on the girth keeps the impulsion, develops the engagement of the inside hind leg, and asks for bend. Your outside leg should be slightly behind the girth preventing the hindquarters from escaping to the outside of the circle and generating some forward movement.

NOTES:

EXERCISE 9C

	INSTRUCTIONS	TIPS/DIRECTIVES
1.	[Start on the left rein] C — Working trot. HXF — Medium trot. F — Working trot.	• If your horse is inexperienced, aim for a few medium trot strides and build up to them gradually. This will help to keep the horse balanced and the rhythm regular. Once the medium trot is more established, you can then ride the movement from marker to marker. • Although your horse should be working with good impulsion during the medium trot, he should not hurry or lose rhythm and must remain in a good uphill balance.
2.	A — 15-meter circle in working trot. A — Halt. Immobility 4 seconds. Proceed in medium walk.	• Keep the bend uniform throughout the exercise. That will help to engage the horse's inside hind leg and make the halt transition more balanced. • Count to 4 in your head so that the halt is maintained for the correct length of time.
3.	KXM — Free walk on a long rein. M — Medium walk. C — Working trot.	• In the free walk, allow the horse to gradually take the rein from you as he stretches forward and down. Keep your leg on so that your horse continues to march forward into the bridle. Take back the contact over a couple of strides by gradually shortening the reins.
4.	C — 15-meter circle in working trot. [Repeat the exercise on both reins]	• The circle must be accurate in order to demonstrate that the horse is supple and connected enough to negotiate the movement without losing his balance and rhythm.

NOTES:

EXERCISE 9D

	INSTRUCTIONS	TIPS/DIRECTIVES
1.	[Start on the left rein] C Working canter left. HXF Medium canter. Just before F, working canter. F Working trot. A Collected trot.	• You will only have enough space for a few strides of medium canter. Aim for a clear transition from working canter into medium, and collect the canter as you approach F ready for the downward transition to working trot. • When riding the medium canter, maintain the regularity and lightness of the canter strides
2.	A 10-meter circle in collected trot. A Working trot.	• Collected trot demands greater self-carriage from the horse. The horse should remain 'on the bit', with his hocks engaged and flexed, stepping well under his center of gravity, and he should move forward, uphill, and with good impulsion. • Use your outside aids to guard the shoulder and quarters so that the horse doesn't drift out.
3.	KXM Medium trot. Just before M, working trot. M/C Working canter left.	• During the medium trot the horse's frame should lengthen so that he carries his head slightly in front of the vertical. • Ensure that you give yourself enough space and time to collect the horse after the medium trot ready for the canter transition in the M/C corner. • Use the corner to encourage the horse to take more weight onto his hindquarters for an uphill transition into canter.

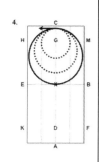	C	15-meter circle in working canter. When crossing the center line give and retake the inside rein. [Repeat the exercise on both reins]	• When riding the give and retake of rein, be sure to release the contact completely. There must be a visible loop in the rein. • The give and retake is a test of the horse's self-carriage. The frame should remain the same throughout and the horse should not lose his balance on to his forehand.

NOTES:

....
....
....
....
....
....
....
....
....
....
....
....
....
....
....
....
....
....
....
....
....

EXERCISE 9E

	INSTRUCTIONS	TIPS/DIRECTIVES
1.	[Start on the left rein] C Working trot. HXF Leg yield left. A Halt. Immobility 4 seconds. Rein-back one horse's length. Proceed in collected canter right.	• Make the horse straight for a couple of strides before asking him to leg-yield. • Ride forwards into the halt, otherwise the horse will not step underneath himself in the transition, and the halt will probably be crooked and not square. • The horse should stay relaxed and calm during the rein-back. There should be no resistance to the contact, and he shouldn't rush backwards or lose his rhythm. • Allow the horse a few walk steps out of the rein-back before asking for the transition to collected canter.
2.	A 10-meter circle in collected canter.	• Collection should be thought of as a rebalancing of the weight carriage towards the haunches, and NOT as a shortening of the stride. • Remember that the degree of collection required is only so much as to be able to perform the 10-meter circle with ease.
3.	A Working canter. KXM Working canter. Simple change over X. M Collected canter.	• When riding the simple change, maintain the relaxation and the clarity of the walk steps. • Try to avoid the horse staying too upright in the walk to canter and hence not really covering enough ground forward.

| 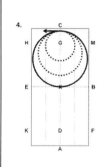 | C   10-meter circle in collected canter.

C   Working trot.

[Repeat the exercise on both reins] | • The collected canter should have shorter and higher steps due to the horse carrying more of the weight towards its haunches, not because you've kept the handbrake on.

• When completing the circle there should be no tilting of the horse's head. |

NOTES:

....

....

....

....

....

....

....

....

....

....

....

....

....

....

....

....

....

....

....

....

....

EXERCISE 9F – Make Your Own

	INSTRUCTIONS
1.	
2.	
3.	
4.	

NOTES:

EXERCISE 9G – Make Your Own

	INSTRUCTIONS
1.	
2.	
3.	
4.	

NOTES:

EXERCISE 9H – Make Your Own

	INSTRUCTIONS
1.	
2.	
3.	
4.	

NOTES:

"You can't be afraid
of power. You need to
learn to use it."

FLOORPLAN #10
'Double-back on Yourself'

PRACTICE LOG – Note the dates when you last practiced this floorplan.

....
....
....
....
....
....
....
....
....
....
....
....
....
....
....
....
....
....
....
....
....
....
....

#10 'DOUBLE-BACK ON YOURSELF' - 20X40 DIAGRAMS

1.

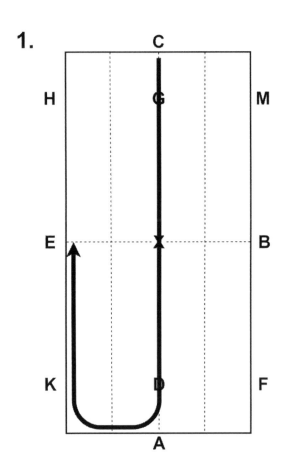

2.

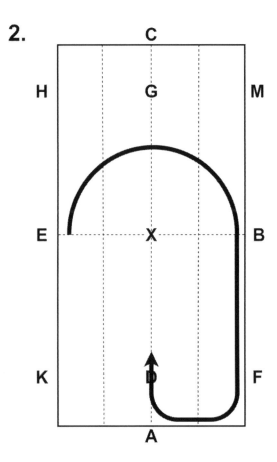

3.

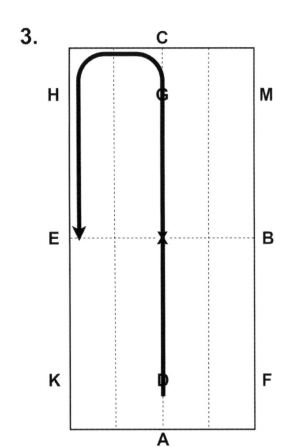

4.

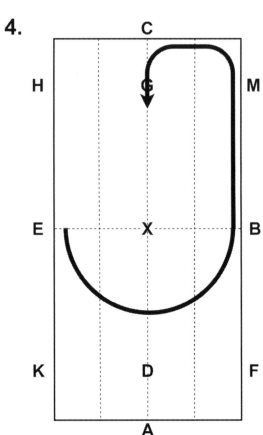

#10 'DOUBLE-BACK ON YOURSELF' - 20X60 DIAGRAMS

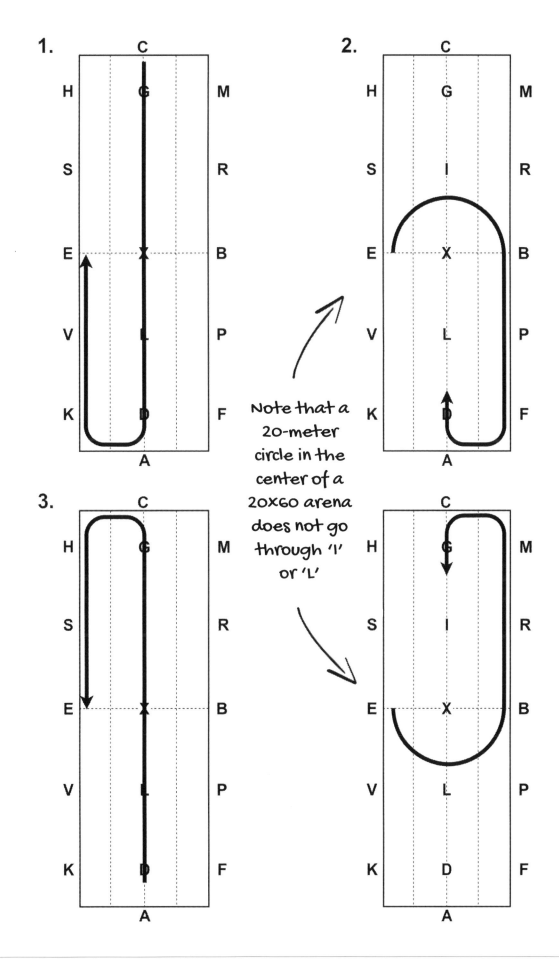

Note that a 20-meter circle in the center of a 20x60 arena does not go through 'I' or 'L'

EXERCISE 10A

	INSTRUCTIONS	TIPS/DIRECTIVES
1.	**C** Down the center line in working trot. **A** Track right. **K/E** Transition to medium walk for one horse's length and then proceed in working trot.	• If you have a young or 'green' horse, always ride rising trot so that he can use his back • When riding the center line, make sure that your horse is working from both your legs into both reins equally. It can be helpful to envisage that your horse is working along a tunnel created by your leg and rein. • Remember to use a half-halt as you approach the downward transition to walk and look for a reactive upward transition back into working trot.
2.	**E** Half 20-meter circle in working trot. **B/F** Transition to medium walk for one horse's length and then proceed in working trot. **A** Turn right onto the center line	• The half circle must be accurate in order to demonstrate that the horse is supple and connected enough to negotiate the movement without losing his balance and rhythm. • When transitioning to walk, there must be the correct number of walk steps, and they must be clearly walked, rather than jogged.
3.	**G** Halt. Immobility 4 seconds. Proceed in medium walk. **H** Working trot.	• Give the horse plenty of notice of your intention to halt by using a half-halt before making the transition. Don't just slam the handbrake on when you're on top of G! • During the halt, the horse should remain still and relaxed but attentive whilst waiting for his rider's next instruction.

4. 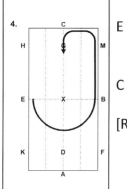	E	Half 20-meter circle in working trot.	• When completing the half circle there should be no tilting of the horse's head.
	C	Turn left down the center line.	
		[Repeat the exercise on both reins]	• When turning onto the center line, look towards A when coming around the corner to make sure that you don't overshoot your turn.

NOTES:

....
....
....
....
....
....
....
....
....
....
....
....
....
....
....
....
....
....
....
....
....
....
....
....

EXERCISE 10B

		INSTRUCTIONS		TIPS/DIRECTIVES
1.	C	Down the center line in working trot.		• If your horse begins to step backwards during the halt, ride forwards immediately. Ride the halt again and ease your hand as you do so. Be positive with your legs and keep thinking forwards.
	X	Halt. Immobility 4 seconds. Proceed in working trot.		
	A	Track right.		• Ask for a sharp, reactive transition into trot from halt. If your horse is young or inexperienced, allow him to take one walk step before the trot transition.
	A/K	Working canter right.		
				• When riding the trot-canter transition, emphasis should be on the horse pushing from the hind legs that are placed under the body rather than launching off the shoulders.
2.	E	Half 20-meter circle in working canter.		• During the half circle, your horse should continue to work forwards, in a good rhythm, and show a clear uniform bend along his body around the circle.
	F	Working trot.		
	A	Turn right onto the center line.		• Look towards C as you prepare to turn onto the center line. If your eyes are glued to the horse's neck, you'll probably overshoot the marker!
3.	X	Medium walk.		• Ride forwards into the downward transition to keep the horse engaged and straight.
	G	Working trot.		
	C	Track left.		• Any tension during the walk may disrupt the rhythm and regularity of the steps, so you should prioritize relaxation in the walk.

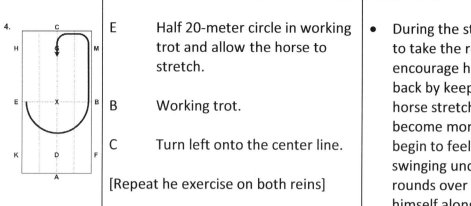	E	Half 20-meter circle in working trot and allow the horse to stretch.	•	During the stretch, allow your horse to take the reins gradually and encourage him to work through his back by keeping your leg on. As the horse stretches his steps should become more elevated. You should begin to feel the horse's back swinging underneath you as he rounds over his topline and pushes himself along from behind.
	B	Working trot.		
	C	Turn left onto the center line.		
		[Repeat he exercise on both reins]		

NOTES:

....

....

....

....

....

....

....

....

....

....

....

....

....

....

....

....

....

....

....

....

EXERCISE 10C

	INSTRUCTIONS		TIPS/DIRECTIVES
1.	C	Down the center line in working trot.	• On the center line the horse's poll should be the highest point, and the contact should be quiet, elastic and steady, without any tilting or swinging of the horse's head.
	G	Medium trot.	
	D	Working trot.	• During the medium trot the horse's frame should lengthen so that he carries his head slightly in front of the vertical.
	A	Track left.	
	E	Halt. Immobility 4 seconds. Rein-back one horse's length. Proceed in working trot.	• In a good halt, the horse should be straight and square. Each leg should bear the same weight evenly so that the horse has 'a leg at each corner'.
			• The rein-back at E is helped by the fence line on one side. However, you must still guard the quarters on the inside to prevent the horse from coming crooking as he steps back.
			• During the rein-back, the horse should remain 'on the bit' with the poll as the highest point. He shouldn't drop his head down or curl up behind the bit.
2.	E	Half circle 20-meters in working trot.	• When riding the half circle, the horse should be supple enough to be able to negotiate the circle accurately, whilst maintaining his rhythm and balance. He should show an adequate degree of bend without losing his quarters to the outside of the circle.
	F	Medium walk.	
	A	Turn right onto the center line	
			• When transitioning to medium walk, ensure that the horse continues to work forwards and doesn't just collapse in a heap!

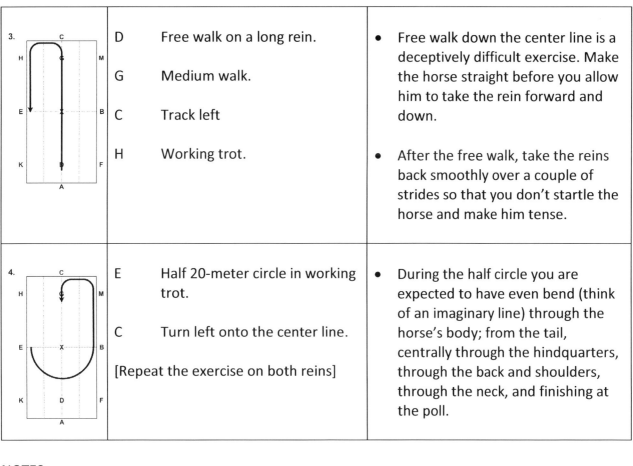

3.	D	Free walk on a long rein.	•	Free walk down the center line is a deceptively difficult exercise. Make the horse straight before you allow him to take the rein forward and down.
	G	Medium walk.		
	C	Track left		
	H	Working trot.	•	After the free walk, take the reins back smoothly over a couple of strides so that you don't startle the horse and make him tense.
4.	E	Half 20-meter circle in working trot.	•	During the half circle you are expected to have even bend (think of an imaginary line) through the horse's body; from the tail, centrally through the hindquarters, through the back and shoulders, through the neck, and finishing at the poll.
	C	Turn left onto the center line.		
		[Repeat the exercise on both reins]		

NOTES:

....

....

....

....

....

....

....

....

....

....

....

....

....

....

....

EXERCISE 10D

	INSTRUCTIONS		TIPS/DIRECTIVES
1.	C	Down the center line in working trot.	• During the trot, the horse's hind feet should step clearly into the prints left by the fore feet.
	D	Medium walk.	
	A	Track right.	• Riding a smart walk to canter transition involves having an energized walk, knowledge of the correct aids, and asking for canter in the appropriate moment.
	A/K	Working canter right.	
2.	E	Half 20-meter circle in working canter.	• Your goal during the canter is to develop regularity and lightness of the strides, an uphill tendency, and the natural ability of the horse to carry himself whilst maintaining active well-placed hind legs.
	A	Turn right onto the center line.	
			• Use a half-halt to balance the horse ready for the turn at A.
3.	X	Change of lead through trot.	• In the change of lead, ride forward in the downward transition to trot and remember to change the flexion over 2-3 trot strides before asking for the transition back into canter.
	C	Track left.	
4.	E	Half 20-meter circle in working canter.	• Use the bend on the circle and a half-halt to bring the horse's quarters underneath him before asking for the canter-walk transition at B.
	B	Medium walk.	
	M	Working trot.	
	C	Turn left onto the center line.	• Use your back, core, and seat to hold the horse in a good balance during the downward transition from canter to walk.
	[Repeat the exercise on both reins]		

NOTES:

EXERCISE 10E

		INSTRUCTIONS	TIPS/DIRECTIVES
1.	C	Down the center line in working canter left.	• Remember to collect the canter before asking for the downward transition to walk at A.
	X	Medium walk.	
	D	Working trot.	• Keep the impulsion through the turn at A and through the A-K corner. If you have plenty of energy in the trot, you'll find it easier to keep the angle and fluency in the shoulder-in.
	A	Track right.	
	K-E	Shoulder-in right.	
			• Ride the corner as though you are about to ride a 10-meter circle. That will give you the correct bend and angle for the shoulder-in.
2.	E	Half 20-meter circle in working trot.	• Use the bend from the half-circle to help position your horse for travers.
	B-F	Travers right.	• Maintain the impulsion so that the position and fluency of the travers is maintained.
	A	Turn right onto the center line	
3.	D	Extended trot.	• In the extended trot, the horse covers the maximum amount of ground he can without hurrying and losing his balance. His fore feet should touch the ground on the spot towards which they're pointing. The movement of the hind and fore legs should reach equally forward in the moment of extension. The whole movement should be spectacular, yet remain balanced and smooth. If your horse lacks experience and balance, don't go for too much ground cover in the extension. Instead, gradually build the stride length.
	G	Working trot.	
	C	Track left.	
	H	Working canter left.	

4. 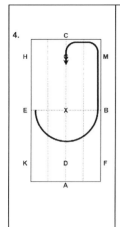	E Half 20-meter circle in working canter. C Turn left onto the center line. [Repeat the exercise on both reins]	• The canter is a pace of 3-beat. It should have 'uphill' cadenced strides, followed by a moment of suspension. • The half circle must be accurate in order to demonstrate that the horse is supple and connected enough to negotiate the movement without losing his balance and rhythm.

NOTES:

....
....
....
....
....
....
....
....
....
....
....
....
....
....
....
....
....
....
....
....
....
....
....

EXERCISE 10F – Make Your Own

	INSTRUCTIONS
1. 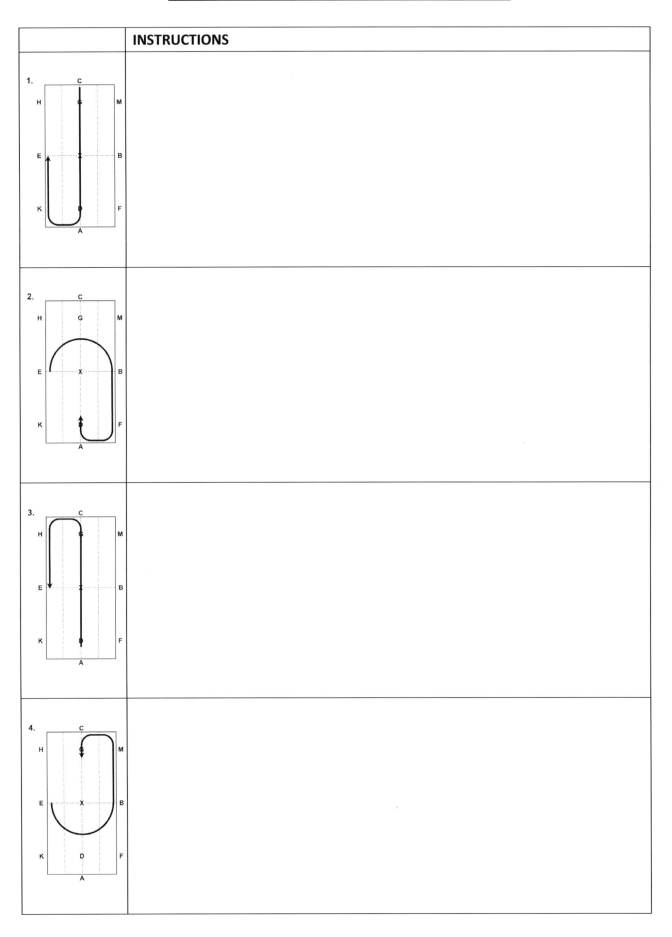	
2.	
3.	
4.	

NOTES:

....

....

....

....

....

....

....

....

....

....

....

....

....

....

....

....

....

....

....

....

....

....

....

....

....

....

....

....

....

....

....

....

EXERCISE 10G – Make Your Own

	INSTRUCTIONS
1.	
2.	
3.	
4.	

NOTES:

EXERCISE 10H – Make Your Own

	INSTRUCTIONS
1.	
2.	
3.	
4.	

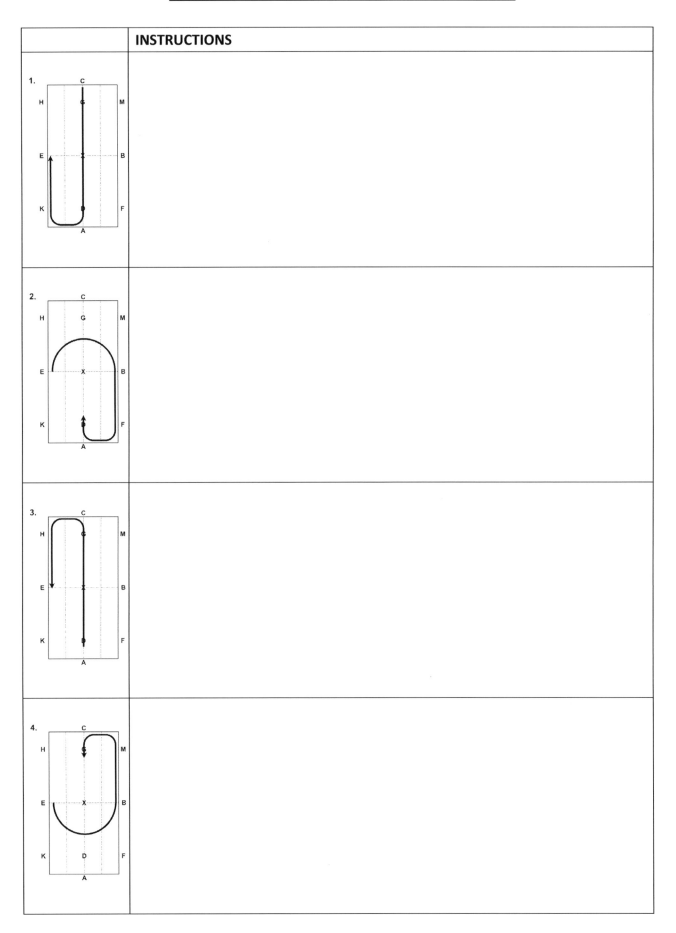

NOTES:

"Acceptance of the bit happens in the hindquarters, not in the mouth."

FLOORPLAN #11

'Around the World'

PRACTICE LOG – Note the dates when you last practiced this floorplan.

#11 'AROUND THE WORLD' - 20X40 DIAGRAMS

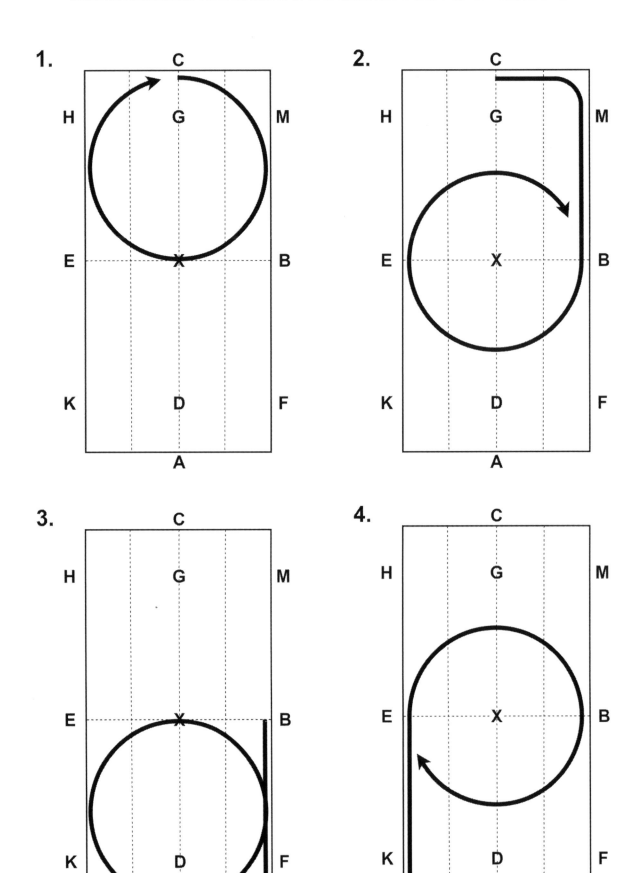

5.

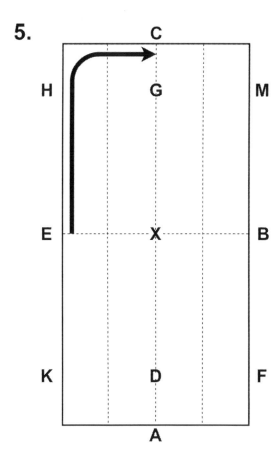

Note that the 20-meter circles at A and C do not go into the corners of the arena. When you ride this exercise make it very clear to distinguish when you are riding a circle, when you are riding a corner, and when you are riding straight.

#11 'AROUND THE WORLD' - 20X60 DIAGRAMS

1.

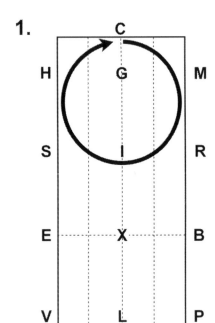

2.

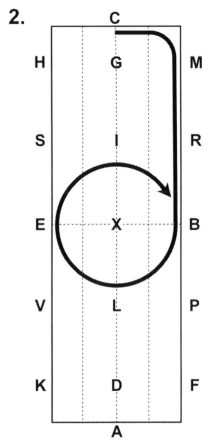

3.

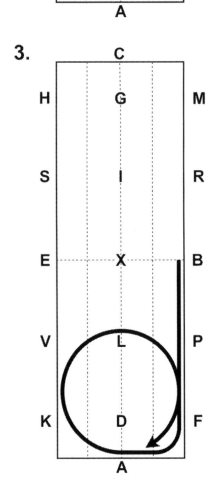

4.

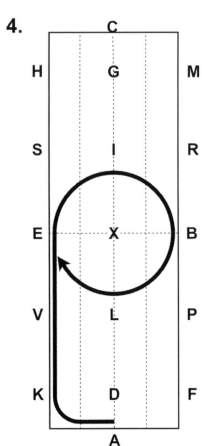

5.

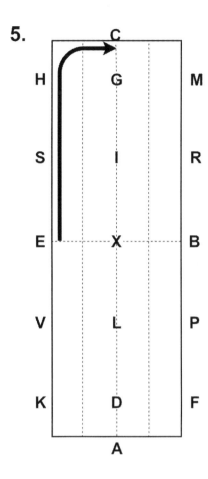

20-meter circles in a 20x60 arena can be a little trickier to ride accurate due to the dimensions and placement of the letters. Study the diagram on page 6 so that you know exactly where to place and center your circle.

EXERCISE 11A

	INSTRUCTIONS	TIPS/DIRECTIVES
1.	[Start on the right rein] C Working trot. 20-meter circle right.	• The horse should be supple enough to be able to negotiate the circle accurately, whilst maintaining his rhythm and balance. He should show an adequate degree of bend without losing his quarters to the outside of the circle. • Your goal is to develop a good, rhythmical and active working trot.
2.	C Medium walk. M Free walk on a long rein. B Medium walk. 20-meter circle right.	• When transitioning to medium walk, ensure that the horse continues to work forwards and doesn't just collapse in a heap! Keep the activity so that the horse then follows the contact forward and down when transitioning to the free walk. • The rhythm during the free walk should remain in a clear four beat, correct sequence, and the horse should clearly over-track, covering maximum ground, and demonstrating complete freedom of his shoulder.
3.	B Working trot. A 20-meter circle right. Over X give and retake the inside rein.	• When riding the circle, keep your hips and shoulders parallel with your horse's shoulders, keep your body upright, and look ahead of you around the circle. • To show a clear give and retake, you must present a visible looping of the rein for a couple of strides. To make the exercise more challenging, give and retake with both reins.

4.	A E	Medium walk. Halt. Immobility 4 seconds. Proceed in medium walk. 20-meter circle right.	• Use the fence line to keep the horse straight in halt. • Count slowly to four in your head to make sure that you maintain the halt for long enough. • When completing the circle there should be no tilting of the horse's head, and your contact should remain still and elastic.
5.	E	Working trot. [Repeat the exercise on both reins]	• During the trot, maintain and active and clear rhythm. If there are any signs of irregularity in the rhythm, or stepping short behind, this can be indicative of tension and stiffness (or injury/accident) and will be penalized during a dressage test.

NOTES:

....
....
....
....
....
....
....
....
....
....
....
....
....
....
....

EXERCISE 11B

	INSTRUCTIONS	TIPS/DIRECTIVES

1.	[Start on the right rein]
	
	C Working canter right.
	     20-meter circle right.
	     Over X give and retake the
	     inside rein.
		• Your goal during the canter is to develop regularity and lightness of the strides, an uphill tendency, and the natural ability of the horse to carry himself whilst maintaining active well-placed hind legs.
		
		• During the give and retake, the horse should remain in the same rhythm and balance and should not speed up or fall onto the forehand. To make the movement more challenging, give and retake both reins.

2.	C Working canter right. B Working trot. 20-meter circle right.	• Ask for the bend as you make the downward transition to trot. That will bring the horse's inside hind leg underneath him, helping him to keep balanced. • During the circle, your horse should continue to work forwards, in a good rhythm, and show a clear uniform bend along his body around the circle.
3.	B/F Transition to walk for one horse's length then proceed in working trot. A 20-meter circle right.	• One horse's length is measured at three to four strides. • Upward transitions should be sharp and crisp. Downward transitions should be balanced and obedient. • The horse should remain in the same outline throughout the whole trot-walk-trot movement, and the trot rhythm and energy following the transition should be the same as it was prior to the walk steps.

4.	A/K	Working canter right.	•	Use the bend around the circle to bring the horse's inside hind leg underneath him to lift his shoulders and improve his balance.
	E	20-meter circle right.	•	Circles are designed to test the horse's balance, suppleness to the bend, and straightness.
5.	E	Proceed in working canter right. [Repeat the exercise on both reins]	•	Maintain the engagement and balance in the canter whilst on the straight side.

NOTES:

....

....

....

....

....

....

....

....

....

....

....

....

....

....

....

....

EXERCISE 11C

		INSTRUCTIONS	TIPS/DIRECTIVES

1.		[Start on the right rein]
		
		C Working trot.
		        Half 20-meter circle to X.
		
		X Working canter right.
		        Half 20-meter circle to C.
			• Make sure the horse is working securely forward into your outside rein when you ask for canter. That will prevent the horse from hollowing through the transition.

2.		C Working canter right. B Half 20-meter circle to E. E Working trot. Half 20-meter circle to B	• Use a half-halt to balance the horse before the downward transition. Keep your leg on into the transition and ride forward into your outside rein to keep the transition balanced and fluent.

3.		B Medium walk.
		
		F Halt. Immobility 4 seconds.
		        Rein-back one horse's length.
		        Proceed in working trot.
		
		A 20-meter circle.
		        Over X give and retake the reins.
			• Whilst in halt, the horse should remain still and relaxed but attentive whilst waiting for his rider's next instruction.
			
			• The rein-back is defined as a rearward movement of diagonal pairs. It has a two-beat rhythm and no moment of suspension. Each pair of legs is raised and returned to the ground alternately, while the horse stays straight and moves on one track.
			
			• During the give and retake, your goal is that the horse does not change his way of going before, during, or after the movement is completed.

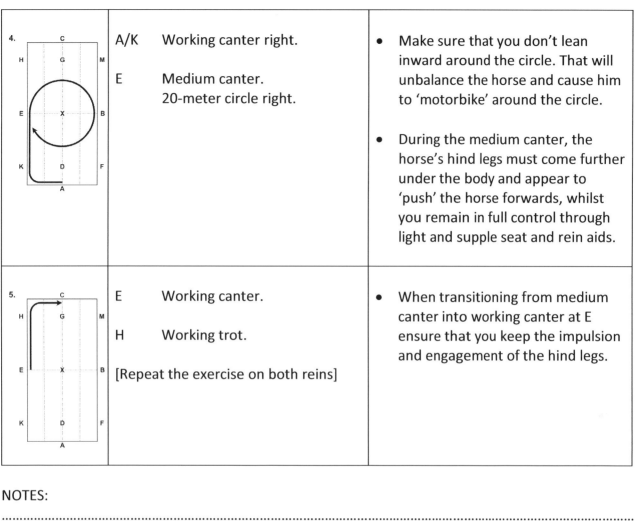

4.	A/K Working canter right. E Medium canter. 20-meter circle right.	• Make sure that you don't lean inward around the circle. That will unbalance the horse and cause him to 'motorbike' around the circle. • During the medium canter, the horse's hind legs must come further under the body and appear to 'push' the horse forwards, whilst you remain in full control through light and supple seat and rein aids.
5.	E Working canter. H Working trot. [Repeat the exercise on both reins]	• When transitioning from medium canter into working canter at E ensure that you keep the impulsion and engagement of the hind legs.

NOTES:

....
....
....
....
....
....
....
....
....
....
....
....
....
....
....

EXERCISE 11D

	INSTRUCTIONS	TIPS/DIRECTIVES

1.	[Start on the right rein]
	
	C Working canter right.
	      20-meter circle right.
	      Over X, give and retake both
	      reins.
		• During the circles you are expected to have even bend (think of an imaginary line) through the horse's body; from the tail, centrally through the hindquarters, through the back and shoulders, through the neck, and finishing at the poll.
		
		• Before the give and retake, use a half-halt to balance the horse.
		
		• During the give and retake there should be a visible loop in the reins for a couple strides.

2.	C Collected canter. B Working trot. 20-meter circle right.	• The shorter, higher steps of collected canter are the result of horse carrying more of the weight towards its haunches. Shortening the strides artificially will result in stiffening and loss of activity, which is exactly what judges do not want to see. • Take up a slight shoulder-fore position before the downward transition to working trot to engage the horse's hind legs and to help keep his balance.
3.	B Extended walk. F Medium walk. A Walk to working canter right 20-meter circle right.	• When riding extended walk, keep your leg on and allow the horse freedom of his neck and shoulder. Don't allow too much rein though or the poll will come too low. • Keep the hind legs active and engaged in the medium walk ready for the transition to canter.

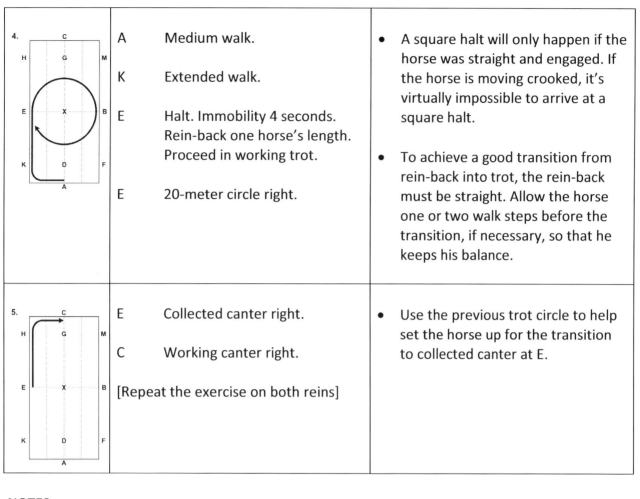

4.	A	Medium walk.	• A square halt will only happen if the horse was straight and engaged. If the horse is moving crooked, it's virtually impossible to arrive at a square halt.
	K	Extended walk.	
	E	Halt. Immobility 4 seconds. Rein-back one horse's length. Proceed in working trot.	• To achieve a good transition from rein-back into trot, the rein-back must be straight. Allow the horse one or two walk steps before the transition, if necessary, so that he keeps his balance.
	E	20-meter circle right.	
5.	E	Collected canter right.	• Use the previous trot circle to help set the horse up for the transition to collected canter at E.
	C	Working canter right.	
		[Repeat the exercise on both reins]	

NOTES:

....

....

....

....

....

....

....

....

....

....

....

....

....

....

EXERCISE 11E

	INSTRUCTIONS	TIPS/DIRECTIVES
1.	[Start on the right rein] C Working trot. 20-meter circle right.	• When riding the circle, remember that your inside leg on the girth keeps the impulsion, develops the engagement of the inside hind leg, and asks for bend. Your outside leg should be slightly behind the girth preventing the hindquarters from escaping to the outside of the circle and generating some forward movement.
2.	C Working trot. M/B Working canter left (counter canter). B 20-meter circle right in working canter left.	• When asking for left canter on the right rein, ask for a little left flexion for the desired leading leg, but no more that what would be asked for true canter. • When riding counter canter on a large circle, ensure you maintain a good riding position – keep your weight onto your left seat bone and your right leg slightly behind the girth to protect the hindquarters from swinging out.

3.	B Working canter left.
	
	F Medium walk.
	
	A Working canter right.
	       20-meter circle.
	       Over X, give and retake both reins.
		• Use your back, core, and seat to hold the horse in a good balance during the downward transition from canter to walk.
		
		• Keep the walk active and engaged to help ensure a smooth and obedient transition into working canter at A.
		
		• When you relinquish your rein contact in a give and retake there should be no change in your horse's outline, speed, size of stride, balance, or alignment to the figure.

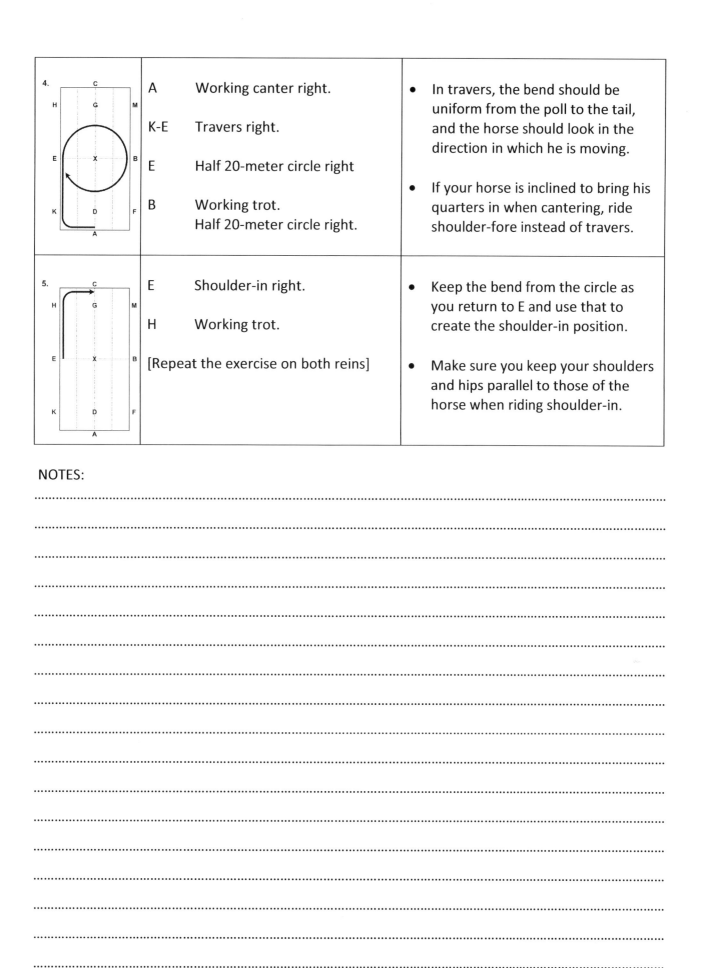

4.	A	Working canter right.	• In travers, the bend should be uniform from the poll to the tail, and the horse should look in the direction in which he is moving.
	K-E	Travers right.	
	E	Half 20-meter circle right	
	B	Working trot. Half 20-meter circle right.	• If your horse is inclined to bring his quarters in when cantering, ride shoulder-fore instead of travers.
5.	E	Shoulder-in right.	• Keep the bend from the circle as you return to E and use that to create the shoulder-in position.
	H	Working trot.	
		[Repeat the exercise on both reins]	• Make sure you keep your shoulders and hips parallel to those of the horse when riding shoulder-in.

NOTES:

....

....

....

....

....

....

....

....

....

....

....

....

....

....

....

....

....

....

EXERCISE 11F – Make Your Own

	INSTRUCTIONS
1.	
2.	
3.	
4.	

5.

NOTES:

....

....

....

....

....

....

....

....

....

....

....

....

....

....

....

....

....

....

....

....

....

....

....

....

....

EXERCISE 11G – Make Your Own

	INSTRUCTIONS
1.	
2.	
3.	
4.	

5.

NOTES:

....

....

....

....

....

....

....

....

....

....

....

....

....

....

....

....

....

....

....

....

....

....

....

....

....

EXERCISE 11H – Make Your Own

	INSTRUCTIONS
1.	
2.	
3.	
4.	

5.

C
H G M
E X B
K D F
A

NOTES:

....
....
....
....
....
....
....
....
....
....
....
....
....
....
....
....
....
....
....
....
....
....
....

"You are only in competition with yourself."

FLOORPLAN #12

'Straight as a Die'

PRACTICE LOG – Note the dates when you last practiced this floorplan.

#12 'STRAIGHT AS A DIE' - 20X40 DIAGRAMS

1.

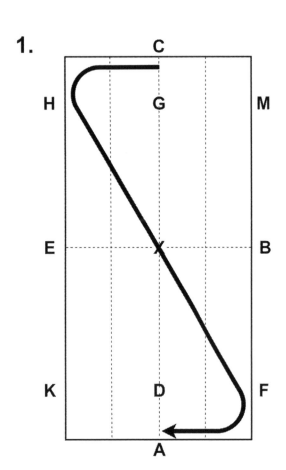

2.

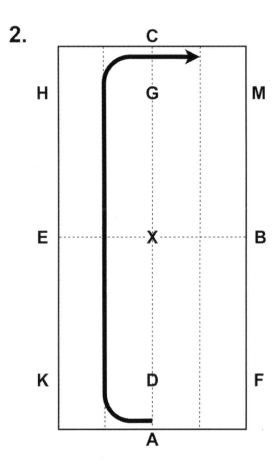

3.

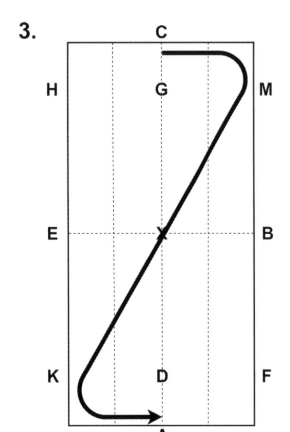

4.

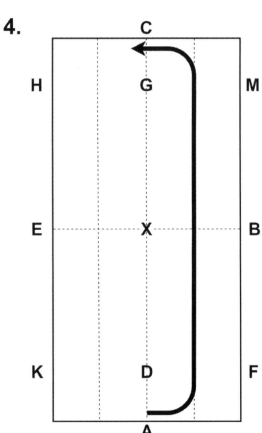

#12 'STRAIGHT AS A DIE' - 20X40 DIAGRAMS

1.

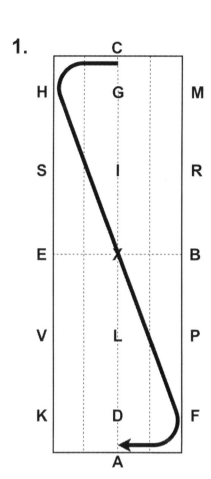

2.

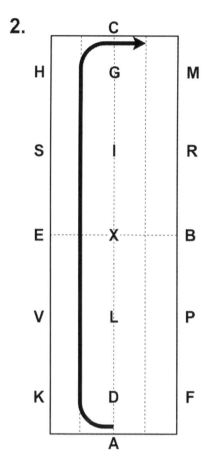

3.

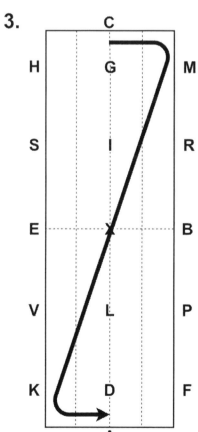

4.

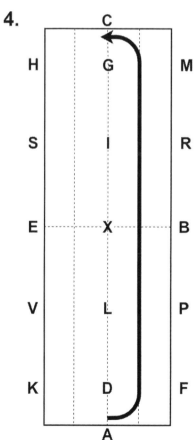

EXERCISE 12A

	INSTRUCTIONS	TIPS/DIRECTIVES
1.	[Start on the left rein] C Working trot. HXF Working trot. F Medium Walk. A Working trot.	• Your goal is to develop a good, rhythmical and active working trot. • As you change the rein HXF, remember to change the horse's flexion. This will help you to ride the horse into the outside rein before the corner, keeping him balanced and supple to the bend ready for your downwards transition to medium walk at F.
2.	A Turn right on to the ¾ line and proceed in working trot. C Medium walk.	• Remember that the ¾ line is half-way between the center line and the outside track. As you transition to working trot at A, you should be looking for this line to make sure you don't overshoot it. • Pick something to focus on at the C end of the arena, and ride forward toward it. This will help you keep the horse straight. Horses that are dawdling behind their riders' leg are far more likely to wander.
3.	MXK Free walk on a long rein. K Medium walk. A Working trot.	• In free walk, allow the horse to gradually take the bit forward, round, and down. Keep the horse straight and marching forward. • The transition from free walk back to medium walk should be smooth, with no loss of rhythm or signs of tension.

4. 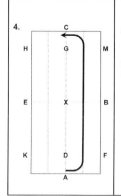	A Turn left onto the ¾ line. [Repeat exercise on both reins]	• On the ¾ line the horse's poll should be the highest point, and the contact should be quiet, elastic and steady, without any tilting or swinging of the horse's head. He should travel forwards and straight, as though he is on railway tracks.

NOTES:

....

....

....

....

....

....

....

....

....

....

....

....

....

....

....

....

....

....

....

....

....

....

....

....

EXERCISE 12B

	INSTRUCTIONS	TIPS/DIRECTIVES
1.	[Start on the left rein] C — Working trot. C/H — Working canter left. HXF — Working canter. F — Working trot.	• If it's difficult for your horse to maintain a balanced canter all the way to F, ride a transition to working trot over X. As the balance improves, you can go a bit further each time before transitioning to trot.
2.	A — Turn right onto the ¾ line. C — Medium walk.	• Pick something to focus on at the C end of the arena, and ride forward toward it. This will help you keep the horse straight. • When joining the track, get ready for the transition to medium walk at C. Use the corner as you come off the ¾ line to help encourage the horse to step under with his hind legs to help create a forward downwards transition.
3.	MXK — Free walk on a long rein. K — Medium walk. A — Halt. Immobility 4 seconds.	• In the free walk, although the horse is relaxed, he should march purposefully forward and look as though he is 'going somewhere'. • The transition from free walk back to medium walk should be smooth, with no loss of rhythm or signs of tension. • It's important to 'think forward' when riding into the halt. If you just close the reins and fail to use enough leg, the horse will lose engagement as he halts. The halt will become unbalanced, and he will probably not be square behind.

| 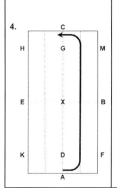 4. | A | Working trot.

Turn left on the ¾ line and show some medium trot strides.

[Repeat the exercise on both reins] | • | Don't fire your horse straight into a full-bore medium trot! Ask him to gradually lengthen his stride, and then come back to working trot. This will prevent the horse from losing his balance, which could affect the regularity of the trot. |

NOTES:

....

....

....

....

....

....

....

....

....

....

....

....

....

....

....

....

....

....

....

....

....

....

....

....

EXERCISE 12C

	INSTRUCTIONS	TIPS/DIRECTIVES
1.	[Start on the left rein] C Working trot. HXF Medium trot. F Working trot. A Halt. Immobility 4 seconds. Rein-back one horse's length. Proceed in working trot.	• Change your horse's flexion and your diagonal either before you ask for medium trot, or after. Don't try to do it during the medium trot as this can upset your horse's balance. • Make sure that the halt is square before asking for rein-back. Keep both legs on and be ready to catch the quarters if they swing to the inside.
2.	A Turn right onto the ¾ line. Show some medium trot strides. Transition to working trot before reaching the track.	• Remember that the ¾ line is half-way between the center line and the outside track. As you transition to working trot after the rein-back, you should be looking for this line to make sure you don't overshoot it. • The preparation for the medium trot is the most important part of the movement. If your horse is not balanced and engaged, he will fall onto his forehand, break into canter or lose the rhythm as he attempts to lengthen his stride.
3.	C/M Working canter right. MXK Show some medium canter strides. K Working trot. A Medium walk.	• Gradually build the canter stride length. If you go for too much, your horse will lose his balance and may fall onto his forehand. A few good strides are better than lots of unbalanced ones. • When transitioning to medium walk, ensure that the horse continues to work forwards and doesn't just collapse in a heap!

| 4. 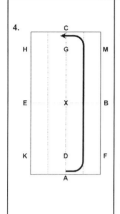 | A | Turn left onto the ¾ line.

Free walk on a long rein.

Medium walk before reaching the track. | • Keep your horse marching forward in the free walk. If the horse drops behind your leg, he will probably wander off the ¾ line. Maintain a light contact, and ride from both legs into both reins to keep the horse focused and straight. |
| | C | Working trot.

[Repeat the exercise on both reins] | • When transitioning to medium walk, slowly shorten the reins over a few strides to keep the horse relaxed and prevent him from jogging. |

NOTES:

....
....
....
....
....
....
....
....
....
....
....
....
....
....
....
....
....
....
....
....

EXERCISE 12D

	INSTRUCTIONS	TIPS/DIRECTIVES

1.	[Start on the left rein]
	
	C Halt. Immobility 4 seconds.
	      Rein-back one horse's length.
	      Proceed in medium walk.
	
	C Walk to working canter left.
	
	HXF Working canter.
	
	F Simple change.
		• The horse should stay relaxed and calm during the rein-back. There should be no resistance to the contact, and he shouldn't rush backwards or lose his rhythm.
		
		• Make sure the horse is marching forward in medium walk before you ask for canter. For training purposes, you may want to give yourself a few more walk strides and ask for the transition after C to ensure a uphill and balanced transition.
		
		• Keep the canter engaged across the diagonal and use your half-halts before transitioning to walk during the simple change.
		
		• When riding the simple change, maintain the relaxation and the clarity of the walk steps.

2.	A Turn right onto the ¾ line.
	
	      Medium canter.
	
	      Working canter before reaching the track.
	
	C Working trot.
		• Although the medium canter should cover more ground than a working canter, it should also clearly demonstrate an uphill tendency.
		
		• Use the corner at the C end of the arena to engage the horse's hind legs during the canter ready for the downward transition to working trot at C. This will encourage the horse to step through into the working trot, rather than 'fall' out of the canter.

3. 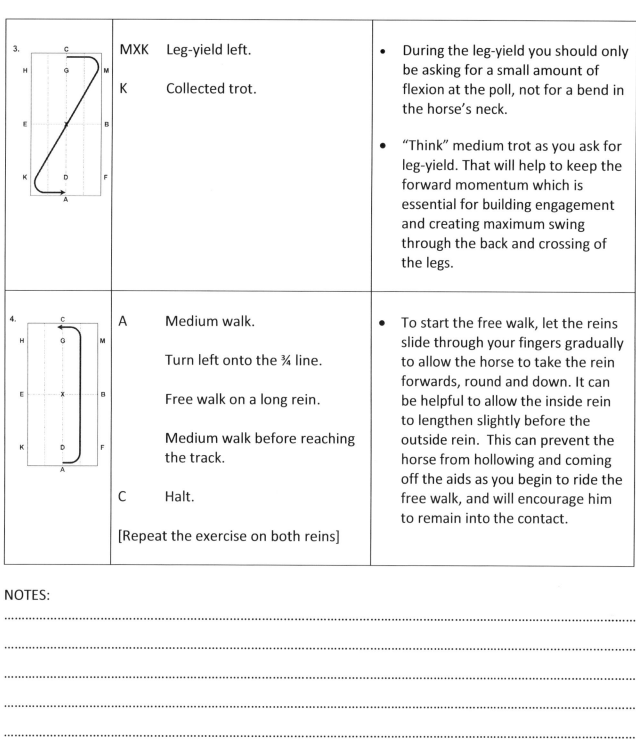	**MXK** Leg-yield left. **K** Collected trot.	• During the leg-yield you should only be asking for a small amount of flexion at the poll, not for a bend in the horse's neck. • "Think" medium trot as you ask for leg-yield. That will help to keep the forward momentum which is essential for building engagement and creating maximum swing through the back and crossing of the legs.
4.	**A** Medium walk. Turn left onto the ¾ line. Free walk on a long rein. Medium walk before reaching the track. **C** Halt. [Repeat the exercise on both reins]	• To start the free walk, let the reins slide through your fingers gradually to allow the horse to take the rein forwards, round and down. It can be helpful to allow the inside rein to lengthen slightly before the outside rein. This can prevent the horse from hollowing and coming off the aids as you begin to ride the free walk, and will encourage him to remain into the contact.

NOTES:

....

....

....

....

....

....

....

....

....

....

....

....

EXERCISE 12E

	INSTRUCTIONS	TIPS/DIRECTIVES
1.	[Start on the left rein] C Working trot. HXF Trot half-pass left. F Medium walk. A Walk to working canter right.	• Use the C/H corner to establish the correct bend for the half-pass. • Riding a smart walk to canter transition involves having an energized walk, knowledge of the correct aids, and asking for canter in the appropriate moment.
2.	A Turn right onto the ¾ line. Proceed in working canter.	• Remember that the ¾ line is half-way between the center line and the outside track. As you transition walk to canter at A, you should be looking for this line to make sure you don't overshoot it. • Your goal during the canter is to develop regularity and lightness of the strides, and an uphill tendency.
3.	MXK Canter half-pass right. K Working trot. A Medium walk.	• Use the C/M corner to establish the correct bend for the half-pass. • During the half-pass, the canter should not change, in terms of energy, elasticity and suspension, nor should the rhythm vary.

4.	A Turn left on the ¾ line.
	
	    Extended walk.
	
	    Medium walk before reaching the track.
	
	C Working trot
	
	[Repeat the exercise on both reins]
		• In extended walk, allow the horse complete freedom to stretch to the bit and open his shoulders. But don't give away the rein completely or the poll will drop too low and the extension will morph into a free walk!

NOTES:

EXERCISE 12F – Make Your Own

	INSTRUCTIONS
1.	
2.	
3.	
4.	

NOTES:

EXERCISE 12G – Make Your Own

	INSTRUCTIONS
1. 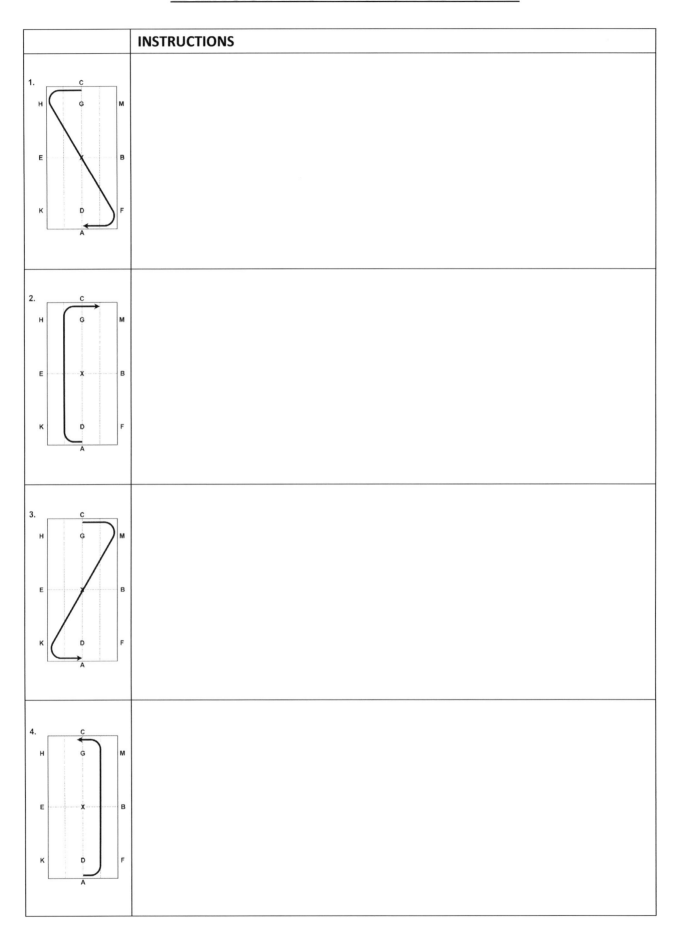	
2.	
3.	
4.	

NOTES:

EXERCISE 12H – Make Your Own

	INSTRUCTIONS
1. 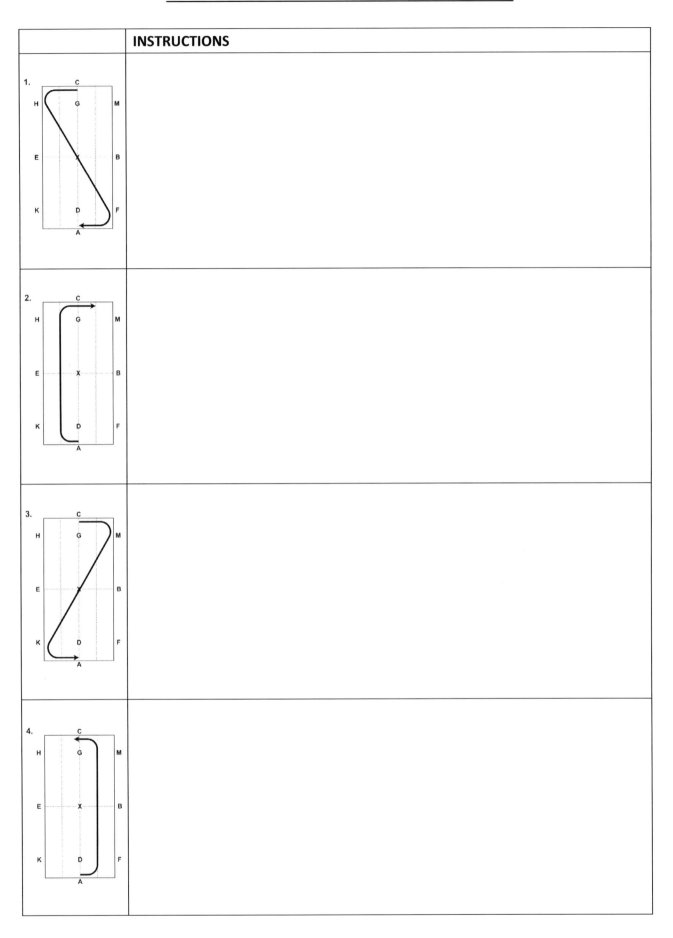	
2.	
3.	
4.	

NOTES:

"Talent without discipline is like an octopus on roller skates. There's plenty of movement, but you never know if it's going to be forwards, backwards, or sideways."

FLOORPLAN #13
'Half-an-Hour Glass'

PRACTICE LOG – Note the dates when you last practiced this floorplan.

....
....
....
....
....
....
....
....
....
....
....
....
....
....
....
....
....
....
....
....
....

#13 'HALF-AN-HOUR GLASS' - 20X40 DIAGRAMS

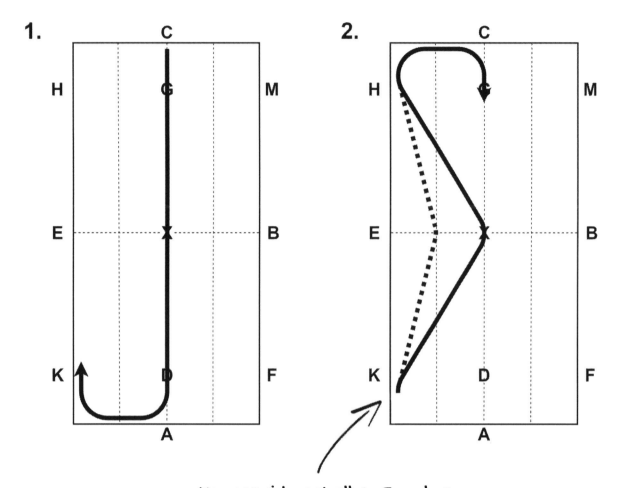

You can ride a shallow 5-meter
loop to the ¾ line, or a deeper
10-meter loop to the center line.

#13 'HALF-AN-HOUR GLASS' 20X60 DIAGRAMS

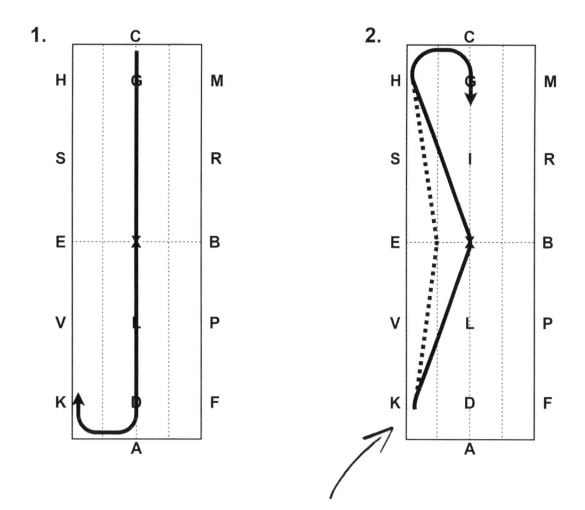

1.

2.

Note that a 10-meter loop in a long arena doesn't ride as deep as in a short arena. This is because the loop is spread out over 60-meters, rather than 40-meters.

EXERCISE 13A

	INSTRUCTIONS	TIPS/DIRECTIVES
1.	[Start on any rein] C Proceed down the center line in working trot. X Medium walk. D Working trot. A Track right.	• Ride your horse forward (not faster) to keep him straight. Riding forward will encourage the horse to step underneath in the transitions too. • Keep the horse's natural rhythm throughout the walk and the trot. This will help your horse maintain balance and fluency.
2.	K 5-meter loop to finish at H. C Turn right onto the center line. [Repeat the exercise on both reins]	• A 5-meter loop should touch the ¾ line, half-way between E and X. • The loop should be a series of gradual curves and changes of bend, not a straight line to a sharp turn.

NOTES:

....
....
....
....
....
....
....
....
....
....
....
....
....

EXERCISE 13B

	INSTRUCTIONS	TIPS/DIRECTIVES
1.	[Start on any rein] C Proceed down the center line in working trot. X Halt. Immobility 4 seconds Proceed in medium walk. D Working trot. A Track right.	• It's important 'think forward' when riding into halt, otherwise the horse will lose engagement. The halt will become unbalanced and the horse may come against the contact. • During the immobility, the horse should remain relaxed but attentive whilst waiting for the next instruction.
2.	K 5-meter loop finishing at H. C Turn right onto the center line. [Repeat the exercise on both reins]	• A 5-meter loop should touch the ¾ line, half-way between E and X. • When riding the loop, do not allow your horse to cling to the track and drift past the marker; you should be leaving the track by the time your own body passes K.

NOTES:

....

....

....

....

....

....

....

....

....

....

....

....

EXERCISE 13C

	INSTRUCTIONS	TIPS/DIRECTIVES
1.	[Start on any rein] C Working trot. G Medium trot. D Working trot. A Track right.	• Medium trot is a pace of moderate lengthening. Whilst maintaining a round frame and working over his back to the contact, the horse should clearly lengthen his stride to cover more ground. • Although your horse should be working with good impulsion during the medium trot, he should not hurry or lose rhythm and must remain in a good uphill balance.
2.	K 10-meter loop finishing at H. C Turn right onto the center line. [Repeat the exercise on both reins]	• A 10-meter loop should touch X. • If you're in a 20x40 arena, you'll need to ride deep into the AK corner to give yourself enough room to get to X. If the corner is ridden too shallow, you won't have enough room to ride the 10-meter loop accurately.

NOTES:

....

....

....

....

....

....

....

....

....

....

....

EXERCISE 13D

	INSTRUCTIONS	TIPS/DIRECTIVES
1.	[Start on any rein] C Working trot. G Extended walk. X Halt. Immobility 4 seconds. Proceed in working trot. A Track right.	• When riding extended walk, allow the horse to lengthen his frame but keep a contact on both reins and don't allow the horse to drop his poll too low. • Remember to use your half-halts to collect the extended walk a few steps before the halt. • Your horse should be straight, square, attentive, relaxed and immobile during the halt, and the move-off should be immediate and obedient.
2.	K-X Leg yield right. X-H Leg yield left. H Working trot. C Turn right onto the center line [Repeat the exercise on both reins]	• After the A/K corner, ride one straight stride before you ask the horse to move sideways away from your leg. • When you reach X, make the horse straight for one stride and change the flexion before asking the horse to leg-yield in the opposite direction.

NOTES:

....

....

....

....

....

....

....

....

....

EXERCISE 13E

	INSTRUCTIONS	TIPS/DIRECTIVES
1. 	[Start on any rein] C Collected canter right. D Working canter. A Track right	• Collection in the canter should be thought of as a rebalancing of the weight carriage towards the haunches, and NOT as a shortening of the stride. • The rhythm should remain the same throughout the whole center line, and the horse should not slow down or anticipate halting.
2. 	K 5-meter loop in working canter right to finish at H. C Turn right down the center line. [Repeat the exercise on both reins]	• This exercise introduces the beginnings of counter-canter. • You can increase the difficulty of this exercise by riding a 10-meter loop instead of a 5-meter loop.

NOTES:

....

....

....

....

....

....

....

....

....

....

....

....

....

EXERCISE 13F – Make Your Own

	INSTRUCTIONS
1.	- 213 -
2.	

NOTES:

....

....

....

....

....

....

....

....

....

....

EXERCISE 13G – Make Your Own

	INSTRUCTIONS
1. C H ⊙ M E ⋯⋯⋯ B K ↑ F A	
2. C H ↓ M E ⋯⋯⋯ B K D F A	

NOTES:

....

....

....

....

....

....

....

....

....

....

EXERCISE 13H – Make Your Own

	INSTRUCTIONS
1.	
2.	

NOTES:

....

....

....

....

....

....

....

....

....

"There are many different types of bits for many different disciplines, but the severity of all bits lies in the hands of who's holding them."

FLOORPLAN #14

'The Boomerang'

PRACTICE LOG – Note the dates when you last practiced this floorplan.

....

....

....

....

....

....

....

....

....

....

....

....

....

....

....

....

....

....

....

....

....

....

#14 'THE BOOMERANG' - 20X40 DIAGRAMS

1.

2.

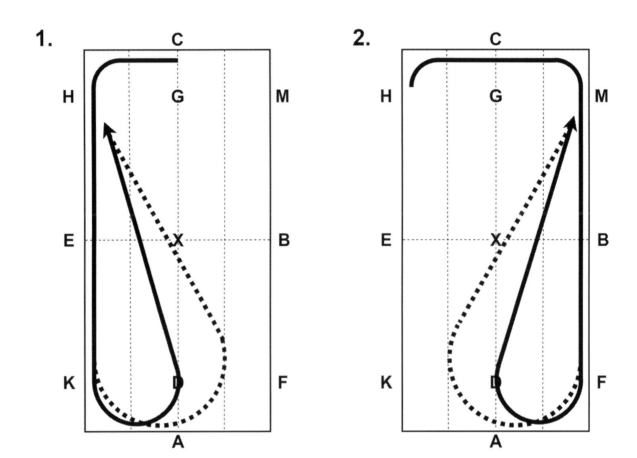

#14 'THE BOOMERANG' - 20X60 DIAGRAMS

1.

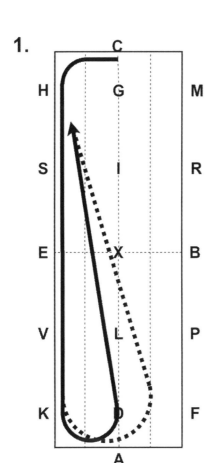

2.

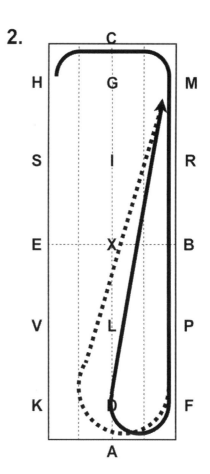

Hi there! We hope you're having
fun trying out some of our
dressage exercises and floorplans!

EXERCISE 14A

	INSTRUCTIONS	TIPS/DIRECTIVES
1.	[Start on the left rein] C Working trot. E Halt. Immobility 4 seconds. Proceed in working trot. K Half 15-meter circle left then re-join the track at H.	• It's important 'think forward' when riding into halt, otherwise the horse will lose engagement. The halt will become unbalanced and the horse may come against the contact. • The 15-meter circle must be accurate in order to demonstrate that the horse is supple and connected enough to negotiate the movement without losing his balance and rhythm.
2.	H Medium walk. M-F Free walk on a long rein. F Medium walk. Half 10-meter circle right. D-M Working trot. [Repeat the exercise on both reins]	• Any tension during the walk may disrupt the rhythm and regularity of the steps, so you should prioritize relaxation in the walk. • A 10-meter circle is quite a small diameter, so it is your job to choose exactly the right tempo (speed of the rhythm), to enable the horse to manage the rhythm and bend without any disturbances or unevenness to the stride length.

NOTES:

....

....

....

....

....

....

....

....

....

....

EXERCISE 14B

	INSTRUCTIONS	TIPS/DIRECTIVES
1.	[Start on the left rein] C Working canter left. K Half 15-meter circle left, then rejoin the track at H, working trot before X.	• The canter is a pace of 3-beat. It should have 'uphill' cadenced strides, followed by a moment of suspension. If the moment of suspension appears only very briefly, or worse, is missing, the beat becomes that of 4-time which is a serious fault and will be heavily penalized in the competitive environment. • Use half-halts to bring the hind legs more underneath the horse and to help balance him for the downward transition to working trot.
2.	H Working trot. C Medium walk. M Working trot. F Half 10-meter circle right. D-M Working trot. M/C Working canter left. [Repeat the exercise on both reins]	• During the half circle, your horse should continue to work forwards, in a good rhythm, and show a clear uniform bend along his body around the circle. • When riding the trot-canter transition, emphasis should be on the horse pushing from the hind legs that are placed under the body rather than launching off the shoulders.

NOTES:

....

....

....

....

....

....

....

....

EXERCISE 14C

	INSTRUCTIONS	TIPS/DIRECTIVES
1. *(arena diagram)*	[Start on the left rein] C Working trot. E Halt. Immobility 4 seconds. Rein-back one horse's length. Proceed in working trot. K Half 10-meter circle. D-H Medium trot.	• Use the fence line to keep the horse straight in the halt. • The rein-back is defined as a rearward movement of diagonal pairs. It has a two-beat rhythm and no moment of suspension. Each pair of legs is raised and returned to the ground alternately, while the horse stays straight and moves on one track. • Keep the impulsion in the half 10-meter circle and encourage the horse to step further under with his hind legs ready for the medium trot.
2. *(arena diagram)*	H Working trot. C/M Working canter right. M-F Medium canter. F Working canter. Half circle right 15-meters and re-join the track at M with a transition to trot after X. [Repeat the exercise on both reins]	• Be careful not to rush the horse in the medium canter and push him onto his forehand. Keep the rhythm, engagement, and uphill tendency during the extended strides. • Half-halt before the transition into working trot to help get a smooth transition rather then the horse 'breaking' from the canter to the trot.

NOTES:

....

....

....

....

....

....

....

EXERCISE 14D

	INSTRUCTIONS	TIPS/DIRECTIVES
1. 	[Start on the left rein] C Working trot. H Medium trot. K Working trot. Half 10-meter circle. D Leg-yield left to H in working trot. *(OR leg-yield to E if you are in a long arena and/or want more sideways movement)*	• During the medium trot the horse's frame should lengthen so that he carries his head slightly in front of the vertical. • As you come around the half circle to D, remember to ride straight for a stride and change the horse's flexion before you ask for leg-yield. • During the leg-yield, the horse should move forwards and sideways on two tracks. His body should remain straight, and there should be a slight flexion of his head and neck away from the direction of travel.
2. 	H/C Working canter right. M Medium canter. F Working canter. Half 15-meter circle then re-join the track at M. M Working trot [Repeat the exercise on both reins]	• The medium canter is a longer version of the working canter. It covers more ground because the horse's frame and strides lengthen. • When riding the medium canter, maintain the regularity and lightness of the canter strides • Maintain the engagement in the working canter as you ride along the diagonal line.

NOTES:

....

....

....

....

....

....

....

EXERCISE 14E

	INSTRUCTIONS	TIPS/DIRECTIVES
1.	[Start on the left rein] C Working trot. H-E Shoulder-in left. E-K Working trot. K Collected canter left. Half 10-meter circle left. D-H Working canter left.	• Use the C/H corner to set up the correct bend and angle for the shoulder-in. • Make sure you keep your shoulders and hips parallel to those of the horse when riding shoulder-in. • Remember that the degree of collection required in the canter is only so much as to be able to perform the half 10-meter circle with ease.

2.	HMF Counter-canter.
	
	F Simple change to collected canter right.
	   Half 10-meter circle right.
	
	D Canter half-pass right to M.
	   (OR half-pass to B if you are in a long arena and/or want more sideways movement)
	
	M Working trot.
	
	[Repeat the exercise on both reins]
		• In counter-canter, maintain a slight flexion. Don't ask for too much neck bend, as that will cause the horse to fall in through his shoulder.
		
		• When riding the simple change, maintain relaxation in the walk and the clarity of the walk steps.
		
		• Create the correct bend and angle for the half-pass as you ride the half 10-meter circle.
		
		• Keep the impulsion in the half-pass to achieve maximum fluency and elasticity in the steps.

NOTES:

....

....

....

....

....

....

....

EXERCISE 14F – Make Your Own

	INSTRUCTIONS
1.	
2.	

NOTES:

....

....

....

....

....

....

....

....

....

....

EXERCISE 14G – Make Your Own

	INSTRUCTIONS
1. 	
2. 	

NOTES:

....

....

....

....

....

....

....

....

....

....

EXERCISE 14H – Make Your Own

	INSTRUCTIONS
1.	
2.	

NOTES:

....

....

....

....

....

....

....

....

....

....

"Fix it forward."

FLOORPLAN #15

'Snake: Level 1'

PRACTICE LOG – Note the dates when you last practiced this floorplan.

#15 'SNAKE: LEVEL 1' - 20X40 DIAGRAMS

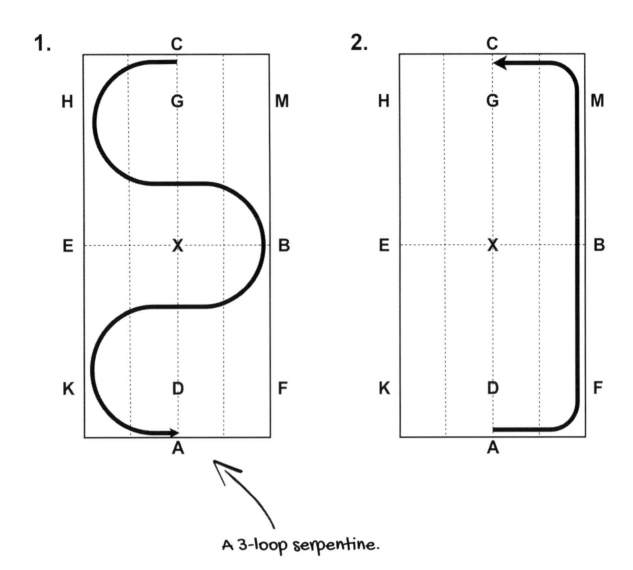

1.

A 3-loop serpentine.

2.

The length of a small arena is 40-meters, therefore, your half circles need to be just a little bigger than 13-meters in diameter.

...But since 13-meters is hard to gauge, just imagine dividing the arena into three equal parts.

#15 'SNAKE: LEVEL 1' - 20X60 DIAGRAMS

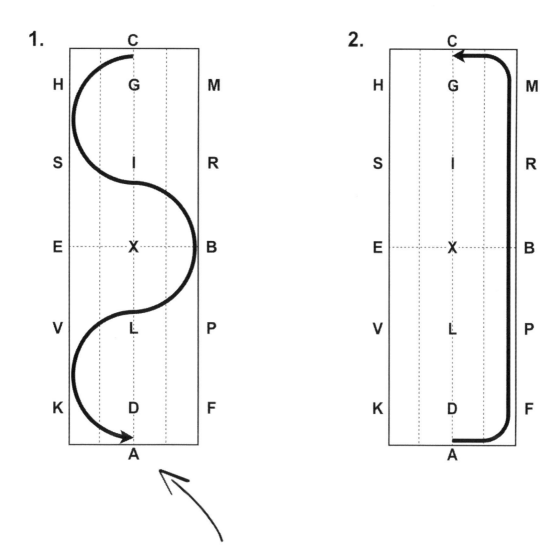

The length of a long arena is 60-meters, therefore, your three half-circles need to be 20-meters in diameters.

EXERCISE 15A

	INSTRUCTIONS	TIPS/DIRECTIVES

1.	[Start on the left rein]
	
	C Working trot.
	      3-loop serpentine to finish
	      at A.
		• Change your diagonal and horse's bend when crossing the center line.
		
		• Keep looking up and around your turns to ensure that you ride an accurate serpentine with all half-circles the same size.

2.	A Working trot. F Medium walk. B Working trot. [Repeat the exercise on both reins]	• When transitioning to medium walk, ensure that the horse continues to work forwards and doesn't just collapse in a heap! • Any tension during the walk may disrupt the rhythm and regularity of the steps, so you should prioritize relaxation in the walk.

NOTES:

....

....

....

....

....

....

....

....

....

....

....

....

....

EXERCISE 15B

	INSTRUCTIONS	TIPS/DIRECTIVES

1.	[Start on the left rein]
	
	C Working trot.
	        3-loop serpentine to finish
	        at A.
	
	        Each time you cross the center
	        line ride a transition to
	        medium walk for 3-4 steps
	        then proceed in working trot.
		• Keep the horse working forwards during the downwards transition and into a purposeful walk. This will help ensure that you have an obedient and forward-thinking transition back to working trot.
		
		• Change your horse's and bend and flexion during the walk steps and establish a new outside rein ready for the next loop of the serpentine.

2.	A Halt. Immobility 4 seconds. Proceed in working trot. B Medium walk. M Working trot. [Repeat the exercise on both reins]	• More advanced horses should be able to step smoothly into and out of the halt directly without losing balance and frame. If your horse is less experienced, allow him a step or two of walk to help him remain in balance and prevent him coming against the hand.

NOTES:

....

....

....

....

....

....

....

....

....

....

....

....

EXERCISE 15C

	INSTRUCTIONS	TIPS/DIRECTIVES

1.	[Start on the left rein]
	
	C Working trot.
	       3-loop serpentine to finish
	       at A.
	
	       When crossing the center line
	       for the first time, halt.
	       Immobility 4 seconds.
	       Proceed in working trot.
	
	       When crossing the center line
	       for the second time, ride a
	       transition to medium walk for
	       3-4 steps then proceed in
	       working trot.
		• Before you ride the transition to halt over the center line, make sure your horse is straight. Otherwise, you could end up with a very crooked halt.
		
		• If your horse begins to step backwards during the halt, ride forwards immediately. Ride the halt again and ease your hand as you do so. Be positive with your legs and keep thinking forwards.
		
		• During the trot-walk-trot movement, make sure you are accurate, ride forwards and keep your horse reactive to your aids

2.	F Medium trot. M Working trot. [Repeat the exercise on both reins]	• The transitions from working trot to medium trot and back to working trot should be balanced, fluent, and clear. • During the medium trot, the horse should lengthen his stride to cover more ground. The horse's frame should also lengthen so that he carries his head slightly in front of the vertical.

NOTES:

....

....

....

....

....

....

....

....

EXERCISE 15D

	INSTRUCTIONS	TIPS/DIRECTIVES

1.	[Start on the left rein]
	
	C Working canter left.
	      3-loop serpentine to finish
	      at A.
	
	When crossing the center line for the first time, ride a change of lead through trot.
	
	When crossing the center line for the second time, ride a simple change (canter-walk-canter)
	
	Proceed in working canter.
		• Before you ride the transitions over the center line, make sure that the horse is straight.
		
		• In the change of lead through trot, ride the downward transition forward and remember to change the flexion over 2-3 trot strides before asking for the transition back into canter.
		
		• When riding the simple change, maintain the relaxation and the clarity of the walk steps.

2.	F Medium canter. M Working canter. [Repeat the exercise on both reins]	• During the medium canter, the horse's hind legs must come further under the body and appear to 'push' the horse forwards, whilst you remain in full control through light and supple seat and rein aids.

NOTES:

....

....

....

....

....

....

....

....

....

....

EXERCISE 15E

	INSTRUCTIONS	TIPS/DIRECTIVES

1.	[Start on the left rein]
	
	C Working canter left.
	      3-loop serpentine to finish
	      at A.
	
	      Stay on the left canter lead and
	      ride counter-canter for your
	      middle loop next to B.
		• If you are riding in a small arena, you can make your middle half-circle larger to help make it easier for your horse to maintain balance in counter-canter.
		
		• During the counter-canter, maintain a little flexion over the leading leg, but no more than what is asked in true canter.

2.	A Medium walk. F Extended walk. B Medium walk. B/M Walk to working canter left. [Repeat the exercise on both reins]	• Collect the canter before asking for the transition to medium walk at A. Think of the canter becoming more elevated rather than covering ground. • Walk to canter on a straight side is a little tricky. Ask for a little inside flexion to help the horse strike off on the correct lead.

NOTES:

....

....

....

....

....

....

....

....

....

....

....

....

EXERCISE 15F – Make Your Own

	INSTRUCTIONS
1.	
2.	

NOTES:

....

....

....

....

....

....

....

....

....

....

EXERCISE 15G – Make Your Own

	INSTRUCTIONS
1.	
2.	

NOTES:

....

....

....

....

....

....

....

....

....

EXERCISE 15H – Make Your Own

	INSTRUCTIONS
1.	
2.	

NOTES:

....

....

....

....

....

....

....

....

....

....

"Poll flexion is not
pull flexion."

FLOORPLAN #16

'Snake: Level 2'

PRACTICE LOG – Note the dates when you last practiced this floorplan.

....
....
....
....
....
....
....
....
....
....
....
....
....
....
....
....
....
....
....
....
....

#16 'SNAKE: LEVEL 2' - 20X40 DIAGRAMS

1.

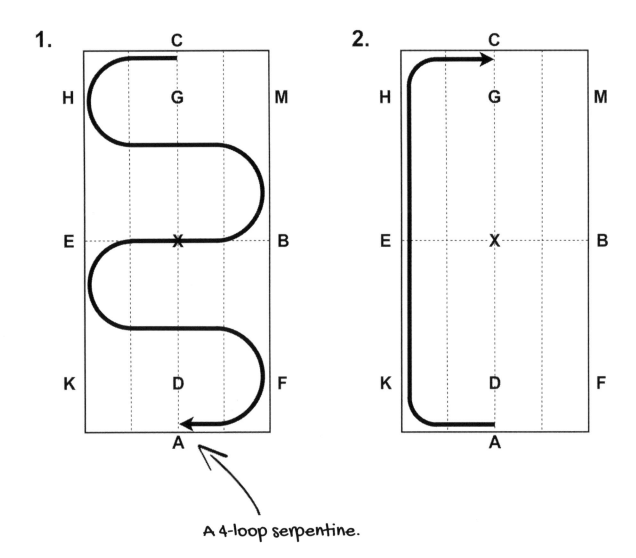

A 4-loop serpentine.

2.

The length of a small arena is 40-meters, therefore, your half circles need to be 10-meters in diameter.

#16 'SNAKE: LEVEL 2' - 20X60 DIAGRAMS

1.

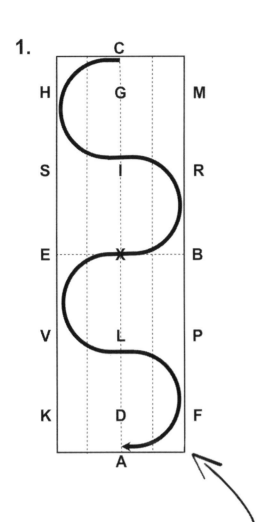

2.

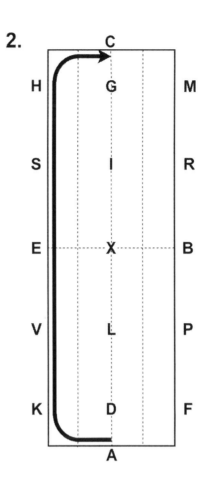

The length of a long arena is 60-meters, therefore, your half circles need to be 15-meters in diameter.

EXERCISE 16A

	INSTRUCTIONS	TIPS/DIRECTIVES
1.	[Start on the left rein] C Working trot. 4-loop serpentine to finish at A.	• Ride straight for a few steps when crossing the center line and change your diagonal and horse's bend. • Keep looking up and around your turns to ensure that you ride an accurate serpentine with all half-circles the same size. • Keep your leg on around the turns to encourage your horse to step under with his inside hind leg.
2.	A Medium walk. KEH Free walk on a long rein. H Medium walk. C Working trot. [Repeat exercise on the other rein]	• As you make the transition into free walk, allow the horse to gradually take the rein and stretch for the contact. Don't suddenly throw the contact away! • As you make the transition back to medium walk, shorten the reins smoothly to prevent the horse coming against the contact and possibly jogging.

NOTES:

....

....

....

....

....

....

....

....

....

....

EXERCISE 16B

	INSTRUCTIONS	TIPS/DIRECTIVES

1.	[Start on the left rein]
	
	C Working trot.
	      4-loop serpentine finishing
	      at A.
	
	      Over X transition to medium
	      walk for 3-4 steps then
	      proceed in working trot.
		• During the serpentine, the horse should continue to work forward over his back to seek the contact, not drop behind the rider's leg, draw back from the hand or stiffen against the new bend of each loop.
		
		• When riding the trot-walk-trot movement, the transitions must be obedient, balanced, and straight, and the horse must be reactive to your aids.

2.	K Medium walk. E Halt. Immobility 4 seconds Proceed in working trot. [Repeat the exercise on both reins]	• In a good halt, the horse should be straight and square. Each leg should bear the same weight evenly so that the horse has 'a leg at each corner'. • If the halt is unbalanced, the horse may tip onto his forehand and drop his poll as he halts, or he might throw his head up against the contact and not halt square.

NOTES:

....

....

....

....

....

....

....

....

....

....

EXERCISE 16C

	INSTRUCTIONS	TIPS/DIRECTIVES

1.	[Start on the left rein]
	
	C Working trot.
	       4-loop serpentine to finish at A.
	
	       Over X, halt. Immobility 4 seconds. Proceed in working trot.
		• During the halt, the horse should remain still and relaxed but attentive whilst waiting for his rider's next instruction.
		
		• When asked to move off from the halt, the horse should step forward immediately and smoothly.

2.	A/K Working canter right. H Working trot. [Repeat the exercise on both reins]	• When riding the trot-canter transition, emphasis should be on the horse pushing from the hind legs that are placed under the body rather than launching off the shoulders. • The canter is a pace of 3-beat. It should have 'uphill' cadenced strides, followed by a moment of suspension.

NOTES:

....

....

....

....

....

....

....

....

....

....

....

....

EXERCISE 16D

	INSTRUCTIONS	TIPS/DIRECTIVES

1.	[Start on the left rein]
	
	C Working canter left.
	        4-loop serpentine finishing
	        at A.
	
	Each time your cross the center line, change the canter lead via a simple change.
		• Simple changes should always be ridden more from the seat and leg than from the hand.
		
		• Keep the horse moving forward in the simple change to avoid the horse staying too upright. Instead, you want to encourage the weight-bearing capacity (in the canter-walk) and the pushing power (in the walk-canter) of the hind legs.

2.	K Medium canter. H Working canter. [Repeat exercise on both reins]	• During the medium canter, the horse's hind legs must come further under the body and appear to 'push' the horse forwards, whilst you remain in full control through light and supple seat and rein aids. • When riding the medium canter, maintain the regularity and lightness of the canter strides

NOTES:

....

....

....

....

....

....

....

....

....

....

....

EXERCISE 16E

	INSTRUCTIONS	TIPS/DIRECTIVES

1.	[Start on the left rein]
	
	C Working canter left.
	     4-loop serpentine finishing
	     at A.
	
	Each time you cross the center line, change the canter lead via a flying change.
		• When riding the flying changes, you must make sure that your horse is sharp to your aids. If he is slow to respond, he may learn to change early or late behind, which is a serious fault that can be difficult to correct.
		
		• The tempo and rhythm of the canter should remain unchanged throughout the whole movement.

2.	A Working trot. K Extended trot. H Working trot. C Working canter right. [Repeat exercise on both reins]	• In the extended trot, the horse covers the maximum amount of ground he can without hurrying and losing his balance. His fore feet should touch the ground on the spot towards which they're pointing. The movement of the hind and fore legs should reach equally forward in the moment of extension. The whole movement should be spectacular, yet remain balanced and smooth.

NOTES:

....

....

....

....

....

....

....

....

....

....

EXERCISE 16F – Make Your Own

	INSTRUCTIONS
1.	
2.	

NOTES:

....

....

....

....

....

....

....

....

....

EXERCISE 16G – Make Your Own

	INSTRUCTIONS
1.	
2.	

NOTES:

....

....

....

....

....

....

....

....

....

....

EXERCISE 16H – Make Your Own

	INSTRUCTIONS
1. 	
2. 	

NOTES:

....

....

....

....

....

....

....

....

....

....

"The goal is not to raise the neck, it is to lower the hips."

FLOORPLAN #17

'Snake: Level 3'

PRACTICE LOG – Note the dates when you last practiced this floorplan.

....
....
....
....
....
....
....
....
....
....
....
....
....
....
....
....
....
....
....
....
....
....

#17 'SNAKE: LEVEL 3' - 20X40 DIAGRAM

1.

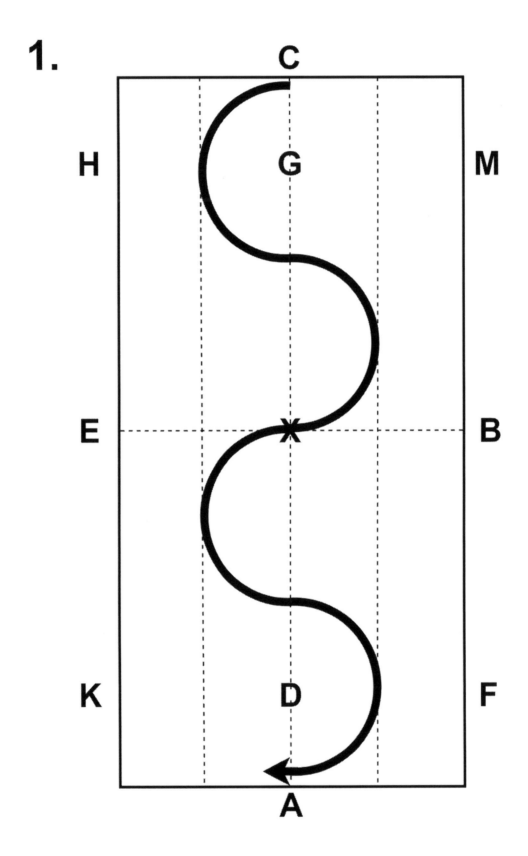

#17 'SNAKE: LEVEL 3' - 20X60 DIAGRAM

1.

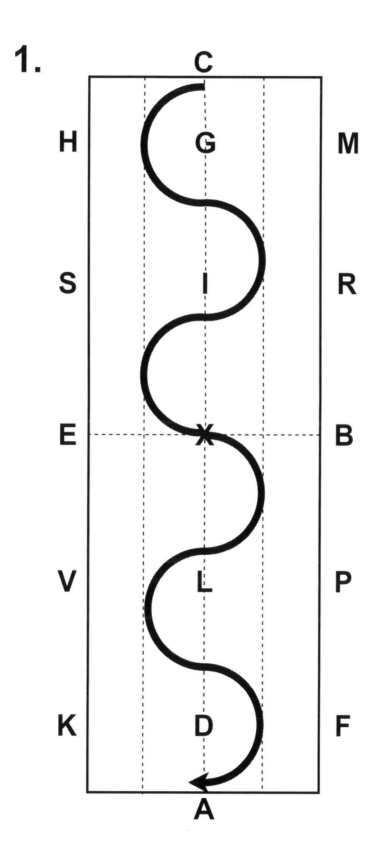

EXERCISE 17A

	INSTRUCTIONS	TIPS/DIRECTIVES

1.	[Start on any rein]
	
	C Medium walk.
	      Half 10-meter circle left.
	      Half 10-meter circle right.
	
	[Repeat until you reach A]
		• A 10-meter circle is quite a small diameter, so it is your job to choose exactly the right tempo (speed of the rhythm), to enable the horse to manage the rhythm and bend without any disturbances or unevenness to the stride length.
		
		• Ask for a smooth change of bend through the horse's body (not just his neck!) each time you cross the center line.
		
		• The horse's walk is a four-beat gait without any suspension. Any tension during the walk may disrupt the rhythm and regularity of the steps, so you should prioritize relaxation in the walk.

NOTES:

....

....

....

....

....

....

....

....

....

....

....

....

....

EXERCISE 17B

	INSTRUCTIONS	TIPS/DIRECTIVES

1.	[Start on any rein]
	
	C Working trot.
	       Half 10-meter circle left.
	       Half 10-meter circle right.
	
	[Repeat until you reach A]
	
	       When passing through X, halt.
	       Immobility 4 seconds.
	       Proceed in working trot
		• The half circles must be accurate in order to demonstrate that the horse is supple and connected enough to negotiate the movement without losing his balance and rhythm.
		
		• Ride straight for one step before asking for the halt. A square halt will only happen if the horse is straight and engaged. If the horse is moving crooked, it's virtually impossible to arrive at a square halt.
		
		• It's important 'think forward' when riding into halt, otherwise the horse will lose engagement as he halts. The halt will become unbalanced and the horse may come against the contact.

NOTES:

....

....

....

....

....

....

....

....

....

....

....

....

....

EXERCISE 17C

	INSTRUCTIONS	TIPS/DIRECTIVES

1.	[Start on the left rein]
	
	C Collected canter left.
	       Half 10-meter circle left.
	       Change the lead through trot.
	       Half 10-meter circle right.
	
	[Repeat until you reach A]
		• Remember that the degree of collection required is only so much as to be able to perform the half 10-meter circles with ease.
		
		• When riding the half circles, remember that your inside leg on the girth keeps the impulsion, develops the engagement of the inside hind leg, and asks for bend. Your outside leg should be slightly behind the girth preventing the hindquarters from escaping to the outside of the circle and generating some forward movement.
		
		• During the change of lead, make sure your aids are clear, with your outside leg well back and your shoulders turning in the new direction.

NOTES:

....

....

....

....

....

....

....

....

....

....

....

....

....

EXERCISE 17D

	INSTRUCTIONS	TIPS/DIRECTIVES

1.
 [diagram of arena with points C, H, G, M, E, B, K, D, F, A showing serpentine pattern]
	[Start on the left rein]
	
	 C Collected canter left.
	         Half 10-meter circle left.
	         Simple change.
	         Half 10-meter circle right.
	
	 [Repeat until you reach A]
		• The collected canter should have shorter and higher steps due to the horse carrying more of the weight towards its haunches, not because you've kept the handbrake on.
		
		 • Keep the horse moving forward in the simple change to avoid the horse staying too upright. Instead, you want to encourage the weight-bearing capacity (in the canter-walk) and the pushing power (in the walk-canter) of the hind legs.

NOTES:

....
....
....
....
....
....
....
....
....
....
....
....
....
....
....
....
....
....

EXERCISE 17E

	INSTRUCTIONS	TIPS/DIRECTIVES

1.
 	
 (arena diagram with serpentine line; points C, H, G, M, E, A, B, K, D, F)
	[Start on the left rein]
	
	 C Collected canter left.
	       Half 10-meter circle left.
	       Flying change.
	       Half 10-meter circle right.
	
	 [Repeat until you reach A]
		• The shorter, higher steps of collected canter are the result of the horse carrying more of the weight towards its haunches. Shortening the strides artificially will result in stiffening and loss of activity, which is exactly what judges do not want to see.
		
		 • Throughout the flying change and during the approach to it, the horse should remain calm and relaxed.
		
		 • The quality of your flying changes will be determined by the suppleness and elasticity of the horse's canter.

NOTES:

....

....

....

....

....

....

....

....

....

....

....

....

....

....

....

EXERCISE 17F – Make Your Own

	INSTRUCTIONS
1. H C M G E ⚬ B K D F A	

NOTES:

....

....

....

....

....

....

....

....

....

....

....

....

....

EXERCISE 17G – Make Your Own

	INSTRUCTIONS
1.	

NOTES:

....

....

....

....

....

....

....

....

....

....

....

....

....

EXERCISE 17H – Make Your Own

	INSTRUCTIONS
1.	

NOTES:

....

....

....

....

....

....

....

....

....

....

....

....

....

....

"Think of riding as a science,
but love it as an art."

FLOORPLAN #18

'Vertical Snake'

PRACTICE LOG – Note the dates when you last practiced this floorplan.

#18 'VERTICAL SNAKE' - 20X40 DIAGRAM

1.

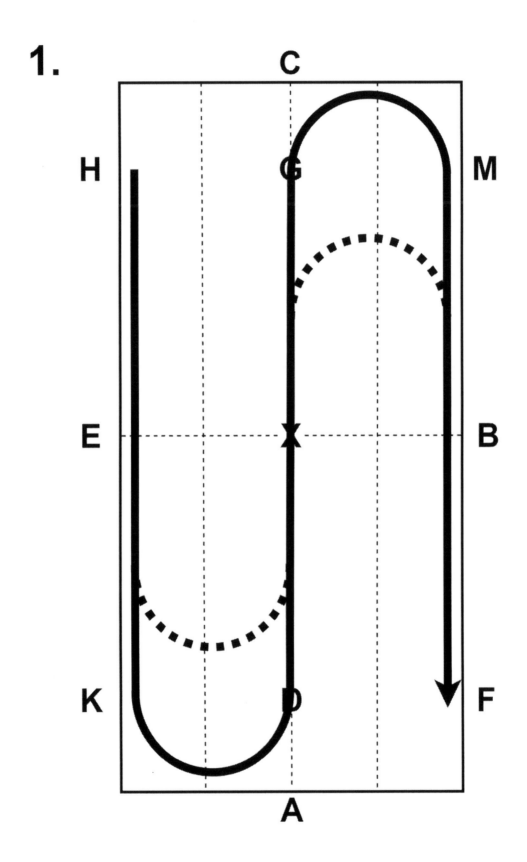

#18 'VERTICAL SNAKE' - 20X60 DIAGRAM

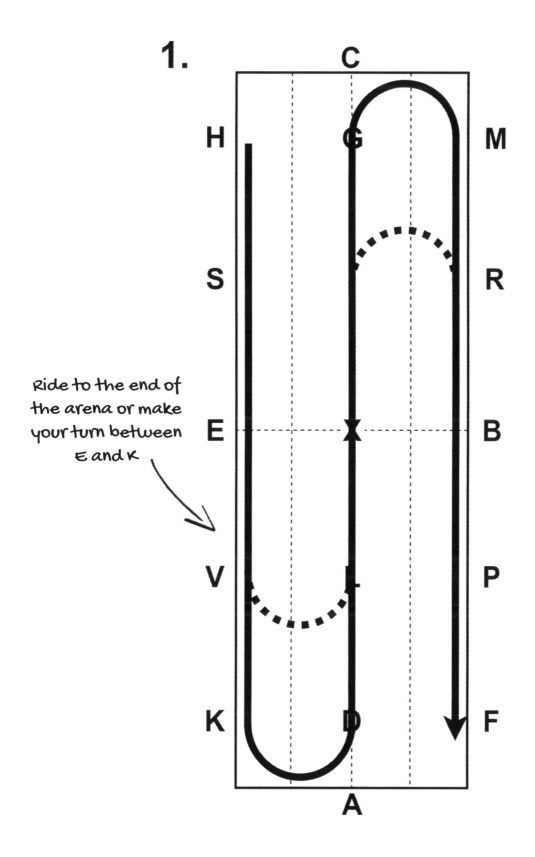

Ride to the end of the arena or make your turn between E and K

EXERCISE 18A

	INSTRUCTIONS	TIPS/DIRECTIVES

1.	[Start on the left rein]
	
	H Working trot.
	
	K Medium walk.
	        Half 10-meter circle left.
	
	D Working trot.
	
	G Medium walk.
	        Half 10-meter circle right.
	
	M Working trot.
	
	F Medium walk.
	
	[Repeat the exercise on both reins]
		• When transitioning to medium walk, ensure that the horse continues to work forwards and doesn't just collapse in a heap!
		
		• Ride forward from your inside leg into the outside rein to maintain the impulsion and bend around the half circles.
		
		• During the trot, the horse's hind feet should step clearly into the prints left by the fore feet.
		
		• When riding the center line, make sure that your horse is working from both your legs into both reins equally. It can be helpful to envisage that your horse is working along a tunnel created by your leg and rein.

NOTES:

....

....

....

....

....

....

....

....

....

....

....

....

EXERCISE 18B

	INSTRUCTIONS	TIPS/DIRECTIVES
1.	[Start on the left rein] H Working trot. E Halt. Immobility 4 seconds. Proceed in working trot. E/K Half 10-meter circle left. X Transition to medium walk for one horse's length then proceed in working trot. X/G Half 10-meter circle right. B Halt. Immobility 4 seconds. Proceed in working trot. [Repeat the exercise on both reins]	• A 10-meter circle is quite a small diameter, so it is your job to choose exactly the right tempo (speed of the rhythm), to enable the horse to manage the rhythm and bend without any disturbances or unevenness to the stride length. • Use the arena fence line to help keep your horse straight into both halts. Guard the horse's hindquarters with your inside leg to prevent them from swinging in. • When riding the trot-walk-trot movement over X, the transitions must be obedient, balanced, and straight, and the horse must be reactive to your aids.

NOTES:

....

....

....

....

....

....

....

....

....

....

....

....

....

....

EXERCISE 18C

	INSTRUCTIONS	TIPS/DIRECTIVES
1.	[Start on the left rein] H Working trot. E Halt. Immobility 4 seconds. Rein-back one horse's length. Proceed in working trot. K Half 10-meter circle left. D Medium trot. G Working trot. Half 10-meter circle right. M Medium walk. B Working trot. [Repeat the exercise on both reins]	• A square halt will only happen if the horse is straight and engaged. If the horse is moving crooked, it's virtually impossible to arrive at a square halt. • The horse should stay relaxed and calm during the rein-back. There should be no resistance to the contact, and he shouldn't rush backwards or lose his rhythm. • Use the first half 10-meter circle at K to encourage the horse to step under with his hind legs. This will help you build some power ready for the medium trot. • Use the second half 10-meter circle to rebalance the trot and prepare the horse for the downward transition to medium walk at M.

NOTES:

....

....

....

....

....

....

....

....

....

....

....

....

EXERCISE 18D

	INSTRUCTIONS	TIPS/DIRECTIVES
1.	[Start on the left rein] H Working canter left. E Collected canter. E/K Half 10-meter circle left in collected canter. X Simple change. X/G Half 10-meter circle right in collected canter. B Working canter. [Repeat the exercise on both reins]	• A collected canter does not mean a slower canter. Keep the jump and the impulsion and ride forward into the simple change. • Use your back, core, and seat to hold the horse in a good balance during the downward transition from canter to walk in the simple change. • Keep the horse moving forward in the simple change to avoid the horse staying too upright. Instead, you want to encourage the weight-bearing capacity (in the canter-walk) and the pushing power (in the walk-canter) of the hind legs.

NOTES:

....
....
....
....
....
....
....
....
....
....
....
....
....
....
....

EXERCISE 18E

	INSTRUCTIONS	TIPS/DIRECTIVES

1.	[Start on the left rein]
	
	H Working trot.
	      Shoulder-in left.
	
	K Half 10-meter circle left.
	
	D Collected walk.
	
	X Half walk pirouette left.
	      Proceed in collected walk.
	
	D Half walk pirouette right.
	      Proceed in collected walk.
	
	X Working trot.
	
	G Half 10-meter circle right.
	
	M Travers right.
	
	[Repeat exercise both reins]
		• When riding the shoulder-in, the horse should have a slight but even bend around your inside leg to create an angle of about 30 degrees.
		
		• In the pirouettes it's crucial that a clear 4-beat walk sequence is maintained, and the tempo of the walk should remain the same before and after the movement.
		
		• If the horse is lazy or becomes 'stuck' in the pirouettes, use your legs throughout the turn in an alternating fashion, matching each of your legs to his hind legs, so that your left leg asks him to lift his left hind and vice versa.
		
		• Use the half 10-meter circle at G to help position the horse ready for travers. The bend should be uniform from the poll to the tail, and the horse should look in the direction in which he is moving.

NOTES:

....

....

....

....

....

....

....

....

....

....

EXERCISE 18F – Make Your Own

	INSTRUCTIONS
1.	

NOTES:

....

....

....

....

....

....

....

....

....

....

....

....

....

....

EXERCISE 18G – Make Your Own

	INSTRUCTIONS
1.	

NOTES:

....

....

....

....

....

....

....

....

....

....

....

....

....

....

EXERCISE 18H – Make Your Own

	INSTRUCTIONS
1. H C M G E X B K D F A	

NOTES:

....

....

....

....

....

....

....

....

....

....

....

....

....

"Ride the horse,
not the plan."

FLOORPLAN #19

'Two of a Kind'

PRACTICE LOG – Note the dates when you last practiced this floorplan.

....

....

....

....

....

....

....

....

....

....

....

....

....

....

....

....

....

....

....

....

....

....

#19 'TWO OF A KIND' - 20X40 DIAGRAMS

1.

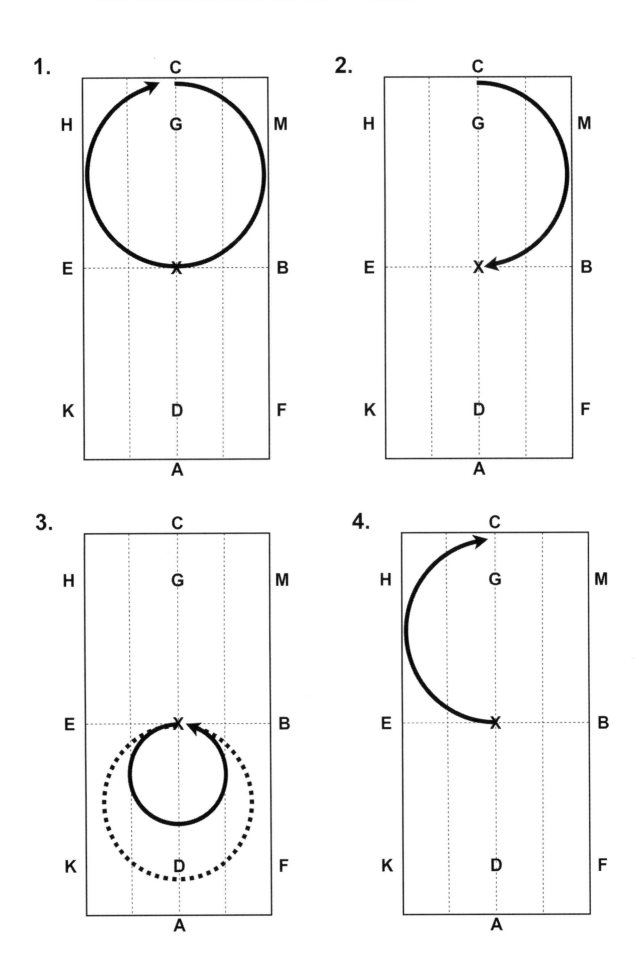

2.

3.

4.

#19 'TWO OF A KIND' - 20X60 DIAGRAMS

1.

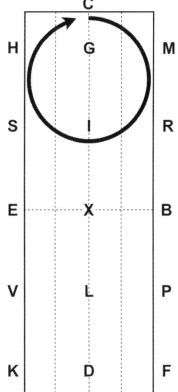

2.

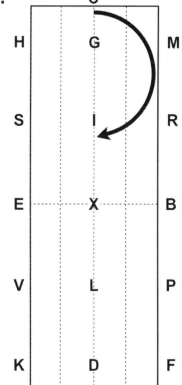

3.

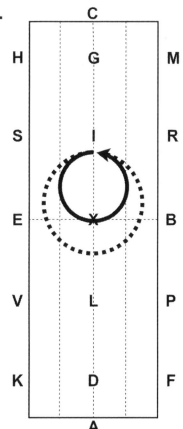

4.

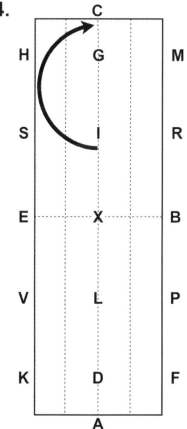

EXERCISE 19A

	INSTRUCTIONS	TIPS/DIRECTIVES
1.	[Start on the right rein] C Working trot. 20-meter circle right.	• Maintain uniform bend around the circle along with your horse's natural rhythm. • Ride from your inside leg to your outside rein to keep your horse straight and moving on one track.
2.	C Half 20-meter circle right in working trot.	• Don't ask for too much neck bend as this will encourage your horse to fall out through his shoulder. • Your goal is to develop a good, rhythmical and active working trot.
3.	X Medium walk. 15-meter circle left.	• A 15-meter circle should touch half-way between the outside track and the ¾ line. • The horse's walk is a four-beat gait without any suspension. • Guard the shoulder with your outside rein to stop the horse from falling out and drifting onto the outside track.
4.	X Working trot. Half 20-meter circle right. [Repeat the exercise on both reins]	• Change the horse's bend and flexion before asking for working trot. • Ride forwards through the transition and onto the circle to encourage the horse to step under with his inside hind leg.

NOTES:

EXERCISE 19B

	INSTRUCTIONS	TIPS/DIRECTIVES
1.	[Start on the right rein] C Working canter right. 20-meter circle right.	• When riding the circle, the horse should be supple enough to be able to negotiate the circle accurately, whilst maintaining his rhythm and balance. He should show an adequate degree of bend without losing his quarters to the outside of the circle.
2.	C Half 20-meter circle right.	• The canter is a pace of 3-beat. It should have 'uphill' cadenced strides, followed by a moment of suspension. • During the canter, if the moment of suspension appears only very briefly, or worse, is missing, the beat becomes that of 4-time which is a serious fault and will be heavily penalized in the competitive environment.
3.	X Working trot. 15-meter circle left.	• Prepare the horse for the downward transition to working trot at X by use of the half-halt. Keep the transition balanced and ride forwards into the trot and around your circle. • A 15-meter circle should touch half-way between the outside track and the ¾ line.
4.	X 20-meter circle right. H/C Working canter right. [Repeat the exercise on both reins]	• Change your horse's bend and flexion at X and establish a new outside rein ready for your canter transition. • Note that the canter transition is on the circle and not in the corner.

NOTES:

EXERCISE 19C

	INSTRUCTIONS	TIPS/DIRECTIVES

1.	[Start on the right rein]
	
	C Halt. Immobility 4 seconds.
	          Rein-back one horse's length.
	          Proceed in working trot.
	          20-meter circle right.
	
	X-C Allow the horse to stretch.
		• Ride a square halt at C making sure that the horse is relax, immobile, and accepting a light contact.
		
		• Use your legs and bodyweight to ask the horse to rein-back whilst keeping your contact elastic. The contact prevents the horse from walking forwards, it should not be used to pull the horse back.
		
		• When allowing the horse to stretch, lengthen the rein to allow the horse to stretch forward and downward, but still maintain an elastic contact.
		
		• If you have a young or 'green' horse, always ride your 'rising' trot so that he can use his back

2.	C Working trot. Half 20-meter circle right.	• During the circle, your horse should continue to work forwards, in a good rhythm, and show a clear uniform bend along his body around the circle. • During the trot, the horse's hind feet should step clearly into the prints left by the fore feet.
3.	X Medium walk. 10-meter circle left.	• When completing the circle there should be no tilting of the horse's head. • When riding the circle, keep your hips and shoulders parallel with your horse's shoulders, keep your body upright, and look ahead of you around the circle.

4. 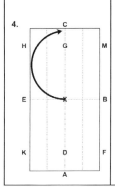	X Working trot Half 20-meter circle right [Repeat the exercise on both reins]	• Change the horse's bend and establish the new outside rein before asking for working trot at X. Otherwise, you may end up wobbling all over the place since you're in the middle of the arena.

NOTES:

....

....

....

....

....

....

....

....

....

....

....

....

....

....

....

....

....

....

....

....

....

....

....

EXERCISE 19D

	INSTRUCTIONS	TIPS/DIRECTIVES
1.	[Start on the right rein] C Working canter right. 20-meter circle right. Over X, give and retake both reins.	• Circles are designed to test the horse's balance, suppleness to the bend, and straightness. • The purpose of the give and retake is to show that you are not holding the horse into an outline solely with your reins and that you are not supporting his balance or controlling his speed with your hands.
2.	C Half 20-meter circle right in working canter.	• Keep the canter engaged and balanced with a clear moment of suspension. • On the last few strides of the circle, use the half-halt to help collect the canter and prepare the horse for the transition to walk in the next movement.
3.	X Simple change. 10-meter circle left in collected canter.	• When riding the simple change, maintain the relaxation and the clarity of the walk steps. • Remember that the degree of collection required is only so much as to be able to perform the 10-meter canter circle with ease.
4.	X Simple change. Half 20-meter circle right in working canter. [Repeat the exercise on both reins]	• Simple changes should always be ridden more from the seat and leg than from the hand. • During the simple change, try to avoid the horse staying too upright in the walk to canter and hence not really covering enough ground forward.

NOTES:

....
....
....
....
....
....
....
....
....
....
....
....
....
....
....
....
....
....
....
....
....
....
....
....
....
....
....
....
....
....

EXERCISE 19E

	INSTRUCTIONS	TIPS/DIRECTIVES
1. 	[Start on the right rein] C Working canter right. 20-meter circle right. X-C Allow the horse to stretch	• The circle must be accurate in order to demonstrate that the horse is supple and connected enough to negotiate the movement without losing his balance and rhythm. • Keep your bum in the saddle but lighten your seat as you allow the horse to stretch. That enables the horse to use his back and helps to keep his hind quarters engaged.
2. 	C Half 20-meter circle right in collected canter.	• During the circle you are expected to have even bend (think of an imaginary line) through the horse's body; from the tail, centrally through the hindquarters, through the back and shoulders, through the neck, and finishing at the poll. • Collection should be thought of as a rebalancing of the weight carriage towards the haunches, and NOT as a shortening of the stride.
3. 	X Flying change. 10-meter circle left in collected canter.	• If the canter is flat, lacking impulsion, or on the forehand, the flying changes will most likely be incorrect. The quality of your flying changes will be determined by the suppleness and elasticity of the horse's canter. • Remember that the degree of collection required is only so much as to be able to perform the 10-meter circle with ease.

4. 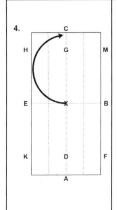	X	Medium walk. Half 20-meter circle right and show some extended walk steps. Walk to working canter right. [Repeat the exercise on both reins]	• Keep your leg on during the downward transition and ride the horse up and out so that his poll doesn't drop too low in the extended walk. • Riding a smart walk to canter transition at C involves having an energized walk, knowledge of the correct aids, and asking for canter in the appropriate moment.

NOTES:

....

....

....

....

....

....

....

....

....

....

....

....

....

....

....

....

....

....

....

....

....

....

....

EXERCISE 19F – Make Your Own

	INSTRUCTIONS
1.	
2.	
3.	
4.	

NOTES:

EXERCISE 19G – Make Your Own

	INSTRUCTIONS
1.	
2.	
3.	
4.	

NOTES:

EXERCISE 19H – Make Your Own

	INSTRUCTIONS
1.	
2.	
3.	
4.	

NOTES:

"As always, everything is connected. Every single exercise or movement influences the other. Which is the reason why we can improve certain movements without riding them at all, but by practicing exercises that improve the necessary ingredients of the movement in question."

FLOORPLAN #20

'Three of a kind'

PRACTICE LOG – Note the dates when you last practiced this floorplan.

....

....

....

....

....

....

....

....

....

....

....

....

....

....

....

....

....

....

....

....

....

....

#20 'THREE OF A KIND' - 20X40 DIAGRAMS

1.

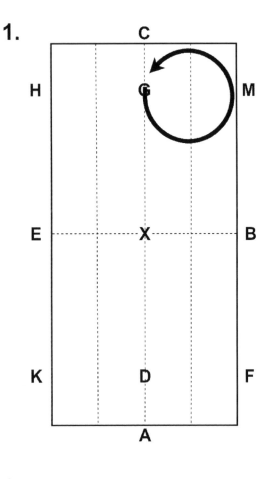

2.

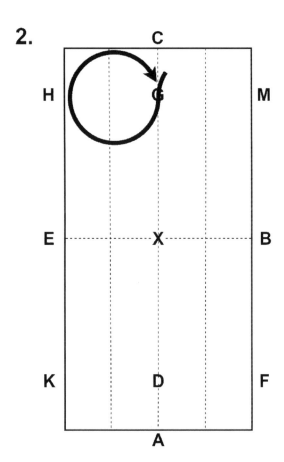

3.

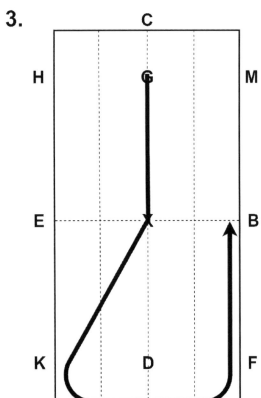

4.

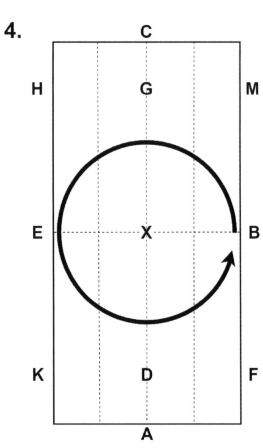

5.

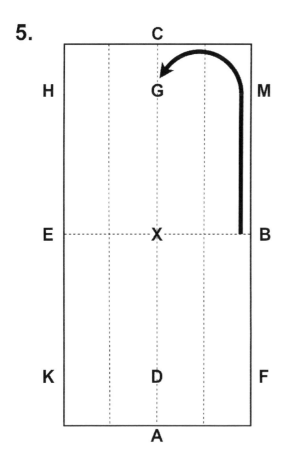

Note that the 10-meter circles at G should touch H and M on the long sides of the arena, but should be 1-meter away from the track on the short side of the arena near C.

#20 'THREE OF A KIND' - 20X60 DIAGRAMS

1.

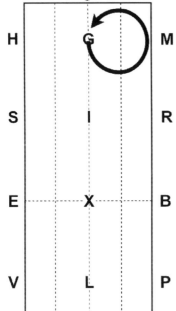

2.

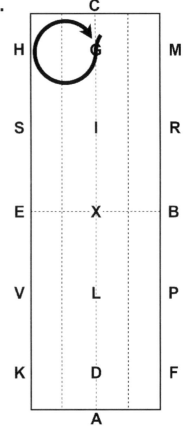

3.

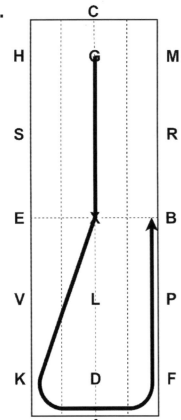

4.

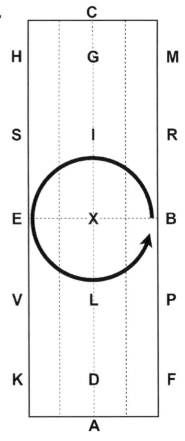

5.

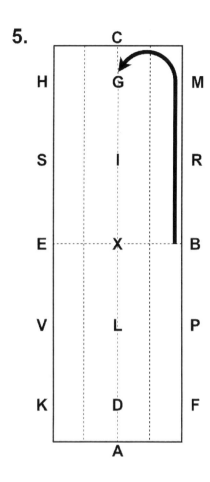

IMPORTANT: Make a note to buy extra
apples and carrots for your horse!

...because we said so! 😊

EXERCISE 20A

	INSTRUCTIONS	TIPS/DIRECTIVES
1.	[Start on any rein] G Medium walk. 10-meter circle left.	• A 10-meter circle is quite a small diameter, so it is your job to choose exactly the right tempo (speed of the rhythm), to enable the horse to manage the rhythm and bend without any disturbances or unevenness to the stride length.
2.	G 10-meter circle right.	• Change the horse's bend when crossing through G. • Guard the quarters with your outside leg to prevent the horse from falling out or crossing behind. • Both circles should be equal in size and the horse's walk should have the same rhythm and ground cover on each rein.
3.	G Medium walk. X-K Free walk on a long rein. K Medium walk. A Working trot.	• In the free walk, although the horse is relaxed, he should march purposefully forward and look as though he is 'going somewhere'. • The transition from free walk back to medium walk should be smooth, with no loss of rhythm or signs of tension.
4.	B 20-meter circle left.	• Circles are designed to test the horse's balance, suppleness to the bend, and straightness. • Your goal is to develop a good, rhythmical and active working trot.

5. 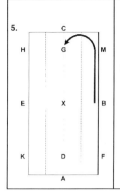	M Medium walk. C Turn left down the center line. [Repeat the exercise on both reins]	• Keep the downward transition forward-thinking and the medium walk active. • Look for center line after you have passed M to make sure you don't overshoot the turn.

NOTES:

....

....

....

....

....

....

....

....

....

....

....

....

....

....

....

....

....

....

....

....

....

....

....

....

EXERCISE 20B

	INSTRUCTIONS	TIPS/DIRECTIVES
1.	[Start on any rein] G Medium walk. 10-meter circle left.	• A 10-meter circle is quite a small diameter, so it is your job to choose exactly the right tempo (speed of the rhythm), to enable the horse to manage the rhythm and bend without any disturbances or unevenness to the stride length.
2.	G 10-meter circle right	• Change the horse's bend when crossing through G. • Guard the quarters with your outside leg to prevent the horse from falling out or crossing behind. • Both circles should be equal in size and the horse's walk should have the same rhythm and ground cover on each rein.
3.	G Medium walk. X Halt. Immobility 4 seconds. Proceed in working trot. X-K Working trot. A/F Working canter left.	• In a good halt, the horse should be straight and square. Each leg should bear the same weight evenly so that the horse has 'a leg at each corner'. • If the halt is unbalanced, the horse may tip onto his forehand and drop his poll as he halts, or he might throw his head up against the contact and not halt square.
4.	B 20-meter circle left in working canter.	• Keep the rhythm and the jump in the canter strides. • Maintain the outside rein contact to stop the horse from falling out through the shoulder and to manage the speed.

5. 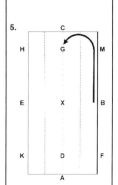	B	Working canter.	• Encourage the horse to step through into the working trot, rather than 'fall' out of the canter.
	M	Working trot.	
	C	Turn left onto the center line.	• Look for center line after you have passed M to make sure you don't overshoot the turn.
		[Repeat the exercise on both reins]	

NOTES:

....
....
....
....
....
....
....
....
....
....
....
....
....
....
....
....
....
....
....
....
....
....
....
....

EXERCISE 20C

	INSTRUCTIONS	TIPS/DIRECTIVES
1. *(arena diagram showing 10m circle left at top near G)*	[Start on any rein] G Working trot. 10-meter circle left.	• When riding the circle, keep your hips and shoulders parallel with your horse's shoulders, keep your body upright, and look ahead of you around the circle. • Make sure that your horse bends equally through his body. • Don't ask for too much neck bend, as that could cause the horse to fall out through his shoulder.
2. *(arena diagram showing 10m circle right at top near G)*	G 10-meter circle right.	• Change the horse's bend when crossing through G. • Both circles should be equal in size and the horse's trot should have the same rhythm and ground cover on each rein.
3. *(arena diagram showing path from G through X to K)*	G-X Working trot. X-K Working trot. K Working canter left.	• In the trot-canter transition at K, emphasis should be on the horse pushing from the hind legs that are placed under the body rather than launching off the shoulders.
4. *(arena diagram showing 20m circle left at B)*	B 20-meter circle left in medium canter	• The circles are designed to test the horse's balance, suppleness to the bend, and straightness. • In the medium canter, the hind legs must come further under the body and appear to 'push' the horse forwards to cover more ground per stride.

5. 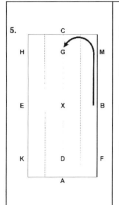	B	Working canter left.	• Half-halt to prepare and balance the horse for the downward transition to trot. The horse should step through into the working trot rather than 'fall' out of the canter.
	M	Working trot.	
	C	Turn left down the center line.	
		[Repeat the exercise on both reins]	• Look for center line after you have passed M to make sure you don't overshoot the turn.

NOTES:

....
....
....
....
....
....
....
....
....
....
....
....
....
....
....
....
....
....
....
....
....
....

EXERCISE 20D

	INSTRUCTIONS	TIPS/DIRECTIVES
1.	[Start on any rein] G 10-meter circle left in collected trot.	• Although the steps are shorter in the collected trot than the working trot, the elasticity and cadence are just as pronounced, and the horse should demonstrate greater mobility in the shoulders. • During the circles, your horse should continue to work forwards, in a good rhythm, and show a clear uniform bend along his body around the circle.
2.	G 10-meter circle right in collected trot. H/C Collected canter right.	• Note that the trot-canter transition is on the circle and not in the corner. • When riding the trot-canter transition, emphasis should be on the horse pushing from the hind legs that are placed under the body rather than launching off the shoulders.
3.	G-X Collected canter right. X-K Collected canter right. K Working trot. B Halt. Immobility 4 seconds. Rein-back one horse's length. Proceed in working canter left.	• The collected canter should have shorter and higher steps due to the horse carrying more of the weight towards its haunches, not because you've kept the handbrake on. • It's important 'think forward' when riding into halt, otherwise the horse will lose engagement as he halts. The halt will become unbalanced and the horse may come against the contact. • Allow the horse a walk step or two forward out of the rein-back before asking for canter.

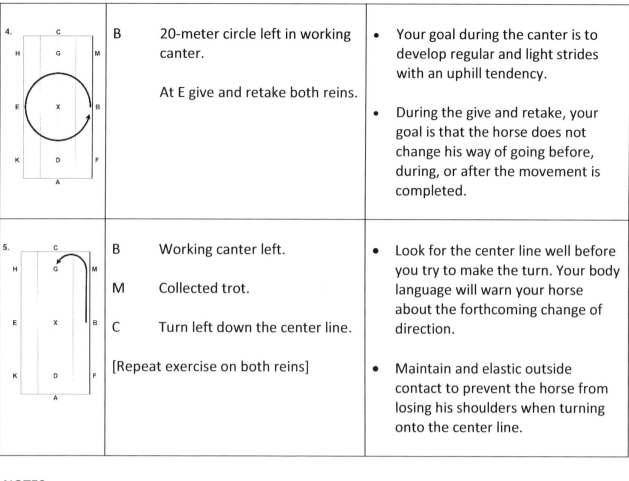

4.	B	20-meter circle left in working canter. At E give and retake both reins.	• Your goal during the canter is to develop regular and light strides with an uphill tendency. • During the give and retake, your goal is that the horse does not change his way of going before, during, or after the movement is completed.
5.	B M C	Working canter left. Collected trot. Turn left down the center line. [Repeat exercise on both reins]	• Look for the center line well before you try to make the turn. Your body language will warn your horse about the forthcoming change of direction. • Maintain and elastic outside contact to prevent the horse from losing his shoulders when turning onto the center line.

NOTES:

....

....

....

....

....

....

....

....

....

....

....

....

....

....

EXERCISE 20E

	INSTRUCTIONS	TIPS/DIRECTIVES
1.	[Start on any rein] G 10-meter circle left in collected canter.	• Collection requires just as much impulsion as working paces. If the canter lacks impulsion, the steps will be flat and labored. • When completing the circle there should be no tilting of the horse's head.
2.	G Simple change. 10-meter circle right in collected canter.	• Keep the horse moving forward in the simple change to avoid the horse staying too upright. Instead, you want to encourage the weight-bearing capacity (in the canter-walk) and the pushing power (in the walk-canter) of the hind legs.
3.	G-X Travers in working canter right. X-K Canter half-pass right. K Working trot. F-B Shoulder-in left.	• Use the 10-meter circle in the previous step to help set your horse up for travers. • Use the travers to help set your horse up for the half-pass. • Use the A/F corner to help set your horse up for the shoulder-in. • During the lateral movements, the energy, elasticity and suspension of the pace should not change, nor should the rhythm vary.
4.	B 20-meter circle left in working trot. After E, allow the horse to stretch.	• Ride forwards into the contact when asking the horse to stretch. That will encourage him to lift his back underneath you. • Ride the stretch exercise in rising trot so that the horse can use his back.

5. 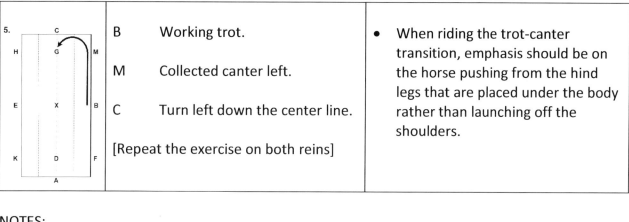	B Working trot. M Collected canter left. C Turn left down the center line. [Repeat the exercise on both reins]	• When riding the trot-canter transition, emphasis should be on the horse pushing from the hind legs that are placed under the body rather than launching off the shoulders.

NOTES:

....

....

....

....

....

....

....

....

....

....

....

....

....

....

....

....

....

....

....

....

....

EXERCISE 20F – Make Your Own

	INSTRUCTIONS
1.	
2.	
3.	
4.	

5.

NOTES:

....
....
....
....
....
....
....
....
....
....
....
....
....
....
....
....
....
....
....
....
....
....
....
....

EXERCISE 20G – Make Your Own

	INSTRUCTIONS
1.	
2.	
3.	
4.	

5.

NOTES:

....
....
....
....
....
....
....
....
....
....
....
....
....
....
....
....
....
....
....
....
....
....
....
....
....

EXERCISE 20H – Make Your Own

	INSTRUCTIONS
1.	
2.	
3.	
4.	

5.

NOTES:

....
....
....
....
....
....
....
....
....
....
....
....
....
....
....
....
....
....
....
....
....
....
....
....

"Anything forced is never beautiful."

FLOORPLAN # 21

'Center Staged'

PRACTICE LOG – Note the dates when you last practiced this floorplan.

#21 'CENTER STAGED' - 20X40 DIAGRAMS

1.

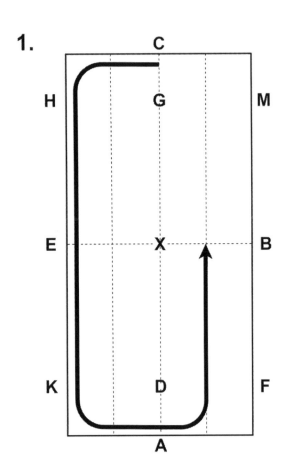

2.

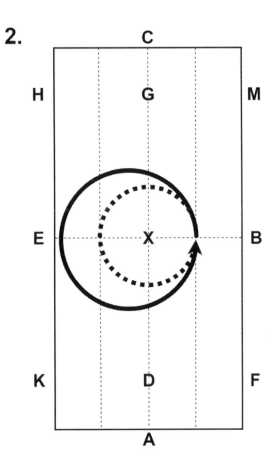

3.

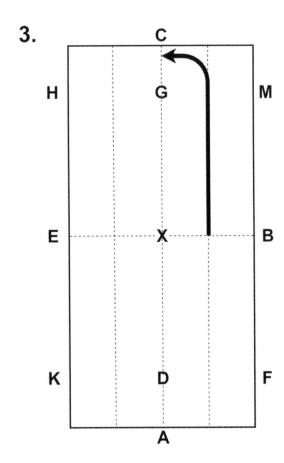

#21 'CENTER STAGED' - 20X60 DIAGRAMS

1.

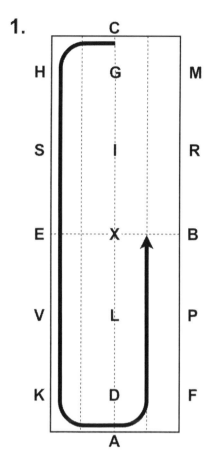

2.

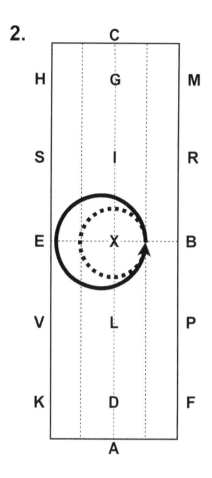

3.

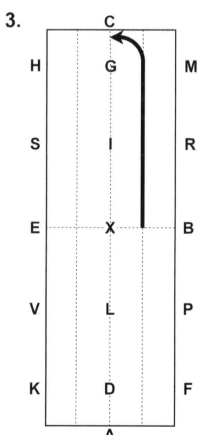

EXERCISE 21A

	INSTRUCTIONS	TIPS/DIRECTIVES
1.	[Start on the left rein] C Working trot. E Transition to medium walk for one horse's length then proceed in working trot. A Turn left onto the ¾ line.	• The horse should remain in the same outline throughout the whole trot-walk-trot movement at E, and the trot rhythm and energy following the transition should be the same as it was prior to the walk steps. • Before turning down the ¾ line, focus on a point at the C end of the arena and ride straight toward it.
2.	X/B 15-meter circle left in working trot.	• An accurate 15-meter circle starting on the ¾ line should touch E and then finish on the ¾ line. • During the circle, your horse should continue to work forwards, in a good rhythm, and show a clear uniform bend along his body around the circle. • Use your outside aids to guard the horse's shoulders and quarters to prevent the horse from drifting out.
3.	X/B Proceed down the ¾ line towards C in working trot then track left. [Repeat the exercise on both reins]	• Ride your horse forward (not faster) to keep him straight. • Keep your outside rein to prevent the horse from falling out into the corner as you make the turn at the C end of the arena.

NOTES:

....

....

....

EXERCISE 21B

	INSTRUCTIONS	TIPS/DIRECTIVES
1.	[Start on the left rein] C Working trot. E Halt. Immobility 4 seconds. Proceed in medium walk. K Working trot. A Turn left down the ¾ line.	• If your horse begins to step backwards during the halt, ride forwards immediately. Ride the halt again and ease your hand as you do so. Be positive with your legs and keep thinking forwards. • Before turning down the ¾ line, focus on one point at the C end of the arena and ride straight toward it.
2.	X/B Medium walk. 10-meter circle left.	• A 10-meter circle is quite a small diameter, so it is your job to choose exactly the right tempo (speed of the rhythm), to enable the horse to manage the rhythm and bend without any disturbances or unevenness to the stride length. • When completing the circle there should be no tilting of the horse's head.

3.	X/B Working trot.
	        Proceed down the ¾ line
	        towards C then track left.
	
	[Repeat the exercise on both reins]
		• Before turning down the ¾ line, focus on one point at the C end of the arena and ride straight toward it.
		
		• Ride your horse forward (not faster) to help keep him straight.

NOTES:

....

....

....

....

EXERCISE 21C

	INSTRUCTIONS	TIPS/DIRECTIVES
1. (diagram)	[Start on the left rein] C Working canter left. HEK Medium canter. K Working canter. A Turn left onto the ¾ line.	• The medium canter is a longer version of the working canter. It covers more ground because the horse's frame and strides lengthen. • Although the medium canter should cover more ground than a working canter, it should also clearly demonstrate an uphill tendency.
2. (diagram)	X/B 15-meter circle left in working canter. When passing E, give and retake the inside rein.	• Make sure that you don't lean inward around the circle. That will unbalance the horse and cause him to 'motorbike' around the circle. • When you relinquish your rein contact in a give and retake there should be no change in your horse's outline, speed, size of stride, balance, or alignment to the circle.
3. (diagram)	X/B Proceed down the ¾ line towards C in working canter then track left. [Repeat the exercise on both reins]	• On the ¾ line the horse should travel forward and straight, as though he is on railway tracks. • The horse's poll should be the highest point, and the contact should be quiet, elastic and steady, without any tilting or swinging of the horse's head.

NOTES:

....

....

....

....

....

....

EXERCISE 21D

	INSTRUCTIONS	TIPS/DIRECTIVES
1.	[Start on the left rein] C Collected canter left. H Medium walk. E Halt. Immobility 4 seconds. Proceed in medium walk. K Walk to working canter left. A Turn left onto the ¾ line.	• Your horse should be straight, square, attentive, relaxed and immobile during the halt, and the move-off should be immediate and obedient. • Establish a clear left flexion before asking for the walk to canter transition. • Keep the outside rein to control the horse's outside shoulder and prevent him from falling out when turning onto the ¾ line.
2.	X/B Collected canter. 10-meter circle left.	• Remember that the degree of collection required in the canter is only so much as to be able to perform the 10-meter circle with ease. • The 10-meter circle should touch both ¾ lines to be accurate.
3.	X/B Proceed down the ¾ line towards C in collected canter then track left.	• Collected canter needs just as much impulsion as working canter! Be sure to keep plenty of energy in the canter so that you don't lose the 3-beat rhythm and moment of suspension.

NOTES:

....

....

....

....

EXERCISE 21E

	INSTRUCTIONS	TIPS/DIRECTIVES
1.	[Start on the left rein] C　　Working trot. HEK　Extended trot. K　　Working trot. A　　Turn left onto the ¾ and proceed in shoulder-in left.	• In the extended trot, the horse covers the maximum amount of ground he can without hurrying and losing his balance • During shoulder-in, the horse's outside foreleg and inside hindleg should work on the same track. The inside foreleg and the outside hindleg should work on their own track.
2.	X/B　10-meter circle left in collected trot.	• The circle should touch both ¾ lines to be accurate. • Collected trot demands greater self-carriage from the horse. The horse should remain 'on the bit', with his hocks engaged and flexed, stepping well under his center of gravity, and should move forward, uphill, and with good impulsion.
3.	X/B　Proceed down the ¾ line towards C in travers left then track left. [Repeat the exercise on both reins]	• In travers, the horse's inside forefoot and outside hindfoot are on the same track, and the angle of the horse's body should be maintained at 35 degrees. The bend should be uniform from the poll to the tail, and the horse should look in the direction in which he is moving.

NOTES:

....

....

....

....

....

EXERCISE 21F – Make Your Own

	INSTRUCTIONS
1. 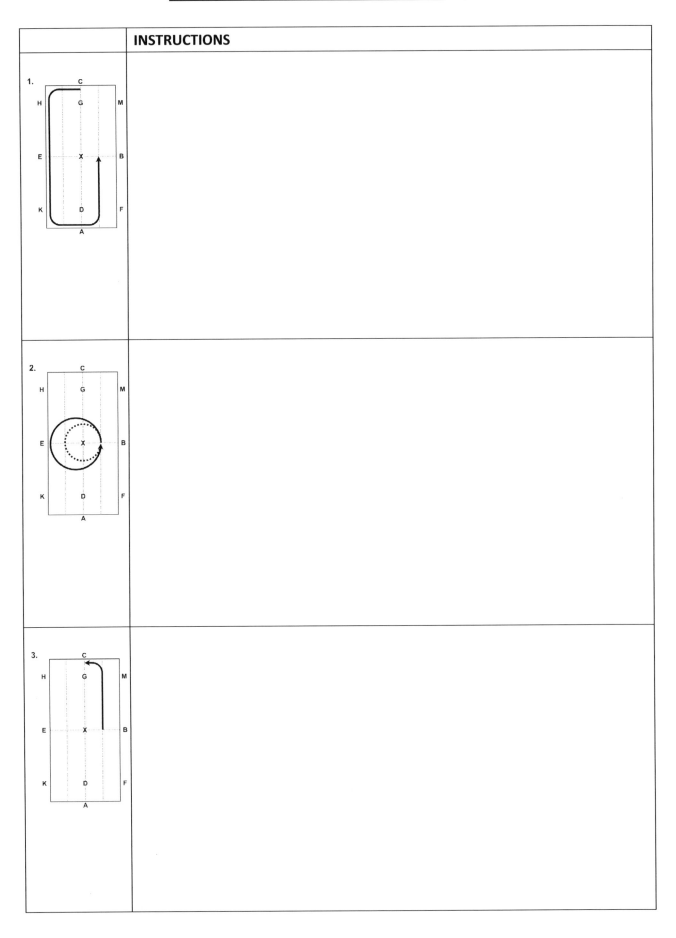	
2.	
3.	

NOTES:

EXERCISE 21G – Make Your Own

	INSTRUCTIONS
1.	
2.	
3.	

NOTES:

EXERCISE 21H – Make Your Own

	INSTRUCTIONS
1.	
2.	
3.	

NOTES:

"The horse reflects
the rider."

FLOORPLAN #22

'Yin and Yang'

PRACTICE LOG – Note the dates when you last practiced this floorplan.

#22 'YIN AND YANG' - 20X40 DIAGRAMS

1.

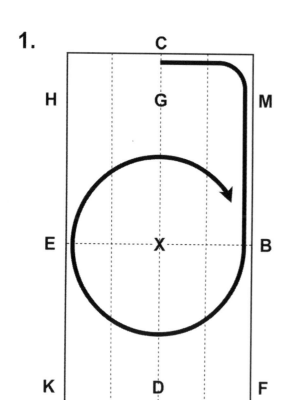

2.

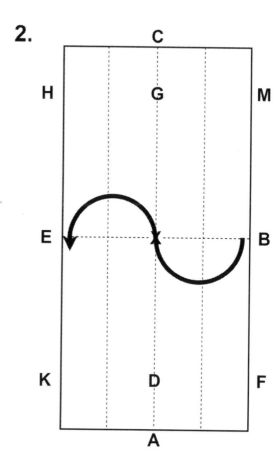

3.

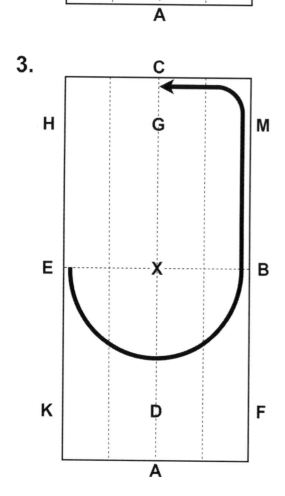

#22 'YIN AND YANG' - 20X60 DIAGRAMS

1.

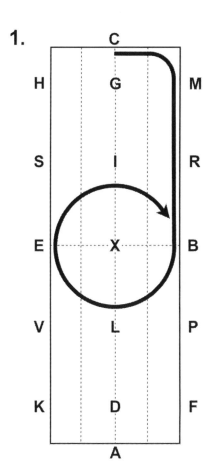

2.

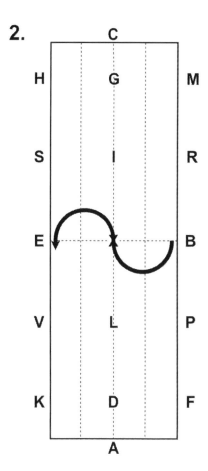

3.

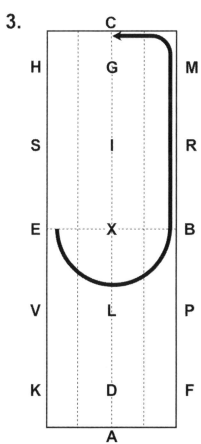

EXERCISE 22A

	INSTRUCTIONS	TIPS/DIRECTIVES
1.	[Start on the right rein] C　　Medium walk. M　　Working trot. B　　20-meter circle right.	• Keep the rhythm and impulsion in the working trot. • During the circle you are expected to have even bend (think of an imaginary line) through the horse's body; from the tail, centrally through the hindquarters, through the back and shoulders, through the neck, and finishing at the poll.
2.	B　　Medium walk. 　　　Half 10-meter circle right. X　　Half 10-meter circle left.	• The walk steps should be purposeful and march forward. • As you change the bend over X, keep the activity so that the horse's new inside hind leg steps underneath him, preventing the horse from falling onto his forehand. • When completing the half circles there should be no tilting of the horse's head.
3.	E　　Working trot. 　　　Half 20-meter circle left. B　　Proceed in working trot. M　　Medium walk. [Repeat the exercise on both reins]	• When riding the half circle, the horse should be supple enough to be able to negotiate the circle accurately, whilst maintaining his rhythm and balance. He should show an adequate degree of bend without losing his quarters to the outside of the circle.

NOTES:

....

....

....

....

EXERCISE 22B

	INSTRUCTIONS	TIPS/DIRECTIVES
1.	[Start on the right rein] C Working canter right. B 20-meter circle right.	• Your goal during the canter is to develop regularity and lightness of the strides, an uphill tendency, and the natural ability of the horse to carry himself whilst maintaining active well-placed hind legs. • On the 20-meter circle, be careful that you don't lean-in to the inside. That will cause your horse to "motorbike" around the circle.
2.	B Working trot. Half 10-meter circle right. X Half 10-meter circle left.	• Use half-halts to balance your horse through the change of bend. • Keep your hips and shoulders parallel with your horse's shoulders, keep your body upright, and look ahead of you around the circle.
3.	E Half 20-meter circle left. Proceed in working trot. M/C Working canter left. [Repeat the exercise on both reins]	• Diligent riding of transitions from trot to canter will build the 'pushing and propulsion' capacity of the horse, enabling him to develop incremental levels of engagement of the hind legs.

NOTES:

....

....

....

....

....

....

EXERCISE 22C

	INSTRUCTIONS	TIPS/DIRECTIVES
1. [diagram]	[Start on the right rein] C Working trot. B Halt. Immobility 4 seconds. Rein-back one horse's length. Proceed in working trot. B 20-meters circle right. When passing E, give and retake the reins.	• If the horse is not moving forwards into the halt, he will not step underneath himself in the transition, and the halt will probably be crooked and not square. • During the rein-back, the horse should remain 'on the bit' with the poll as the highest point. He shouldn't drop his head down or curl up behind the bit. • In the give and retake of reins, you must clearly release the contact so there is a visible loop in both reins. That can happen over one stride, but you will receive a better mark in a dressage test if you can demonstrate that the horse is in self-carriage by releasing your contact over a few strides.
2. [diagram]	B Half 10-meter circle right. X Half 10-meter circle left.	• Use half-halts to balance your horse through the change of bend. • Keep your hips and shoulders parallel with your horse's shoulders, keep your body upright, and look ahead of you around the circle.
3. [diagram]	E Half 20-meter circle left. B Halt. Immobility 4 seconds. Proceed in medium walk. M Working trot. [Repeat the exercise on both reins]	• Count to 4 in your head so that the halt is maintained for the correct length of time. • When asked to move off from the halt, the horse should step forward immediately and smoothly.

NOTES:

EXERCISE 22D

	INSTRUCTIONS	TIPS/DIRECTIVES
1.	[Start on the right rein] C Medium walk. M Walk to working canter right. B 20-meter circle right. When passing E, give and retake the reins.	• When riding the circle, remember that your inside leg on the girth keeps the impulsion, develops the engagement of the inside hind leg, and asks for bend. Your outside leg should be slightly behind the girth preventing the hindquarters from escaping to the outside of the circle and generating some forward movement.

2.	B Collected canter.
	    Half 10-meter circle right.
	
	X Simple change.
	    Collected canter.
	    Half 10-meter circle left.
		• The shorter, higher steps of the collected canter are the result of the horse carrying more of the weight towards its haunches. Shortening the strides artificially will result in stiffening and loss of activity, which is exactly what judges do not want to see.
		
		• During the simple change, try to avoid the horse staying too upright in the walk to canter and hence not really covering enough ground forward.

3.	E Working canter. Half 20-meter circle left. M Medium walk. [Repeat the exercise on both reins]	• Use your back, core, and seat to hold the horse in a good balance during the downward transition from canter to walk. • Ensure that the horse continues to work forwards and doesn't just collapse in a heap!

NOTES:

....

....

....

EXERCISE 22E

	INSTRUCTIONS	TIPS/DIRECTIVES
1.	[Start on the right rein] C Working trot. M-B Shoulder-in right. B Half 20-meter circle right. E Working canter right. Half 20-meter circle right.	• When riding the shoulder-in, the horse should have a slight but even bend around your inside leg to create an angle of about 30 degrees. • Make sure you keep your shoulders and hips parallel to those of the horse when riding shoulder-in.

2.	B Collected canter.
	       Half 10-meter circle right.
	
	X Flying change.
	       Collected canter.
	       Half 10-meter circle left.
		• The collected canter should have shorter and higher steps due to the horse carrying more of the weight towards its haunches, not because you've kept the handbrake on.
		
		• When riding a flying change, you must make sure that your horse is sharp to your aids. If he is slow to respond, he may learn to change early or late behind, which is a serious fault that can be difficult to correct.

3.	E Working trot. Half 20-meter circle left. B-M Travers left. M Working trot. [Repeat the exercise on both reins]	• Position the horse for travers, and then ride him forward. "Think" medium trot to ensure that you get plenty of impulsion to give the steps more elevation, swing, and quality.

NOTES:

....

....

....

EXERCISE 22F – Make Your Own

	INSTRUCTIONS
1. H · C(→) · M E · G · B K · X · F · D · · A ·	
2. H · C · M E · G · B K · D · F · A ·	
3. H · C(←) · M E · G · B K · X · F · D · · A ·	

NOTES:

EXERCISE 22G – Make Your Own

	INSTRUCTIONS
1. 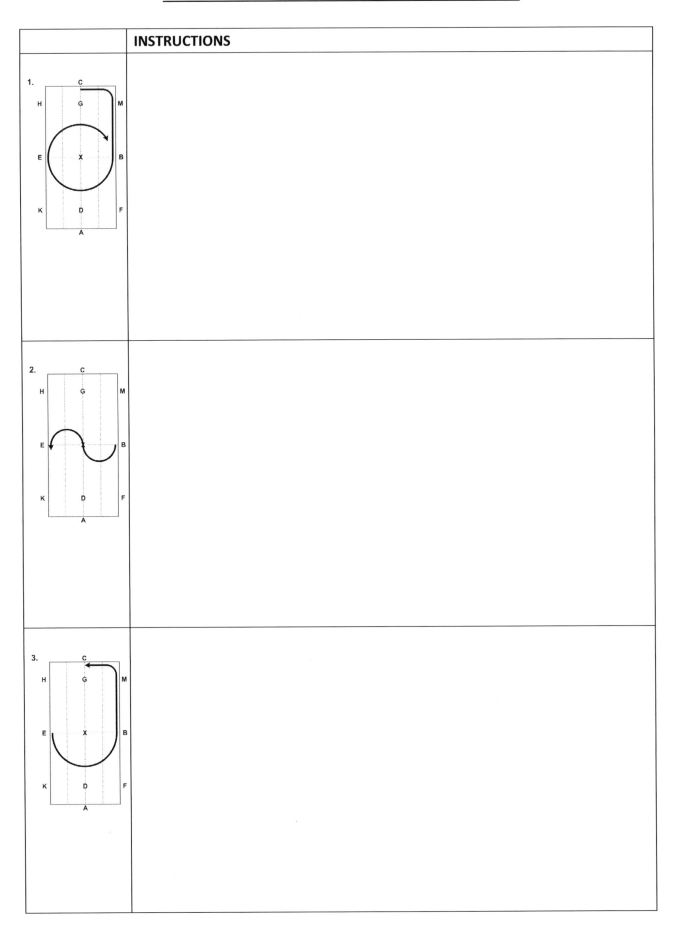	
2.	
3.	

NOTES:

EXERCISE 22H – Make Your Own

	INSTRUCTIONS
1.	
2.	
3.	

NOTES:

"Make the wrong things difficult and the right things easy."

FLOORPLAN #23

'Thread the Needle'

PRACTICE LOG – Note the dates when you last practiced this floorplan.

....
....
....
....
....
....
....
....
....
....
....
....
....
....
....
....
....
....
....
....

#23 'THREAD THE NEEDLE' - 20X40 DIAGRAMS

1.

2.

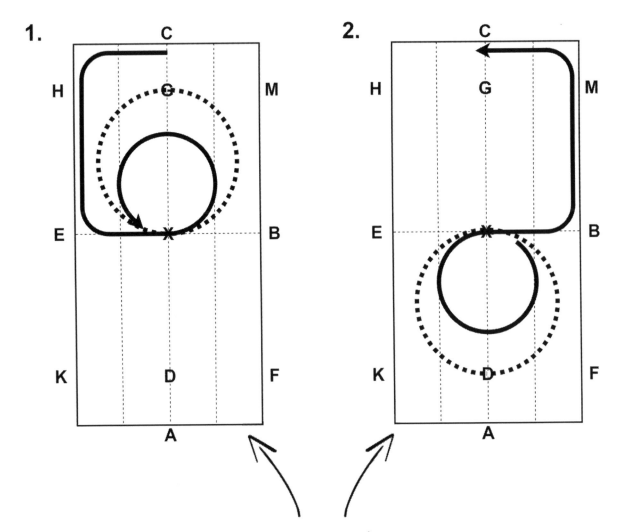

You are riding a figure of eight in the center of the arena.

#23 'THREAD THE NEEDLE' - 20X60 DIAGRAMS

1.

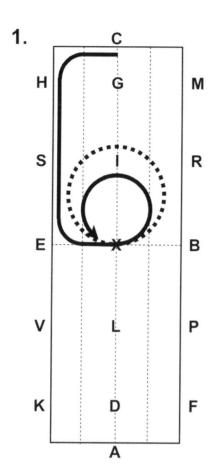

2.

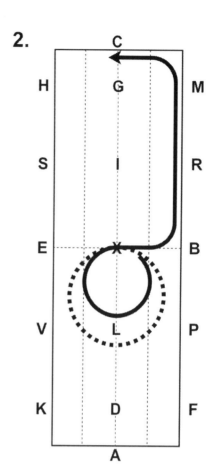

EXERCISE 23A

	INSTRUCTIONS	TIPS/DIRECTIVES
1.	[Start on the left rein] C Working trot. H Medium walk. E Turn left. X 15-meter circle left.	• The horse's walk is a four-beat gait without any suspension. Any tension during the walk may disrupt the rhythm and regularity of the steps, so you should prioritize relaxation in the walk. • A 15-meter circle a X should touch half-way between the ¾ line and the outside track on both sides.
2.	X 15-meter circle right. X-B Working trot. B Track left. [Repeat the exercise on both reins]	• The transition into trot should be obedient and reactive, whilst remaining fluent and calm. • During the trot, the horse's hind feet should step clearly into the prints left by the fore feet.

NOTES:

....

....

....

....

....

....

....

....

....

....

....

....

....

EXERCISE 23B

	INSTRUCTIONS	TIPS/DIRECTIVES
1.	[Start on the left rein] C — Working trot. H/E — Transition to medium walk for one horse's length then proceed in working trot. E — Turn left. X — 15-meter circle left.	• During the trot-walk-trot movement, make sure you are accurate, ride forwards and keep your horse reactive to your aids • When riding the circle, the horse should be supple enough to be able to negotiate the circle accurately, whilst maintaining his rhythm and balance. He should show an adequate degree of bend without losing his quarters to the outside of the circle.
2.	X — 15-meter circle right. X-B — Working trot. B — Track left. M — Halt. Immobility 4 seconds. Proceed in working trot. [Repeat the exercise on both reins]	• More advanced horses should be able to step smoothly into and out of the halt directly without losing balance and frame. If your horse is less experienced, allow him a step or two of walk to help him remain in balance and prevent him coming against the hand.

NOTES:

....

....

....

....

....

....

....

....

....

....

EXERCISE 23C

	INSTRUCTIONS	TIPS/DIRECTIVES
1.	[Start on the left rein] C Working trot. E Turn left. X Medium walk. 10-meter circle left.	• The 10-meter circle should be ridden accurately, five meters in from each side of the arena touching both ¾ lines. • A 10-meter circle is quite a small diameter, so it is the rider's job to choose exactly the right tempo (speed of the rhythm), to enable the horse to manage the rhythm and bend without any disturbances or unevenness to the stride length.

2.	X 10-meter circle right.
	
	X Working trot.
	
	B Track left.
	
	C Halt. Immobility 4 seconds.
	        Rein-back one horse's length.
	        Proceed in working trot.
	
	[Repeat the exercise on both reins]
		• If the horse is not moving forwards into the halt, he will not step underneath himself in the transition, and the halt will probably be crooked and not square.
		
		• Use your bodyweight and your legs to ask for rein-back. Don't try to pull or fiddle the horse backward with your hands.

NOTES:

....

....

....

....

....

....

....

....

....

....

EXERCISE 23D

	INSTRUCTIONS	TIPS/DIRECTIVES
1.	[Start on the left rein] C Medium walk. H Working canter left. E Track left. X 15-meter circle left.	• The canter is a pace of 3-beat. It should have 'uphill' cadenced strides, followed by a moment of suspension. • During the canter, if the moment of suspension appears only very briefly, or worse, is missing, the beat becomes that of 4-time which is a serious fault and will be heavily penalized in the competitive environment.
2.	X Change of lead through trot to working canter right. 15-meter circle right. X Working trot. B Track left. M Medium walk. [Repeat the exercise on both reins]	• In the change of lead, ride the downward transition forward and remember to change the bend over 2-3 trot strides before asking for the transition back into canter. • Encourage the horse to step through into the downward transition to working trot, rather than 'fall' out of the canter.

NOTES:

....

....

....

....

....

....

....

....

....

....

EXERCISE 23E

	INSTRUCTIONS	TIPS/DIRECTIVES
1. 	[Start on the left rein] C Working canter left. E Turn left. X Collected canter. 10-meter circle left.	• Collected canter needs just as much impulsion as working canter! Be sure to keep plenty of energy in the canter so that you don't lose the 3-beat rhythm and moment of suspension. • The circle must be accurate in order to demonstrate that the horse is supple and connected enough to negotiate the movement without losing his balance and rhythm.
2. 	X Simple change OR flying change. 10-meter circle right. X Canter to walk. X-B Medium walk. B Track left. B-M Extended walk. M Medium walk. C Walk to working canter left. [Repeat the exercise on both reins]	• When riding the simple change, maintain the relaxation and the clarity of the walk steps. • When riding a flying change, you must make sure that your horse is sharp to your aids. If he is slow to respond, he may learn to change early or late behind, which is a serious fault that can be difficult to correct. • When transitioning to medium walk, ensure that the horse continues to work forwards and doesn't just collapse in a heap!

NOTES:

....

....

....

....

....

....

....

EXERCISE 23F – Make Your Own

	INSTRUCTIONS
1.	
2.	

NOTES:

....

....

....

....

....

....

....

....

....

....

EXERCISE 23G – Make Your Own

	INSTRUCTIONS
1.	
2.	

NOTES:

....
....
....
....
....
....
....
....
....
....

EXERCISE 23H – Make Your Own

	INSTRUCTIONS
1.	
2.	

NOTES:

....

....

....

....

....

....

....

....

....

....

"Sometimes you win.
Sometimes you learn."

FLOORPLAN #24

'Spirograph'

PRACTICE LOG – Note the dates when you last practiced this floorplan.

#24 'SPIROGRAPH' - 20X40 DIAGRAMS

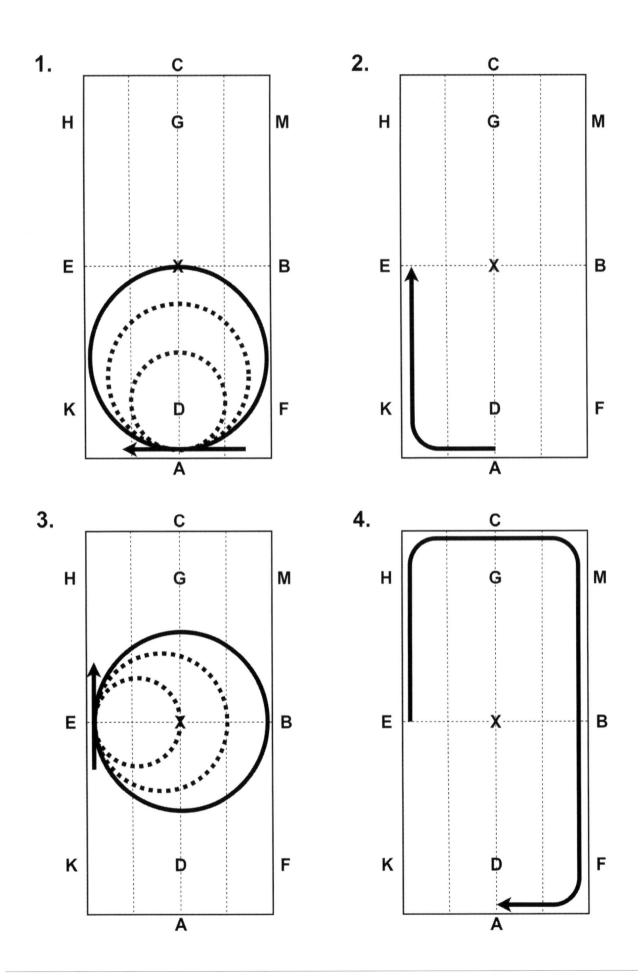

#24 'SPIROGRAPH' - 20X60 DIAGRAMS

1.

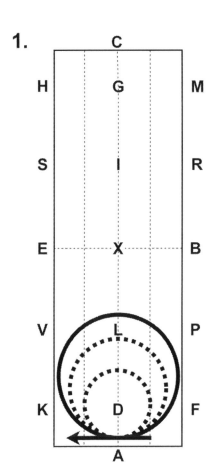

2.

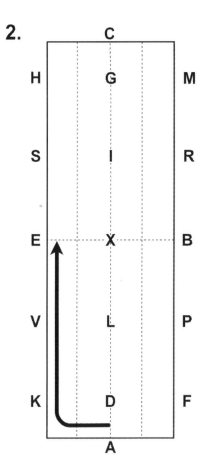

3.

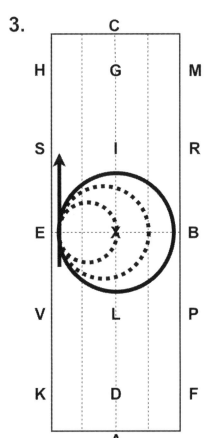

4.

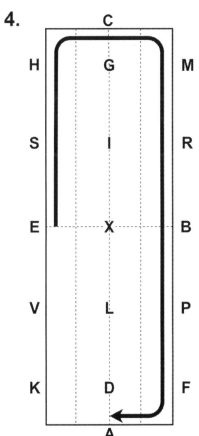

EXERCISE 24A

	INSTRUCTIONS	TIPS/DIRECTIVES
1.	[Start on the right rein] A Working trot. 20-meter circle right.	• Your goal is to develop a good, rhythmical and active working trot. • When riding the circle, keep your hips and shoulders parallel with your horse's shoulders, keep your body upright, and look ahead of you around the circle.
2.	A Medium walk. K Working trot.	• The horse's walk is a four-beat gait without any suspension. • Any tension during the walk may disrupt the rhythm and regularity of the steps, so you should prioritize relaxation in the walk.
3.	E 20-meter circle right in working trot.	• During the circle you are expected to have even bend (think of an imaginary line) through the horse's body; from the tail, centrally through the hindquarters, through the back and shoulders, through the neck, and finishing at the poll.
4.	E Working trot. H Medium walk. C Halt. Immobility 4 seconds. Proceed in medium walk. M Working trot. B/F Transition to medium walk for one horse's length then proceed in working trot. [Repeat the exercise on both reins]	• In a good halt, the horse should be straight and square. Each leg should bear the same weight evenly so that the horse has 'a leg at each corner'. • In the trot-walk-trot movement, the rhythm and frame should remain constant and correct throughout the exercise, and the whole thing should appear fluent and effortless.

NOTES:

EXERCISE 24B

	INSTRUCTIONS	TIPS/DIRECTIVES
1.	[Start on the right rein] A Working canter right. 20-meter circle right.	• When riding the circle, remember that your inside leg on the girth keeps the impulsion, develops the engagement of the inside hind leg, and asks for bend. Your outside leg should be slightly behind the girth preventing the hindquarters from escaping to the outside of the circle and generating some forward movement.
2.	A Working canter right. K Working trot.	• Encourage the horse to step through into the working trot, rather than 'fall' out of the canter.
3.	E 15-meter circle right in working trot.	• A 15-meter circle at E should touch the ¾ line on the other side of the arena. • Make sure the horse has equal bend throughout his whole body. Don't ask for too much neck bend as this will encourage him to fall out through his shoulder.
4.	E Working trot. C Halt. Immobility 4 seconds. Proceed in medium walk. M Working trot. F/A Working canter right. [Repeat the exercise on both reins]	• During the halt, the horse should remain still and relaxed but attentive whilst waiting for his rider's next instruction. • When riding the trot-canter transition, emphasis should be on the horse pushing from the hind legs that are placed under the body rather than launching off the shoulders.

NOTES:

EXERCISE 24C

	INSTRUCTIONS	TIPS/DIRECTIVES

1.	[Start on the right rein]
	
	A Working trot.
	      15-meter circle right.
	      10-meter circle right.
		• Circles are designed to test the horse's balance, suppleness to the bend, and straightness.
		
		• When riding the circles, keep your hips and shoulders parallel with your horse's shoulders, keep your body upright, and look ahead of you around the circle.

2.	A/K Working canter right.	• The canter transition should be reactive, uphill, and balanced. The horse should maintain his round frame. Diligent riding of transitions from trot to canter will build the 'pushing and propulsion' capacity of the horse, enabling him to develop incremental levels of engagement of the hind legs.
3.	E 20-meter circle right. 15-meter circle right.	• Your goal during the canter is to develop regularity and lightness of the strides, an uphill tendency, and the natural ability of the horse to carry himself whilst maintaining active well-placed hind legs.

4.	H Working trot.
	
	C Halt. Immobility 4 seconds.
	      Rein-back one horse's length.
	      Proceed in working trot.
	
	M Medium trot.
	
	F Working trot.
	
	[Repeat the exercise on both reins]
		• The preparation for the medium trot is the most important part of the movement. If your horse is not balanced and engaged, he will fall onto his forehand, break into canter or lose the rhythm as he attempts to lengthen his stride.

NOTES:

EXERCISE 24D

	INSTRUCTIONS	TIPS/DIRECTIVES
1.	[Start on the right rein] A Collected canter. 10-meter circle right.	• The 10-meter circle should touch both ¾ lines. • Remember that the degree of collection required in the canter is only so much as to be able to perform the 10-meter circle with ease.
2.	K Medium walk. E Collected canter right.	• Use your back, core, and seat to hold the horse in a good balance during the downward transition from canter to walk. • When asking for walk to canter at E, create a slight flexion over the desired leading leg and be very clear with your aids.
3.	E 15-meter circle right in collected canter.	• The 15-meter canter circle should touch the ¾ line. • Keep the horse working forward into the bridle. Collected canter should have just as much energy as working canter.
4.	E Collected canter right. H Medium walk. C Working canter right. M Medium canter right. F Collected canter right. [Repeat the exercise on both reins]	• Use half-halts to keep the horse balanced through all the transitions. • Although the medium canter should cover more ground than a working canter, it should also clearly demonstrate an uphill tendency.

NOTES:

EXERCISE 24E

	INSTRUCTIONS	TIPS/DIRECTIVES
1.	[Start on the right rein] A Working trot. 15-meter circle right.	• The trot has a two-beat rhythm during which the horse's legs move in diagonal pairs. There should be a clear moment of suspension when all the horse's feet are off the floor. It's this moment of suspension that gives the trot its expression and lift.
2.	K-E Shoulder-in right.	• When riding the shoulder-in, the horse should have a slight but even bend around your inside leg to create an angle of about 30 degrees.
3.	E 10-meter circle right.	• During the circle you are expected to have even bend (think of an imaginary line) through the horse's body; from the tail, centrally through the hindquarters, through the back and shoulders, through the neck, and finishing at the poll.
4.	E-H Travers right. H Working trot. C Working canter right. M Medium canter. F Working canter. A Working trot. [Repeat the exercise on both reins]	• Position the horse for travers, and then ride him forward. "Think" medium trot to ensure that you get plenty of impulsion to give the steps more elevation, swing, and quality. • During the medium canter, the horse's hind legs must come further under the body and appear to 'push' the horse forwards, whilst you remain in full control through light and supple seat and rein aids.

NOTES:

EXERCISE 24F – Make Your Own

	INSTRUCTIONS
1.	
2.	
3.	
4.	

NOTES:

EXERCISE 24G – Make Your Own

	INSTRUCTIONS
1.	
2.	
3.	
4.	

NOTES:

EXERCISE 24H – Make Your Own

	INSTRUCTIONS
1.	
2.	
3.	
4.	

NOTES:

"Not every victory shows up on the scoreboard."

FLOORPLAN #25

'Aiming for x'

PRACTICE LOG – Note the dates when you last practiced this floorplan.

....

....

....

....

....

....

....

....

....

....

....

....

....

....

....

....

....

....

....

....

....

....

#25 'AIMING FOR X' - 20X40 DIAGRAMS

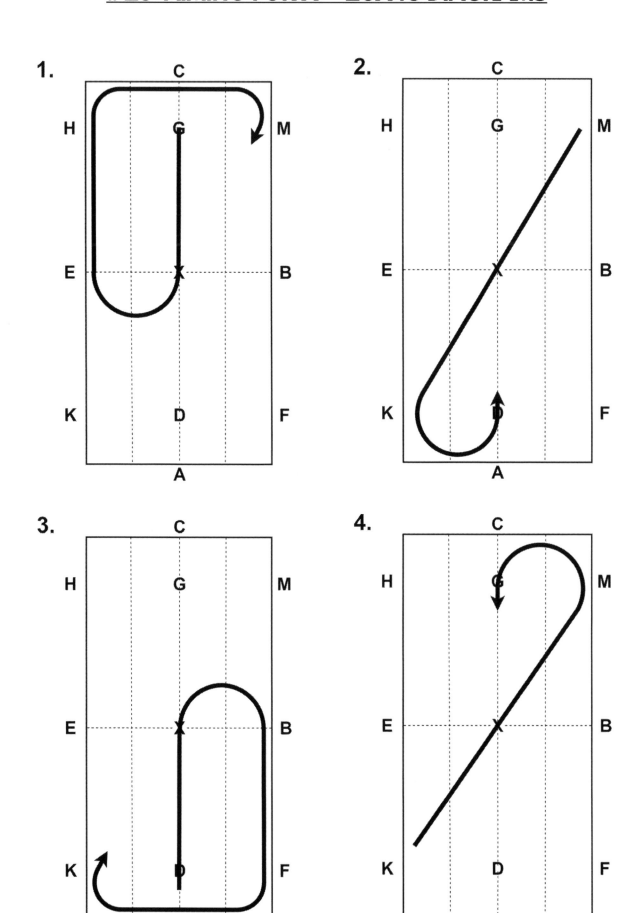

#25 'AIMING FOR X' - 20X60 DIAGRAMS

1.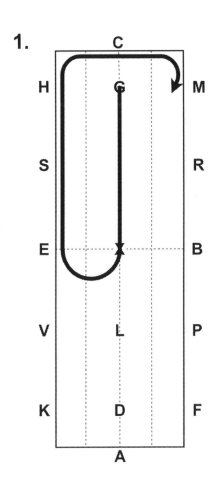

2.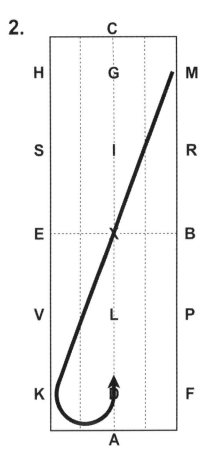

3.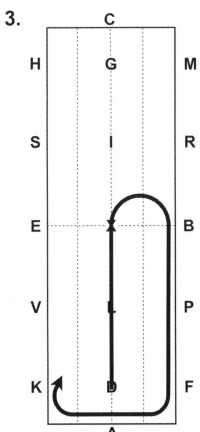

4.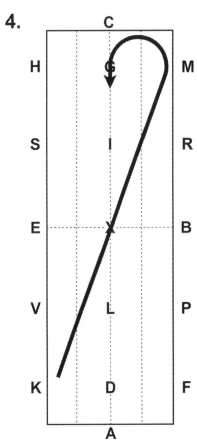

EXERCISE 25A

	INSTRUCTIONS	TIPS/DIRECTIVES
1.	[Start on any rein] C Proceed down the center line in working trot. X Halt. Immobility 4 seconds. Proceed in medium walk. Half 10-meter circle right. E Working trot. C Medium walk.	• Ride your horse forward (not faster) to keep him straight on the center line. • If your horse begins to step backwards during the halt, ride forwards immediately. Ride the halt again and ease your hand as you do so. Be positive with your legs and keep thinking forwards. • When completing the half 10-meter circle there should be no tilting of the horse's head.
2.	MXK Free walk on a long rein. K Medium walk. Half 10-meter circle left. Proceed down the center line.	• The free walk should show the horse in a relaxed state, being allowed total freedom to lower and stretch out his head and neck. • The rhythm during the free walk should remain in a clear four beat, correct sequence, and the horse should clearly over-track, covering maximum ground, and demonstrating complete freedom of his shoulder.
3.	X Half 10-meter circle right. B Working trot .	• Any tension during the walk may disrupt the rhythm and regularity of the steps, so you should prioritize relaxation in the walk. • The transition back into trot should be obedient and reactive, whilst remaining fluent and calm.

4. 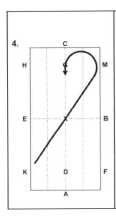	**KXM** Working trot. **M** Medium walk. Half 10-meter circle left. **G** Working trot. [Repeat exercise on both reins]	• During the trot, the horse's hind feet should step clearly into the prints left by the fore feet. • When transitioning to medium walk, ensure that the horse continues to work forwards and doesn't just collapse in a heap!

NOTES:

....
....
....
....
....
....
....
....
....
....
....
....
....
....
....
....
....
....
....
....
....
....

EXERCISE 25B

	INSTRUCTIONS	TIPS/DIRECTIVES
1.	**[Start on any rein]** C Proceed down the center line in working trot. X Half 10-meter circle right. E Working canter right.	• Keep the horse into your outside rein as you ride the half circle, asking for uniform bend through the horse's body around your inside leg. • The canter transition should be reactive, uphill, and balanced.
2.	MXK Working canter right. K Working trot. Half 10-meter circle left. Proceed down the center line.	• If it's difficult for your horse to maintain a balanced canter all the way to F, ride a transition to working trot over X. As the balance improves, you can go a bit further each time before transitioning to trot
3.	X Half 10-meter circle right. B Medium walk. F Halt. Immobility 4 seconds Proceed in medium walk.	• Your horse should be straight, square, attentive, relaxed and immobile during the halt, and the move-off should be immediate and obedient. • The halt should happen when your body is in line with the F marker.
4.	KXM Free walk on a long rein. M Working trot. Half 10-meter circle left. **[Repeat exercise on both reins]**	• In free walk, allow the horse to gradually take the contact from you and stretch down for the bit. Don't throw the contact away completely, as that could cause the horse to hollow and lose focus. • Shorten the reins slowly over a coupe of strides ready for the transition to working trot at M. Breath deeply and stay relaxed so that your horse doesn't anticipate a transition and start to jog.

NOTES:

EXERCISE 25C

	INSTRUCTIONS	TIPS/DIRECTIVES
1.	[Start on any rein] C Proceed down the center line in working trot. X Halt. Immobility 4 seconds. Proceed in medium walk. Half 10-meter circle right. E-H Free walk on a long rein. H Medium walk. C Working trot.	• When riding the half circle, keep your hips and shoulders parallel with your horse's shoulders, keep your body upright, and look ahead of you around the circle. • During the free walk, the horse should follow the contact round and down, stretching his neck and head to show relaxation and suppleness over his back. • In the free walk, although the horse is relaxed, he should march purposefully forward and look as though he is 'going somewhere'.
2.	MXK Show some medium trot strides. K Working trot. Half 10-meter circle left. Proceed down the center line.	• Make sure the horse is straight on the diagonal before asking for medium trot. • Aim for a balanced upward and downward transitions into and out of medium trot. Don't "fire" the horse abruptly into medium trot. That risks the horse losing his balance, breaking rhythm, and falling onto his forehand.
3.	X Half 10-meter circle right. B Working canter right.	• When riding the trot to canter transition at B, use the previous half circle to encourage the horse to push from the hind legs that are placed under the body rather than launching off the shoulders. • The canter is a pace of 3-beat. It should have 'uphill' cadenced strides, followed by a moment of suspension.

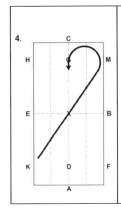	**KXM** Show some strides of medium canter. **M** Working trot. Half 10-meter circle left. [Repeat the exercise on both reins]	• The medium canter is a longer version of the working canter. It covers more ground because the horse's frame and strides lengthen. • When riding the medium canter, maintain the regularity and lightness of the canter strides.

NOTES:

....

....

....

....

....

....

....

....

....

....

....

....

....

....

....

....

....

....

....

....

....

....

....

EXERCISE 25D

	INSTRUCTIONS	TIPS/DIRECTIVES
1.	[Start on any rein] C Proceed down the center line in collected trot. X Half 10-meter circle right. H Halt. Immobility 4 seconds. Rein-back one horse's length. Proceed in medium walk. H/C Walk to working canter right.	• Collected trot demands greater self-carriage from the horse. The horse should remain 'on the bit', with his hocks engaged and flexed, stepping well under his center of gravity, and should move forward, uphill, and with good impulsion. • During the halt, the horse should remain still and relaxed but attentive whilst waiting for his rider's next instruction. • Make sure that you establish the walk steps before asking for the upward transition to canter.
2.	MXK Working canter. K Simple change. Collected canter. Half 10-meter circle left. Proceed down the center line.	• Keep the horse moving forward in the simple change to avoid the horse staying too upright. Instead, you want to encourage the weight-bearing capacity (in the canter-walk) and the pushing power (in the walk-canter) of the hind legs. • Remember that the degree of collection required in the canter is only so much as to be able to perform the half 10-meter circle with ease.
3.	X Medium walk. Half 10-meter circle right. B Extended walk. F Working trot.	• In extended walk, allow the horse sufficient freedom of his neck to stretch, but don't allow him to drop his poll too low as this could morph into a 'stretching on a long rein' movement.

4. 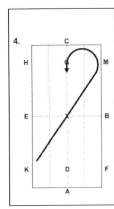	KXM Leg yield right. M Collected trot. Half 10-meter circle left. [Repeat exercise on both reins]	• During the leg-yield, the horse should move forwards and sideways on two tracks. His body should remain straight, and there should be a slight flexion of his head and neck away from the direction of travel.

NOTES:

....
....
....
....
....
....
....
....
....
....
....
....
....
....
....
....
....
....
....
....
....
....
....
....

EXERCISE 25E

	INSTRUCTIONS	TIPS/DIRECTIVES
1.	[Start on the right rein] C Proceed down the center line in collected canter right. X Half 10-meter circle right. E Travers right in working canter. H Working canter.	• The collected canter should have shorter and higher steps due to the horse carrying more of the weight towards its haunches, not because you've kept the handbrake on. • Be careful not to ask for too much angle in the travers or the horse will be unable to maintain impulsion. • If the horse has a tendency to come crooked in canter, ride shoulder-fore, rather than travers.
2.	MXK Canter half-pass right. K Simple change OR flying change to collected canter left. Half 10-meter circle left. Proceed down the center line.	• During the half-pass, the pace should not change, in terms of energy, elasticity and suspension, nor should the rhythm vary. • To create a steeper angle in the half-pass, simply leave the track a few strides after M and/or re-join the track a few strides before K. • When riding a simple change, remember that they should always be ridden more from the seat and leg than from the hand. • When riding a flying change, remember that the quality of your change will be determined by the suppleness and elasticity of the horse's canter.

3. 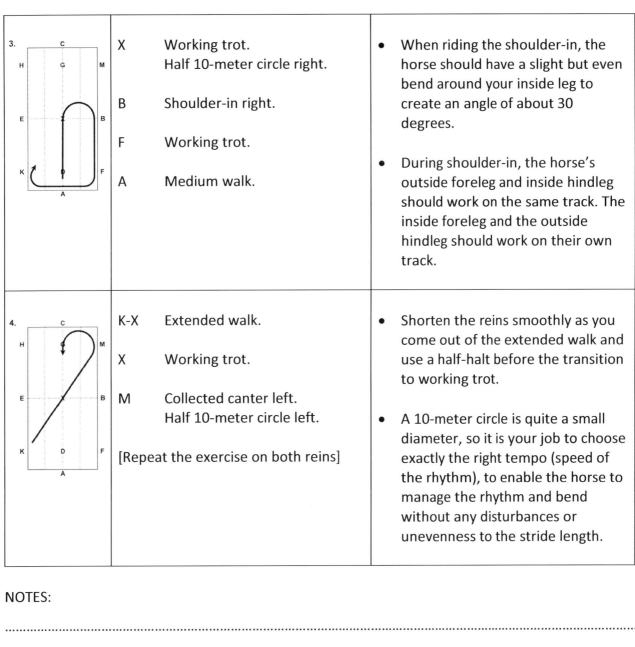	X	Working trot. Half 10-meter circle right.	• When riding the shoulder-in, the horse should have a slight but even bend around your inside leg to create an angle of about 30 degrees.
	B	Shoulder-in right.	
	F	Working trot.	• During shoulder-in, the horse's outside foreleg and inside hindleg should work on the same track. The inside foreleg and the outside hindleg should work on their own track.
	A	Medium walk.	
4.	K-X	Extended walk.	• Shorten the reins smoothly as you come out of the extended walk and use a half-halt before the transition to working trot.
	X	Working trot.	
	M	Collected canter left. Half 10-meter circle left.	• A 10-meter circle is quite a small diameter, so it is your job to choose exactly the right tempo (speed of the rhythm), to enable the horse to manage the rhythm and bend without any disturbances or unevenness to the stride length.
		[Repeat the exercise on both reins]	

NOTES:

....
....
....
....
....
....
....
....
....
....
....
....

EXERCISE 25F – Make Your Own

	INSTRUCTIONS
1.	
2.	
3.	
4.	

NOTES:

EXERCISE 25G – Make Your Own

	INSTRUCTIONS
1.	
2.	
3.	
4.	

NOTES:

EXERCISE 25H – Make Your Own

	INSTRUCTIONS
1.	
2.	
3.	
4.	

NOTES:

"Your corners and short sides are what make your movements. Nine times out of ten you have to do something out of a corner. Ride a bad corner, you ride a bad movement."

FLOORPLAN #26

'Teardrops in Heaven'

PRACTICE LOG – Note the dates when you last practiced this floorplan.

#26 'TEARDROPS IN HEAVEN' - 20X40 DIAGRAMS

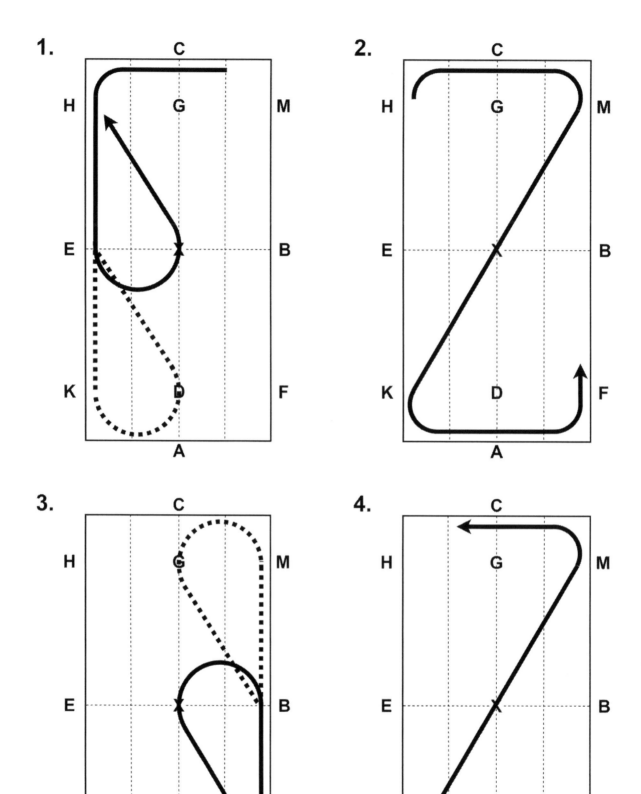

#26 'TEARDROPS IN HEAVEN' - 20X60 DIAGRAMS

1.

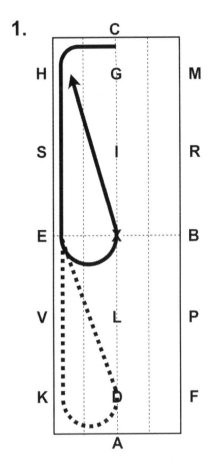

2.

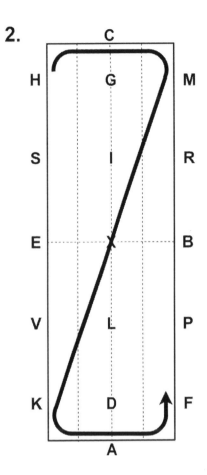

3.

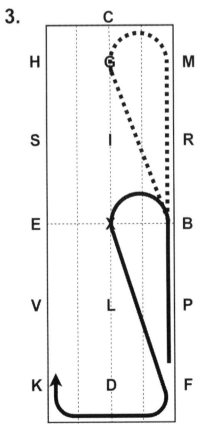

4.

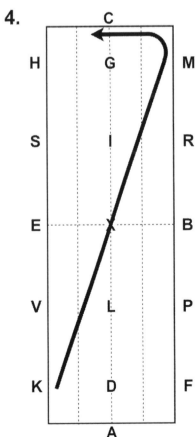

EXERCISE 26A

	INSTRUCTIONS	TIPS/DIRECTIVES

1.	[Start on the left rein]
	
	C Working trot.
	
	E Medium walk.
	       Half 10-meter circle left.
	       Re-join the track at H on the
	       right rein.
		• When transitioning to medium walk, keep the horse working forwards so that he doesn't just fall in a heap!
		
		• When riding the half circle, keep your hips and shoulders parallel with your horse's shoulders, keep your body upright, and look ahead of you around the circle.
		
		• Guard the horse's quarters with your outside leg to prevent them from swinging out on the half circle.

2.	C Medium walk. MXK Free walk on a long rein. K Medium walk. A Working trot.	• In the free walk, although the horse is relaxed, he should march purposefully forward and look as though he is 'going somewhere'. • The transition back into trot should be obedient and reactive, whilst remaining fluent and calm.

3.	FBM Working trot.
	
	M Medium walk.
	       Half 10-meter circle left.
	
	G Working trot.
	       Re-join the track at B on the
	       right rein.
	
	A Halt. Immobility 4 seconds.
	       Proceed in working trot.
		• Maintain the outside rein contact on the half circle to keep control of the horse's outside shoulder and to manage the tempo.
		
		• More advanced horses should be able to step smoothly into and out of the halt directly without losing balance and frame. If your horse is less experienced, allow him a step or two of walk to help him remain in balance and prevent him coming against the hand.

4. 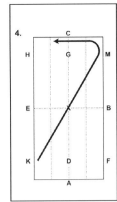	KXM Working trot [Repeat exercise on both reins]	• The trot has a two-beat rhythm during which the horse's legs move in diagonal pairs. There should be a clear moment of suspension when all the horse's feet are off the floor. It's this moment of suspension that gives the trot its expression and lift.

NOTES:

....

....

....

....

....

....

....

....

....

....

....

....

....

....

....

....

....

....

....

....

....

....

....

....

....

EXERCISE 26B

	INSTRUCTIONS	TIPS/DIRECTIVES
1.	[Start on the left rein] C Working trot. E Half 10-meter circle left. Re-join the track at H on the right rein.	• Don't ask for too much neck bend as that can encourage the horse to fall out. Keep the outside rein on the half circle to keep control of the horse's outside shoulder. • The half circle must be accurate in order to demonstrate that the horse is supple and connected enough to negotiate the movement without losing his balance and rhythm.
2.	MXK Working trot. K/A Working canter left.	• Ride your horse forward (not faster) to keep him straight when going across the diagonal. • Use a half-halt to rebalance the horse, and make sure you have the correct bend before asking for canter.
3.	FBM Working canter left. M Working trot. Half 10-meter circle left. Re-join the track at B on the right rein. A Medium walk.	• Keep the horse securely into your outside rein and use a half-halt to balance him before you ride the downward transition at M and the half-circle. • Encourage the horse to step through into the working trot, rather than 'fall' out of the canter.
4.	KXM Free walk on a long rein. M Medium walk. C Working trot. [Repeat the exercise on both reins]	• When riding the free walk, remember to ride your horse forward into the contact; the exercise should be ridden on a LONG rein, not a loose one.

NOTES:

EXERCISE 26C

	INSTRUCTIONS	TIPS/DIRECTIVES
1. 	**[Start on the left rein]** C Working trot. HXK Show some medium trot strides. K Half 10-meter circle left. Re-join the track at E on the right rein.	• Medium trot is a pace of moderate lengthening. Whilst maintaining a round frame and working over his back to the contact, the horse should clearly lengthen his stride to cover more ground. • The transition back to working trot from medium trot should be balanced and smooth, and the rhythm should not change – only the stride length.
2. 	H/C Working canter right. MXK Show some medium canter strides. K Working trot. A Halt. Immobility 4 seconds. Rein-back one horse's length. Proceed in medium walk.	• The medium canter is a longer version of the working canter. It covers more ground because the horse's frame and strides lengthen. • During the rein-back, the horse should remain 'on the bit' with the poll as the highest point. He shouldn't drop his head down or curl up behind the bit.
3. 	FBM Free walk on a long rein. M Medium walk. Half 10-meter circle left. Re-join track at B on the right rein. B Working trot.	• To start the free walk, let the reins slide through your fingers gradually to allow the horse to take the rein forwards, round and down. It can be helpful to allow the inside rein to lengthen slightly before the outside rein. This can prevent the horse from hollowing and coming off the aids as you begin to ride the free walk, and will encourage him to remain into the contact. • The transition back into trot should be obedient and reactive, whilst remaining fluent and calm.

| 4. 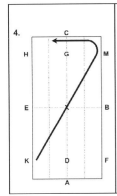 | KXM Working trot.
Over X transition to medium walk for one horse's length then proceed in working trot.

[Repeat the exercise on both reins] | • When transitioning to walk, there must be the correct number of walk steps, and they must be clearly walked, rather than jogged.

• One horse's length is measured at three to four strides. |

NOTES:

....

....

....

....

....

....

....

....

....

....

....

....

....

....

....

....

....

....

....

....

....

....

EXERCISE 26D

	INSTRUCTIONS	TIPS/DIRECTIVES
1.	[Start on the left rein] C Working trot. H Working canter left. K Half 10-meter circle left Re-join the track at E on the right rein. E Simple change. Proceed in working canter right.	• Keep plenty of impulsion in the canter strides and don't slow the rhythm. If you have plenty of jump in the canter steps, your horse will find negotiating the half circle much easier. Slowing the rhythm will put the horse onto his forehand and potentially lose the clear three beat canter sequence. • When riding the simple change, maintain the relaxation and the clarity of the walk steps.
2.	MXK Medium canter. K Working trot. A Medium walk. F Working trot.	• Use a half-halt to balance the horse before the medium canter strides and afterward. • During the medium canter, the horse's hind legs must come further under the body and appear to 'push' the horse forwards, whilst you remain in full control through light and supple seat and rein aids.
3.	B Half 10-meter circle left. X Leg-yield left to re-join the track at F.	• After the half circle, remember to make the horse straight before you commence leg-yielding. • During the leg-yield, if the horse doesn't move away from your leg, or trails its quarters to avoid stepping through and underneath its body, re-emphasize the aid. Don't try to compensate for the horse's lack of response by leaning to one side, or wriggling around in the saddle!

| 4. 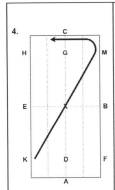 | KXM Medium trot.

M Working trot.

[Repeat the exercise on both reins] | • Although your horse should be working with good impulsion during the medium trot, he should not hurry or lose rhythm and must remain in a good uphill balance. |

NOTES:

....

....

....

....

....

....

....

....

....

....

....

....

....

....

....

....

....

....

....

....

....

EXERCISE 26E

	INSTRUCTIONS	TIPS/DIRECTIVES
1.	**[Start on the left rein]** C Working trot. H Working canter left. K Half 10-meter circle left. Re-join the track at E on the right rein. E-H Counter canter. H Working trot.	• During the half circle you are expected to have even bend (think of an imaginary line) through the horse's body; from the tail, centrally through the hindquarters, through the back and shoulders, through the neck, and finishing at the poll. • During the counter-canter, maintain a little flexion over the leading leg, but no more than what is asked in true canter. • Encourage the horse to step through into the working trot, rather than 'fall' out of the canter.
2.	MXK Extended trot. K Working trot. F Working canter left.	• In the extended trot, the horse covers the maximum amount of ground he can without hurrying and losing his balance. • If your horse is inexperienced, aim to ride a few balanced extended trot strides, rather than trying to cover the whole diagonal. If your horse is more experienced, aim for clear, balanced transitions in and out of the extended trot and ride the pace from marker to marker.
3.	FBM Working canter. M Half 10-meter circle left. G Canter half-pass left to re-join the track at B. B Working trot. A Medium walk.	• During the half-pass, the horse must be bent towards the direction he is traveling in. A good guide to the amount of bend is simply to ensure that his face is looking at the point on the track (in this case B) where you are aiming to arrive at the end of the movement.

4. 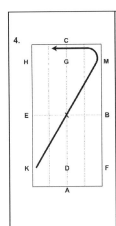	KXM	Extended walk.	• Allow the horse to stretch to the bit and give him freedom of his shoulders during the extended walk, but don't let him drop his poll too low.
	M	Medium walk.	
	C	Working trot.	
	[Repeat the exercise on both reins]		• The transition back to medium walk from extended walk should be balanced and smooth, with no tension or jogging.

NOTES:

....

....

....

....

....

....

....

....

....

....

....

....

....

....

....

....

....

....

....

....

....

....

EXERCISE 26F – Make Your Own

	INSTRUCTIONS
1. 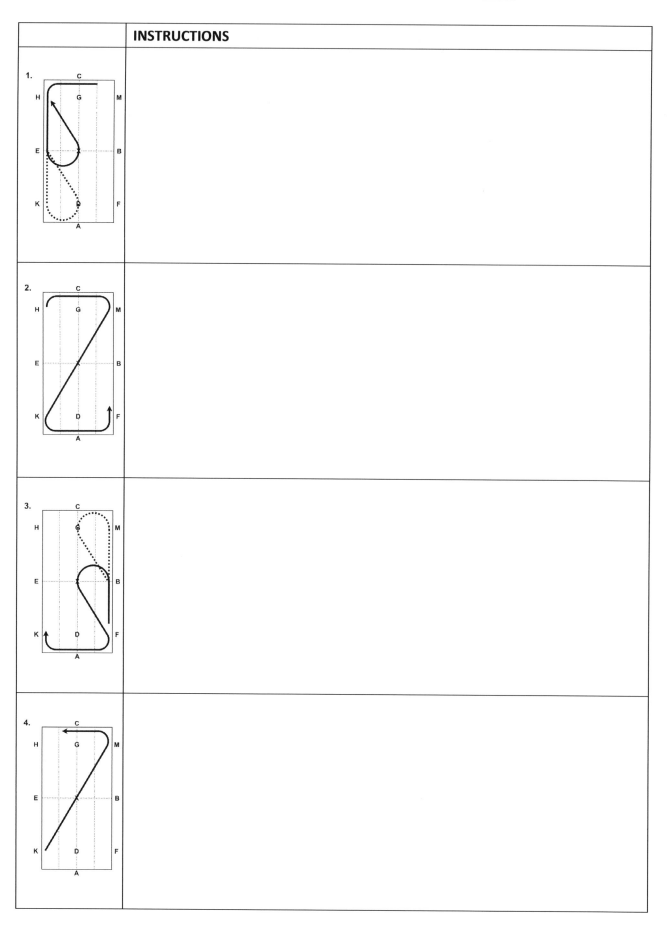	
2.	
3.	
4.	

NOTES:

EXERCISE 26G – Make Your Own

	INSTRUCTIONS
1. 	
2.	
3.	
4.	

NOTES:

EXERCISE 26H – Make Your Own

	INSTRUCTIONS
1. 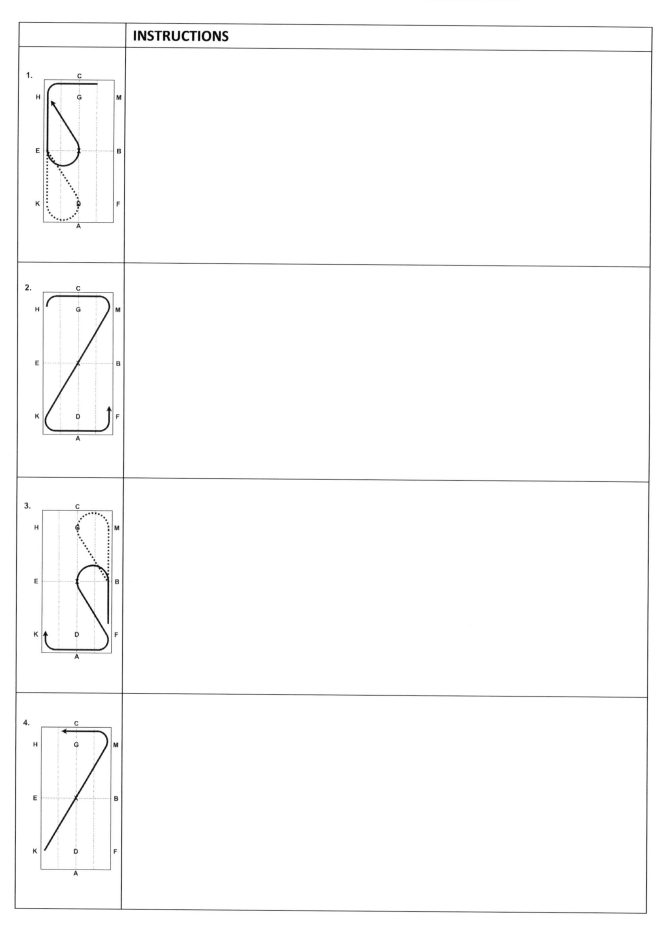	
2.	
3.	
4.	

NOTES:

"Feel the ride,
don't think the ride."

FLOORPLAN #27

'The Bow Tie'

PRACTICE LOG – Note the dates when you last practiced this floorplan.

....
....
....
....
....
....
....
....
....
....
....
....
....
....
....
....
....
....
....
....
....
....
....

#27 'THE BOW TIE' - 20X40 DIAGRAMS

1.

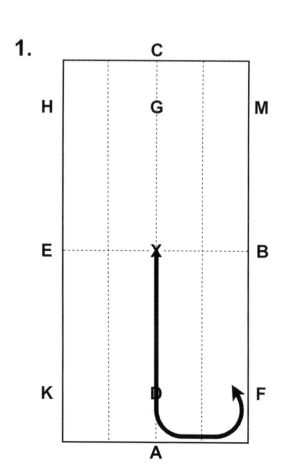

2.

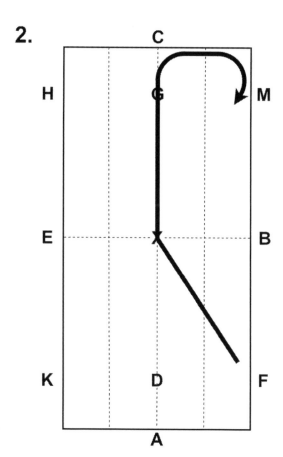

3.

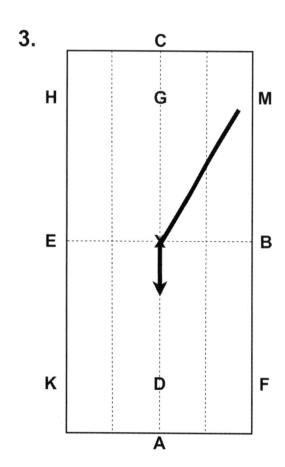

#27 'THE BOW TIE' - 20X60 DIAGRAMS

1.

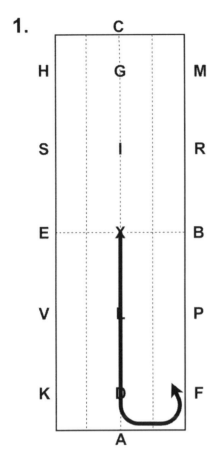

2.

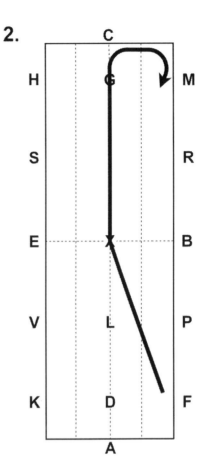

3.

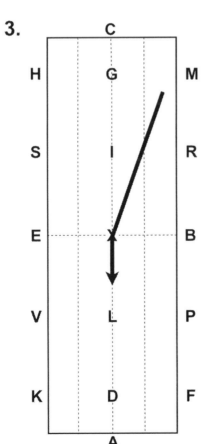

EXERCISE 27A

	INSTRUCTIONS	TIPS/DIRECTIVES
1.	[Proceed down the center line] X Halt. Immobility 4 seconds. Proceed in working trot. A Track left	• Your horse should be straight, square, attentive, relaxed and immobile during the halt, and the move-off should be smooth and obedient. • On the center line the horse should travel forward and straight, as though he is on railway tracks.
2.	F-X Working trot. X-G Medium walk. G Working trot. C Track right.	• When riding the F-X line, keep your eye on C so that you finish up on the center line and don't overshoot X. • When transitioning to medium walk, ensure that the horse continues to work forwards and doesn't just collapse in a heap! • The transition back into trot should be obedient and reactive, whilst remaining fluent and calm.
3.	M-X Working trot. X Halt. Immobility 4 seconds. [Repeat on both reins]	• Before halting at X, make the horse straight for one stride. This will help you get a straight and square halt. • In a good halt, the horse should be straight and square. Each leg should bear the same weight evenly so that the horse has 'a leg at each corner'. • If the halt is unbalanced, the horse may tip onto his forehand and drop his poll as he halts, or he might throw his head up against the contact and not halt square.

NOTES:

EXERCISE 27B

	INSTRUCTIONS	TIPS/DIRECTIVES
1.	[Proceed down the center line] X Working trot. A Track left. F Medium walk.	• On the center line, ride your horse forward (not faster) to help keep him straight. • Your goal is to develop a good, rhythmical and active working trot. • When transitioning to medium walk, ensure that the horse continues to work forwards and doesn't just collapse in a heap!
2.	F-X Medium walk. X-G Free walk on a long rein. G Medium walk. C Track right. M Working trot.	• When asking the horse for free walk, allow him to take the reins gradually. Open your fingers and keep riding forward into the contact so that the horse stretches down the rein. • To ride a good transition from free walk back to medium walk, shorten your reins gradually. Keep your leg on to maintain the impulsion and engagement and to encourage the horse's hind legs to remain active.
3.	M-X Working trot, [Repeat the exercise on both reins]	• Your horse will stay straighter if he is working nicely forward; horses that are dawdling behind their riders' leg are far more likely to wander. • Keep the outside rein so that the horse doesn't drift and miss X.

NOTES:

....

....

....

EXERCISE 27C

	INSTRUCTIONS	TIPS/DIRECTIVES
1.	[Proceed down the center line] X Working trot. D Halt. Immobility 4 seconds. Rein-back one horse's length. Proceed in working trot. A Track left.	• The rein-back is defined as a rearward movement of diagonal pairs. It has a two-beat rhythm and no moment of suspension. Each pair of legs is raised and returned to the ground alternately, while the horse stays straight and moves on one track.
2.	F-X Medium trot. X-G Working trot. G Halt. Immobility 4 seconds. Proceed in medium walk. C Track right. M Working trot.	• Keep the horse into your outside rein as you ride the medium trot. If you allow the horse to drift through his outside shoulder, you'll overshoot X. • A square halt will only happen if the horse was straight and engaged. If the horse is moving crooked, it's virtually impossible to arrive at a square halt.
3.	M-X Working trot. [Repeat the exercise on both reins]	• Keep your eye on A as you ride the diagonal line so that you don't overshoot X. • The horse should travel forward and straight, as though he is on railway tracks.

NOTES:

....

....

....

....

....

....

EXERCISE 27D

	INSTRUCTIONS	TIPS/DIRECTIVES
1.	[Proceed down the center line] X Working trot. A Track left.	• During the trot, the horse's hind feet should step clearly into the prints left by the fore feet. • If you have a young or 'green' horse, always ride rising trot so that he can use his back
2.	F-X Leg-yield left. X-G Working trot. G Halt. Immobility 4 seconds. Proceed in medium walk. C Track right.	• The key to correct leg-yielding is to have the horse moving forwards, and stepping sideways away from your leg aid, whilst maintaining a slight flexion from the poll – not a bend in the neck! • During the halt, the horse should remain still and relaxed but attentive whilst waiting for his rider's next instruction.
3.	M-X Extended walk. X Working trot. [Repeat the exercise on both reins]	• During the extended walk, allow the horse to lengthen his frame and have complete freedom of his shoulder, but don't allow the reins to get too long as he may drop his poll too low and the movement may morph into a stretch exercise.

NOTES:

....

....

....

....

....

....

EXERCISE 27E

	INSTRUCTIONS	TIPS/DIRECTIVES
1. (diagram)	[Proceed down the center line] X Working canter left. A Track left.	• The canter is a pace of 3-beat. It should have 'uphill' cadenced strides, followed by a moment of suspension. • Your goal during the canter is to develop regularity and lightness of the strides, an uphill tendency, and the natural ability of the horse to carry himself whilst maintaining active well-placed hind legs.
2. (diagram)	F-X Canter half-pass left. X-G Working canter. G Halt. Immobility 4 seconds. Proceed in collected trot. C Track right.	• In the half-pass, the bend should be through the length of horse's body, around the rider's inside leg, not just in the neck. • During the half-pass, the canter should not change, in terms of energy, elasticity and suspension, nor should the rhythm vary. • It's important 'think forward' when riding into halt, otherwise the horse will lose engagement as he halts. The halt will become unbalanced and the horse may come against the contact.
3. (diagram)	M-X Working trot. X Working canter left. [Repeat the exercise on both reins]	• Make the horse straight for a stride as you approach X and pick up a slight left flexion before asking for the canter transition.

NOTES:

EXERCISE 27F – Make Your Own

	INSTRUCTIONS
1. 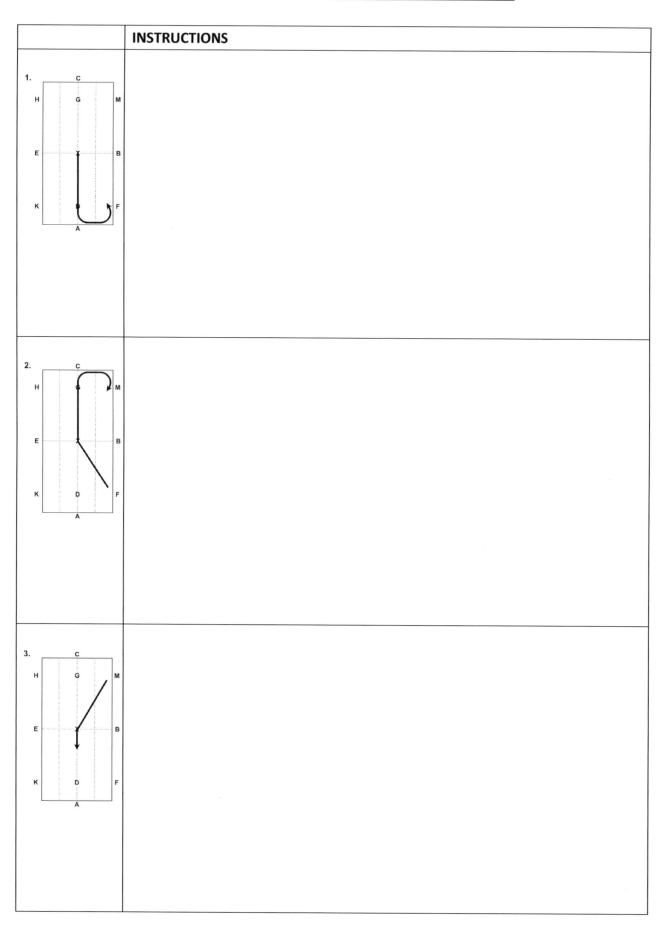	
2.	
3.	

NOTES:

EXERCISE 27G – Make Your Own

	INSTRUCTIONS
1. 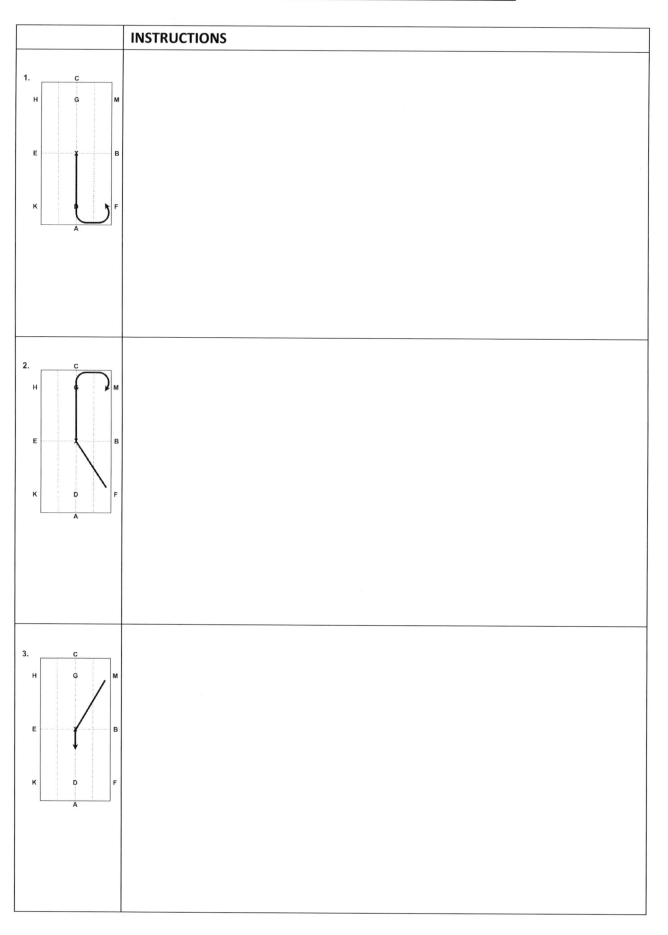	
2.	
3.	

NOTES:

EXERCISE 27H – Make Your Own

	INSTRUCTIONS
1. 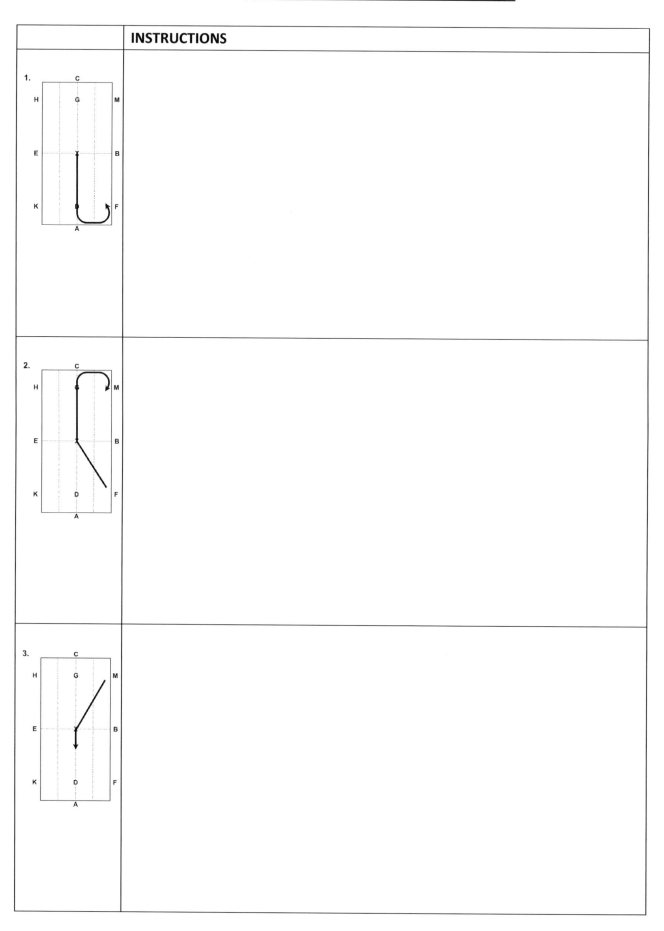	
2.	
3.	

NOTES:

"Ride him to the contact but be careful not to drive him <u>through</u> the contact."

FLOORPLAN #28

'The Hook'

PRACTICE LOG – Note the dates when you last practiced this floorplan.

#28 'THE HOOK' - 20X40 DIAGRAMS

1.

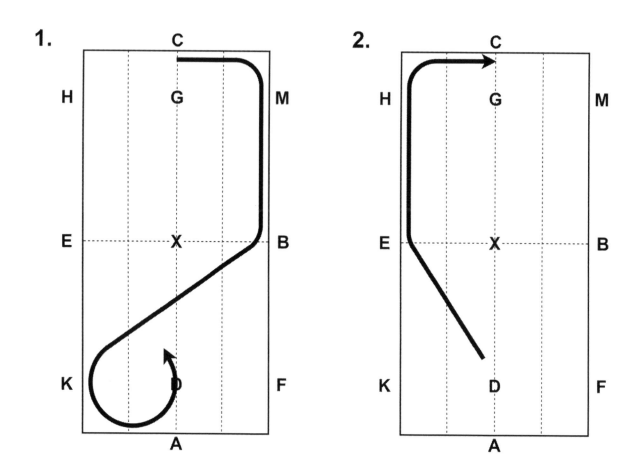

2.

#28 'THE HOOK' - 20X60 DIAGRAMS

1.

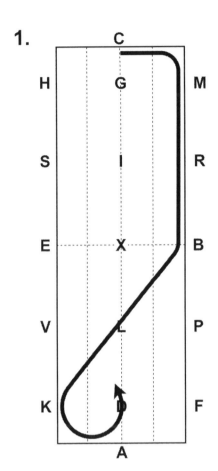

2.

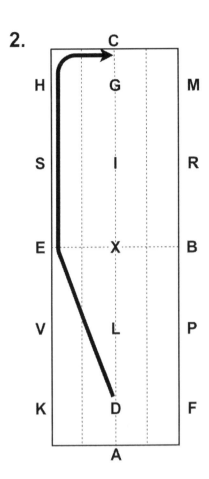

EXERCISE 28A

	INSTRUCTIONS	TIPS/DIRECTIVES
1.	[Start on the right rein] C Working trot. M Medium walk. B-K Free walk on a long rein. K Medium walk. Half 10-meter circle left.	• To ride a good transition from free walk back to medium walk, shorten your reins gradually. Keep your leg on to maintain the impulsion and engagement and to encourage the horse's hind leg to remain active. • When completing the half circle there should be no tilting of the horse's head.
2.	D-E Medium walk. H Halt. Immobility 4 seconds. Proceed in working trot. [Repeat the exercise on both reins]	• The halt should happen when your body is in line with the H marker. • Count to 4 in your head so that the halt is maintained for the correct length of time.

NOTES:

....
....
....
....
....
....
....
....
....
....
....
....
....

EXERCISE 28B

	INSTRUCTIONS	TIPS/DIRECTIVES
1.	[Start on the right rein] C Working canter right. B Working trot. B-K Working trot. K Half 10-meter circle left.	• Prepare well ahead for the transition to trot at B. Keep the horse supported in your outside rein through the transition, and be ready to change the bend as you approach K. • During the circle, your horse should continue to work forwards, in a good rhythm, and show a clear uniform bend along his body around the circle.
2.	D-E Working trot. E Working canter right. [Repeat the exercise on both reins]	• Take up a slight right flexion on the diagonal line, supporting the horse with your outside rein. That will help prepare and balanced the horse for the correct canter strike off. • The canter transition should be reactive, uphill, and balanced. The horse should maintain his round frame.

NOTES:

....

....

....

....

....

....

....

....

....

....

....

EXERCISE 28C

	INSTRUCTIONS	TIPS/DIRECTIVES
1.	[Start on the right rein] C Medium walk. M Working trot. B-K Medium trot. K Half 10-meter circle left in working trot.	• During the medium trot the horse's frame should lengthen so that he carries his head slightly in front of the vertical. • Leave enough space to get your horse back from the medium trot and balanced ready for the half-10-meter circle.
2.	D-E Working trot. H Halt. Immobility 4 seconds. Rein-back one horse's length. Proceed in medium walk. [Repeat exercise on both reins]	• Use the fence line to keep your horse straight in the halt and rein-back. If the horse does not halt square, ask him to walk forward one step to correct the halt. If the halt is crooked, it's highly likely that the rein-back will be crooked too.

NOTES:

....
....
....
....
....
....
....
....
....
....
....
....
....

EXERCISE 28D

	INSTRUCTIONS	TIPS/DIRECTIVES
1.	[Start on the right rein] C — Working canter right. B-K — Working canter right. K — Medium walk. Half 10-meter circle left.	• As the horse makes the transition to walk, ease your hand and keep your leg on to maintain the engagement and keep the transition fluent and balanced. • The circle is designed to test the horse's balance, suppleness to the bend, and straightness.
2.	D-E — Extended walk. E — Medium walk. H — Walk to working canter right. [Repeat the exercise on both reins]	• Keep the extended walk marching forward. • The transition back to medium walk from extended walk should be balanced and smooth, and the rhythm should not change – only the stride length.

NOTES:

....

....

....

....

....

....

....

....

....

....

....

....

....

....

EXERCISE 28E

	INSTRUCTIONS	TIPS/DIRECTIVES
1. [diagram]	[Start on the right rein] C Working trot. B-K Trot half-pass right. K Collected canter left. Half 10-meter circle left.	• Give yourself enough time to re-join the track and change bend ready for the canter transition at K. • The collection in the canter should be thought of as a rebalancing of the weight carriage towards the haunches, and NOT as a shortening of the stride.
2. [diagram]	D-E Working canter left. E-H Counter canter. H Working trot. [Repeat the exercise on both reins]	• During the counter-canter, maintain a little flexion over the leading leg, but no more than what is asked in true canter. • Encourage the horse to step through into the working trot, rather than 'fall' out of the canter.

NOTES:

....

....

....

....

....

....

....

....

....

....

....

....

....

....

EXERCISE 28F – Make Your Own

	INSTRUCTIONS
1.	
2.	

NOTES:

....

....

....

....

....

....

....

....

....

....

EXERCISE 28G – Make Your Own

	INSTRUCTIONS
1. 	
2. 	

NOTES:

....

....

....

....

....

....

....

....

....

....

EXERCISE 28H – Make Your Own

	INSTRUCTIONS
1.	
2.	

NOTES:

....

....

....

....

....

....

....

....

....

....

"Success is the sum of small efforts repeated day in and day out."

FLOORPLAN #29

'Mirrored Droplets'

PRACTICE LOG – Note the dates when you last practiced this floorplan.

#29 'MIRRORED DROPLETS' - 20X40 DIAGRAMS

1.

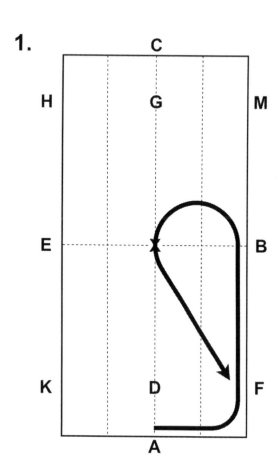

2.

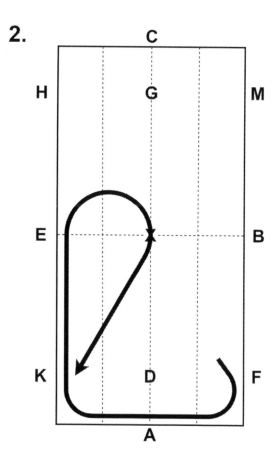

3.

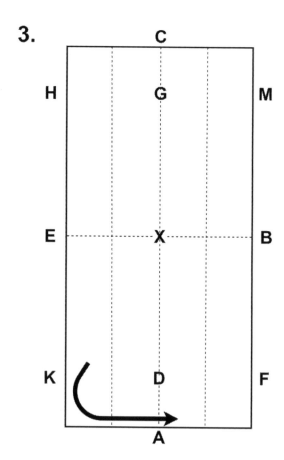

#29 'MIRRORED DROPLETS' - 20X60 DIAGRAMS

1.

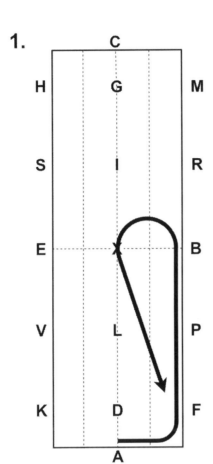

2.

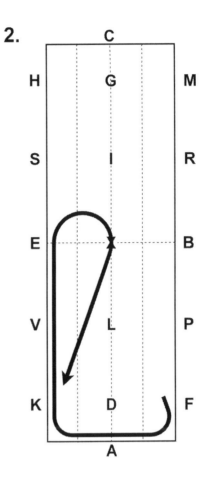

3.

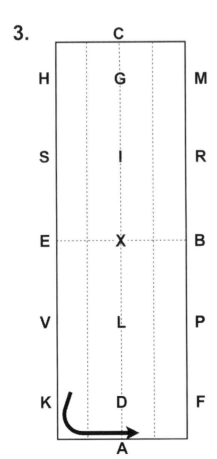

EXERCISE 29A

	INSTRUCTIONS	TIPS/DIRECTIVES
1. [diagram: arena with markers C, H, G, M, E, B, K, D, F, A showing a half circle from B to X to F]	[Start on the left rein] A Working trot. B Medium walk. Half 10-meter circle left. X-F Working trot.	• When riding the circle, the horse should be supple enough to be able to negotiate the circle accurately, whilst maintaining his rhythm and balance. He should show an adequate degree of bend without losing his quarters to the outside of the circle.
2. [diagram: arena with markers C, H, G, M, E, B, K, D, F, A showing path from E looping to X down to K]	FKE Working trot. E Medium walk. Half 10-meter circle right. X-K Free walk on a long rein.	• To start the free walk, let the reins slide through your fingers gradually to allow the horse to take the rein forwards, round and down. It can be helpful to allow the inside rein to lengthen slightly before the outside rein. This can prevent the horse from hollowing and coming off the aids as you begin to ride the free walk, and will encourage him to remain into the contact.
3. [diagram: arena with markers C, H, G, M, E, X, B, K, D, F, A showing path along bottom to A]	K Medium walk. A Halt. Immobility 4 seconds. Proceed in working trot. [Repeat the exercise on both reins]	• To ride a good transition from free walk back to medium walk, shorten your reins gradually. Keep your leg on to maintain the impulsion and engagement and to encourage the horse's hind leg to remain active. • More advanced horses should be able to step out of the halt directly into working trot without losing balance and frame. If your horse is less experienced, allow him a step or two of walk to help him remain in balance and prevent him coming against the hand.

NOTES:

....

....

EXERCISE 29B

	INSTRUCTIONS	TIPS/DIRECTIVES
1.	[Start on the left rein] A Working trot. F/B Transition to medium walk for one horse's length and proceed in working trot. B Half 10-meter circle left. X-F Working trot.	• Make sure that you show a few clear walk steps in the trot-walk-trot movement. The horse should clearly walk, rather than jog. • One horse's length is measured at three to four strides. • During the half circle, your horse should continue to work forwards, in a good rhythm, and show a clear uniform bend along his body around the circle.
2.	A Halt. Immobility 4 seconds. Proceed in medium walk. K Working trot. E Half 10-meter circle right. X-K Working trot.	• Wait until the halt is completely established, then count to 4 before proceeding in medium walk. • When riding the half circle, keep your hips and shoulders parallel with your horse's shoulders, keep your body upright, and look ahead of you around the circle.
3.	KA Working trot. [Repeat the exercise on both reins]	• Make sure you change the bend before you reach the KA corner. Keep the horse securely in your outside rein to help balance him through the turn. • Your goal during working trot is for it to be active and rhythmical.

NOTES:

....

....

....

....

....

EXERCISE 29C

	INSTRUCTIONS	TIPS/DIRECTIVES
1.	[Start on the left rein] A Working canter left. B Half 10-meter circle left. X-F Working canter left. F Working trot.	• When riding the half circle, remember that your inside leg on the girth keeps the impulsion, develops the engagement of the inside hind leg, and asks for bend. Your outside leg should be slightly behind the girth preventing the hindquarters from escaping to the outside of the circle and generating some forward movement. • If it's difficult for your horse to maintain a balanced canter all the way to F, ride a transition to working trot a few strides earlier. As the balance improves, you can go a bit further.
2.	FKE Working trot. E Half 10-meter circle right. X-K Working trot.	• A 10-meter circle is quite a small diameter, so it is your job to choose exactly the right tempo (speed of the rhythm), to enable the horse to manage the rhythm and bend without any disturbances or unevenness to the stride length. • If you have a young or 'green' horse, always ride rising trot so that he can use his back.
3.	K/A Working canter left. [Repeat exercise on both reins]	• Change the bend before you reach the KA corner. That will help to ensure that your horse strikes off on the correct lead. • The canter transition should be reactive, uphill, and balanced. The horse should maintain his round frame.

NOTES:

EXERCISE 29D

	INSTRUCTIONS	TIPS/DIRECTIVES
1.	[Start on the left rein] A Medium walk. F Walk to collected canter left. B Half 10-meter circle left. X-F Collected canter left.	• The shorter, higher steps of the collected canter are the RESULT of the horse carrying more of the weight towards its haunches. Shortening the strides artificially will result in stiffening and loss of activity, which is exactly what judges do not want to see.
2.	F Medium walk. A Halt. Immobility 4 seconds. Rein-back one horse's length. Proceed in medium walk. K Working trot. E Half 10-meter circle right. X-K Leg yield right.	• The horse should stay relaxed and calm during the rein-back. There should be no resistance to the contact, and he shouldn't rush backwards or lose his rhythm. • When riding the rein-back, it's important that the halt is square. If the horse is trailing a hind leg at the start, he won't be able to keep his balance or step back clearly in diagonal pairs. • During the leg-yield, the horse should move forwards and sideways on two tracks. His body should remain straight, and there should be a slight flexion of his head and neck away from the direction of travel.
3.	K Working trot. A Medium walk. [Repeat the exercise on both reins]	• Make the transition into medium walk a crisp, direct one. The horse should not jog into the downward transition.

NOTES:

EXERCISE 29E

	INSTRUCTIONS	TIPS/DIRECTIVES
1.	[Start on the left rein] A Working trot. F-B Shoulder-in left. B Half 10-meter circle left. X-F Leg yield left.	• Establish the correct bend for shoulder-in as you come through the A/F corner. Ride out of the corner as if you are about to commence a 10-meter circle. That will give you the correct bend and position for shoulder-in. • The key to correct leg-yielding is to have the horse moving forwards, and stepping sideways away from your inside leg aid, whilst maintaining a slight inside flexion from the poll.
2.	F Working trot. K-E Travers right. E Half 10-meter circle right. X-K Trot half-pass right.	• As you come out of travers, make the horse straight before the 10-meter half circle. That will prevent the quarters from coming in around the circle. • During the half-pass, the horse must be bent towards the direction he is traveling in. A good guide to the amount of bend is simply to ensure that his face is looking at the point on the track (in this case K) where you are aiming to arrive at the end of the movement.
3.	KA Working trot. [Repeat the exercise on both reins]	• Keep the impulsion and rhythm in the trot. Use the extra engagement created by the previous lateral work and feed it into the working trot to improve the quality of the pace.

NOTES:

EXERCISE 29F – Make Your Own

	INSTRUCTIONS
1.	
2.	
3.	

NOTES:

EXERCISE 29G – Make Your Own

	INSTRUCTIONS
1.	
2.	
3.	

NOTES:

EXERCISE 29H – Make Your Own

	INSTRUCTIONS
1.	
2.	
3.	

NOTES:

"To learn to succeed,
you must first learn to fail."

FLOORPLAN #30

'The Catherine Wheel'

PRACTICE LOG – Note the dates when you last practiced this floorplan.

....
....
....
....
....
....
....
....
....
....
....
....
....
....
....
....
....
....
....
....
....

1.

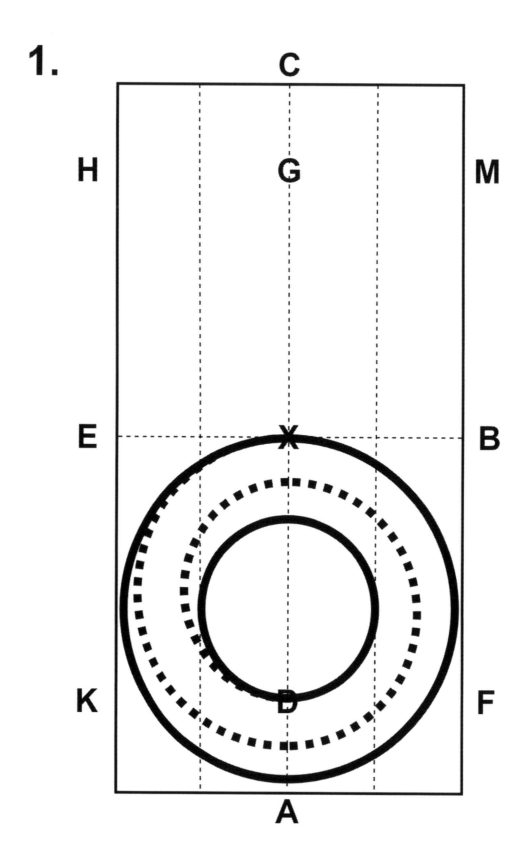

#30 'THE CATHERINE WHEEL' - 20X60 DIAGRAM

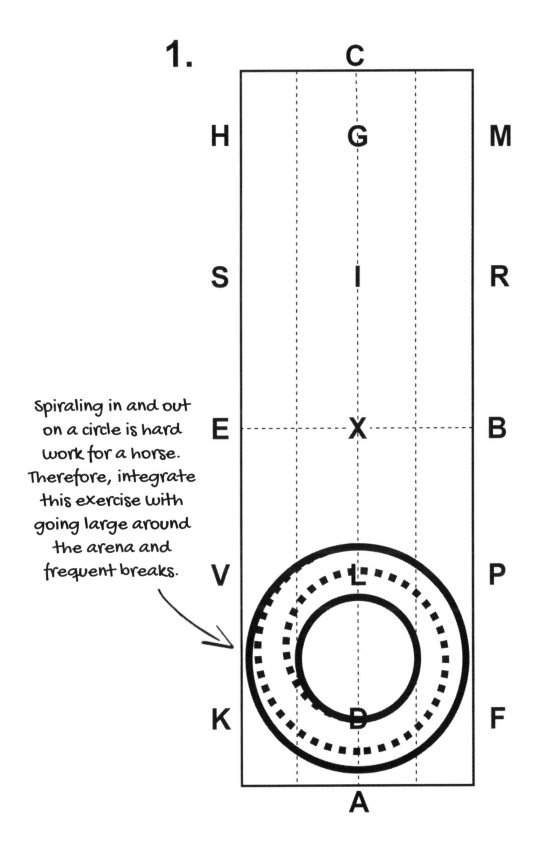

1.

Spiraling in and out on a circle is hard work for a horse. Therefore, integrate this exercise with going large around the arena and frequent breaks.

EXERCISE 30A

	INSTRUCTIONS	TIPS/DIRECTIVES

1.	[Start on the left rein]
	
	X Working trot.
	       20-meter circle left.
	
	X Transition to medium walk.
	       Spiral down to a 10-meter
	       circle OR 15-meter circle.
	
	       Spiral back up to a 20-meter
	       circle and then transition back
	       into working trot.
	
	[Repeat the exercise on both reins]
		• As you ride the spiral, aim to gradually make the circle smaller. Don't push the horse sideways.
		
		• Only go down to a 10-meter circle if your horse can keep a uniform bend and remain relaxed in the walk with a clear 4-beath rhythm. If the horse becomes tense, jogs, or struggles to work on one track, go back to a larger circle.

NOTES:

....

....

....

....

....

....

....

....

....

....

....

....

....

....

....

....

....

....

EXERCISE 30B

	INSTRUCTIONS	TIPS/DIRECTIVES
1. *(arena diagram with circles, points C, H, G, M, E, B, K, F, A, X)*	[Start on the left rein] X Working canter left. 20-meter circle left. X Working trot. Spiral down to a 10-meter circle OR 15-meter circle. Give and retake the inside rein. Spiral back up to a 20-meter circle and then transition back into working canter left. [Repeat the exercise on both reins]	• Encourage the horse to step through into the working trot, rather than 'fall' out of the canter. • When you relinquish your rein contact in a give and retake there should be no change in your horse's outline, speed, size of stride, balance, or alignment to the figure. • Diligently riding the transition from trot back into canter will build the 'pushing and propulsion' capacity of the horse, enabling him to develop incremental levels of engagement of the hind legs.

NOTES:

....

....

....

....

....

....

....

....

....

....

....

....

....

....

....

....

EXERCISE 30C

	INSTRUCTIONS	TIPS/DIRECTIVES

1.
(diagram of dressage arena with spiral circles)
	[Start on the left rein]
	
	X Working trot.
	      20-meter circle left.
	
	X Spiral down to a 10-meter circle.
	      Spiral back up to a 20-meter circle.
	
	X Working canter left.
	      20-meter circle left.
	
	X Spiral down to a 15-meter circle.
	      Give and retake the inside rein.
	      Spiral back up to a 20-meter circle.
	
	X Working trot.
	
	[Repeat the exercise on both reins]
		• When riding the circles, keep your hips and shoulders parallel with your horse's shoulders, keep your body upright, and look ahead.
		
		• Your goal during the canter is to develop regularity and lightness of the strides, an uphill tendency, and the natural ability of the horse to carry himself whilst maintaining active well-placed hind legs.
		
		• The purpose of the give and retake is to show that you are not holding the horse into an outline solely with your reins and that you are not supporting his balance or controlling his speed with your hands. To show a clear give and retake, you must present a visible looping of the reins for a couple of strides.

NOTES:

....

....

....

....

....

....

....

....

....

....

....

....

EXERCISE 30D

	INSTRUCTIONS	TIPS/DIRECTIVES

1.
 (arena diagram with circles, markers C, H, G, M, E, B, K, F, A)
	[Start on the left rein]
	
	 X Working trot.
	          20-meter circle left.
	
	 X Leg-yield left down to a 10-meter circle.
	          Leg-yield right back up to a 20-meter circle.
	
	 X Transition to canter left.
	          20-meter circle in medium canter.
	
	          Spiral down to a 10-meter circle in collected canter.
	
	          Give and retake the inside rein.
	
	          Spiral back to up a 20-meter circle in medium canter.
	
	 X Working trot.
	
	 [Repeat the exercises on both reins]
		• In the leg-yield, the horse should move forwards and sideways. There should be a slight flexion at the poll away from the direction of travel.
		
		 • During the leg-yield, if the horse doesn't move away from your leg, or trails his quarters to avoid stepping through and underneath his body, re-emphasize the aid. Don't try to compensate for the horse's lack of response by leaning to one side or wriggling around in the saddle!
		
		 • Although the medium canter should cover more ground than a working canter, it should also clearly demonstrate an uphill tendency.
		
		 • Remember that the degree of collection required in the canter is only so much as to be able to perform the 10-meter circle with ease.
		
		 • During the give and retake, your goal is that the horse does not change his way of going before, during, or after the movement is completed.

NOTES:

....

....

....

....

....

....

....

EXERCISE 30E

	INSTRUCTIONS	TIPS/DIRECTIVES
1.	[Start on the left rein] X Collected canter left. 20-meter circle left. X Spiral down to a 10-meter circle. Transition to medium walk for 5-6 strides. Transition back to collected canter. Spiral back up to a 20-meter circle [Repeat the exercise on both reins]	• When riding the circle, the horse should be supple enough to be able to negotiate the circle accurately, whilst maintaining his rhythm and balance. He should show an adequate degree of bend without losing his quarters to the outside of the circle. • Keep the horse securely connected through your outside rein to help maintain the engagement and balance throughout the transitions. • The shorter, higher steps of the collected canter are the RESULT of the horse carrying more of the weight towards its haunches. Shortening the strides artificially will result in stiffening and loss of activity, which is exactly what judges do not want to see.

NOTES:

....

....

....

....

....

....

....

....

....

....

....

....

EXERCISE 30F – Make Your Own

	INSTRUCTIONS
1. C H G M E X B K D F A	

NOTES:

....
....
....
....
....
....
....
....
....
....
....
....
....
....

EXERCISE 30G – Make Your Own

	INSTRUCTIONS
1. H C M G E ✗ B K D F A	

NOTES:

....

....

....

....

....

....

....

....

....

....

....

....

....

EXERCISE 30H – Make Your Own

	INSTRUCTIONS
1.	

NOTES:

....

....

....

....

....

....

....

....

....

....

....

....

....

"Never assume that your horse remembers anything from one day to the next. Check his responses and use previous lessons as a warm-up before advancing to something new."

FLOORPLANS
WITH POLES

Before doing any exercises in this section,
check out page 12 for some hints and tips on
working with poles.

We lost this page in the washing machine.

...it's currently hanging out with all the odd socks!

FLOORPLAN #31

'Parallel Lines'

PRACTICE LOG – Note the dates when you last practiced this floorplan.

#31 'PARALLEL LINES' - 20X40 DIAGRAMS

1.

2.

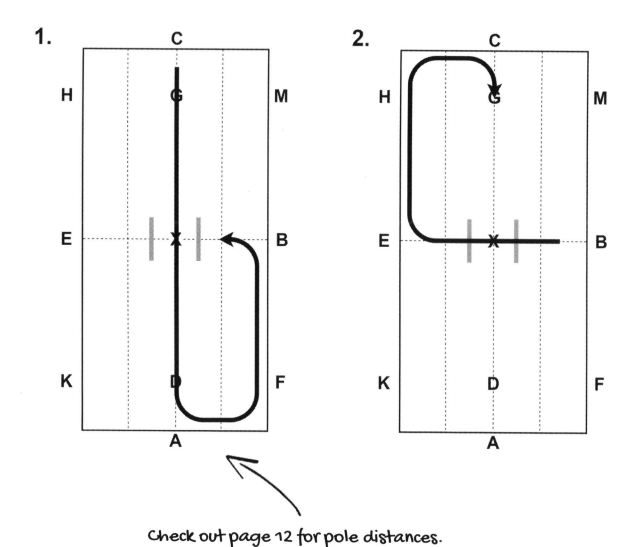

Check out page 12 for pole distances.

#31 'PARALLEL LINES' - 20X60 DIAGRAMS

1.

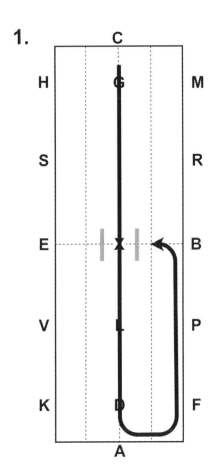

2.

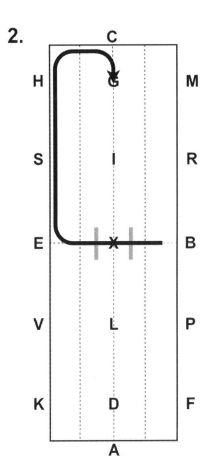

EXERCISE 31A

	INSTRUCTIONS	TIPS/DIRECTIVES
1.	[Proceed down the center line] G Free walk on a long rein. D Medium walk. A Track left. F Working trot. B Turn left.	• Free walk on the center line is deceptively difficult. Keep the walk marching purposely forward and look towards A to help maintain straightness. • The transition from free walk back to medium walk should be smooth, with no loss of rhythm or signs of tension.
2.	E Track right. H Medium walk. C Turn left onto the center line. [Repeat the exercise on both reins]	• Change your horse's bend and your diagonal either before or after the poles. Don't try to change them over X as this could upset your horse's balance as he tried to negotiate the poles. • When transitioning to medium walk, ensure that the horse continues to work forwards and doesn't just collapse in a heap!

NOTES:

....

....

....

....

....

....

....

....

....

....

....

EXERCISE 31B

	INSTRUCTIONS	TIPS/DIRECTIVES
1.	[Proceed down the center line] G Working trot. X Halt. Immobility 4 seconds. Proceed in working trot. A Track left. F/B Transition to medium walk for one horse's length then proceed in working trot. B Track left.	• Use the poles to help you ride a straight halt. • Count to 4 in your head so that the halt is maintained for the correct length of time. • When asked to move off from the halt, the horse should step forward immediately and smoothly. • When transitioning to walk, there must be the correct number of walk steps, and they must be clearly walked, rather than jogged.
2.	E Track right. H Medium walk. C Turn right onto the center line. G Working trot. [Repeat the exercise on both reins]	• When riding across the school from B to E, keep the activity and rhythm in the trot steps. • Don't look down at the poles. • Allow the horse a little freedom of his neck so that he can negotiate the poles.

NOTES:

....

....

....

....

....

....

....

....

....

....

EXERCISE 31C

	INSTRUCTIONS	TIPS/DIRECTIVES

1.	[Proceed down the center line]
	
	G Medium trot.
	
	D Working trot.
	
	A Track left.
	
	B Halt. Immobility 4 seconds.
	       Rein-back one horse's length
	       Proceed in working trot.
	
	B Turn left.
		• Aim for a balanced upward and downward transitions into and out of medium trot. Don't "fire" the horse abruptly into medium trot. That risks the horse losing his balance, breaking rhythm, and falling onto his forehand.
		
		• Use your legs and bodyweight to ask the horse to rein-back whilst keeping your contact elastic. The contact prevents the horse from walking forwards, it should not be used to pull the horse back.
		
		• The upward transition to working trot after the rein-back must be swift, balanced, and obedient because you only have a few strides before turning left for the poles.

2.	E Turn right. E/H Transition to medium walk for one horse's length then proceed in working trot. C Turn left down the center line. [Repeat the exercise on both reins]	• Make sure that the walk steps are clear. Don't allow the horse to jog in anticipation of the trot transition. • The horse should remain in the same outline throughout the whole trot-walk-trot movement, and the trot rhythm and energy following the transition should be the same as it was prior to the walk steps.

NOTES:

....

....

....

....

....

....

....

EXERCISE 31D

	INSTRUCTIONS	TIPS/DIRECTIVES
1.	[Proceed down the center line] G Working canter right. X Simple change to working canter left. A Track left. F/B Working trot. B Turn left.	• Use the poles to help keep the horse straight during the simple change. • In the simple change, the transitions into and out of walk should be direct. However inexperienced horses often lose their balance in the downward transition, therefore, you can make the exercise easier for your horse until he's better balanced by riding step of trot into walk, before proceeding back into the canter.
2.	E Track right. H Working canter right. C Turn right onto the center line. [Repeat the exercise on both reins]	• The canter transition should be reactive, uphill, and balanced. The horse should maintain his round frame. • Maintain your outside rein contact to prevent the horse from drifting out through his shoulder as you make the turn at C.

NOTES:

....

....

....

....

....

....

....

....

....

....

EXERCISE 31E

	INSTRUCTIONS	TIPS/DIRECTIVES
1.	[Proceed down the center line] G Extended trot. D Working trot. A Track left. F-B Renvers OR shoulder-in. B Turn left.	• If your horse is inexperienced, aim to ride a few balanced extended trot strides, rather than trying to cover the whole center line. If your horse is more experienced, aim for clear, balanced transitions in and out of the extended trot and ride the pace from marker to marker. • If riding renvers you'll need to have the horse very attentive to your aids so that you can position the horse and create the bend correctly PLUS straighten him in time for the left turn at B.
2.	E Track right. E-H Renvers OR shoulder-in C Turn right onto the center line. [Repeat exercise on both reins]	• During the renvers or shoulder-in, the pace should not change, in terms of energy, elasticity and suspension, nor should the rhythm vary.

NOTES:

....

....

....

....

....

....

....

....

....

....

EXERCISE 31F – Make Your Own

	INSTRUCTIONS
1.	
2.	

NOTES:

....

....

....

....

....

....

....

....

....

....

EXERCISE 31G – Make Your Own

	INSTRUCTIONS
1.	
2.	

NOTES:

....

....

....

....

....

....

....

....

....

....

EXERCISE 31H – Make Your Own

	INSTRUCTIONS
1.	
2.	

NOTES:

....

....

....

....

....

....

....

....

....

....

"Through gaining
competence, we gain
confidence."

FLOORPLAN #32

'Wider Parallel Lines'

PRACTICE LOG – Note the dates when you last practiced this floorplan.

#32 'WIDER PARALLEL LINES' - 20X40 DIAGRAM

1.

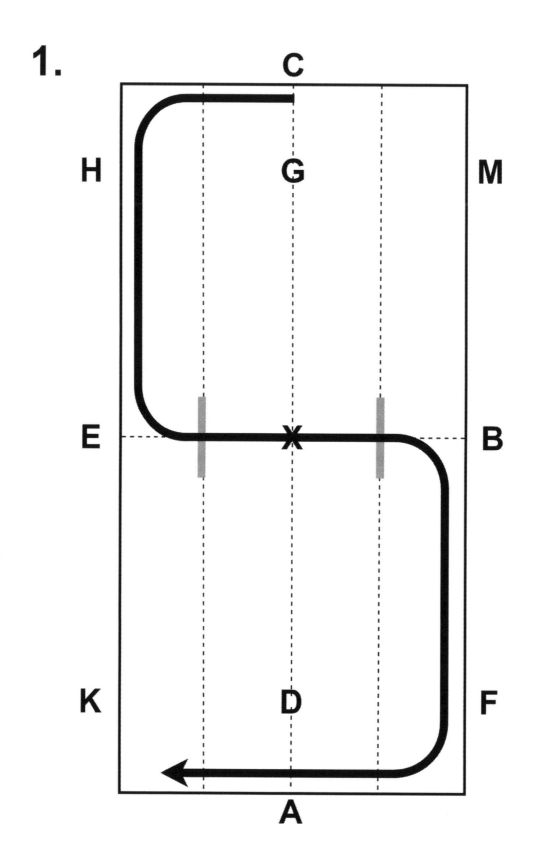

#32 'WIDER PARALLEL LINES' - 20X60 DIAGRAM

1.

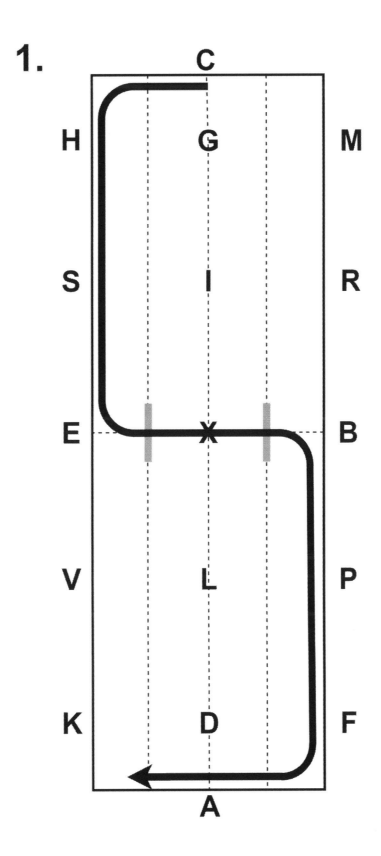

EXERCISE 32A

	INSTRUCTIONS	TIPS/DIRECTIVES
1. [diagram of arena with markers C, H, G, M, E, X, B, K, D, F, A]	[Start on the left rein] C Working trot. H/E Medium walk. E Turn left. X Halt. Immobility 4 seconds. Proceed in medium walk. B Track right. B/F Working trot. [Repeat the exercise on both reins]	• Ask for the transition to halt well before you reach the second pole. If you get too close to the pole, the horse will drop his head to look at it, the poll will drop, and he'll lose his balance onto his forehand. • During the halt, the horse should remain still and relaxed but attentive whilst waiting for his rider's next instruction. • When asked to move off from the halt, the horse should step forward immediately and smoothly. • The transition back into trot should be obedient and reactive, whilst remaining fluent and calm.

NOTES:

....

....

....

....

....

....

....

....

....

....

....

....

....

....

EXERCISE 32B

	INSTRUCTIONS	TIPS/DIRECTIVES
1.	[Start on the left rein] C Medium walk. H Working trot. E Turn left. B Track right. F Halt. Immobility 4 seconds. Proceed in medium walk. [Repeat the exercise on both reins]	• Change the horse's bend, and change your diagonal, over X in the middle of the poles as there won't be much space to do it before or after the poles. • Keep the impulsion in the trot and ride the pace in the same tempo and rhythm over the poles. • In a good halt, the horse should be straight and square. Each leg should bear the same weight evenly so that the horse has 'a leg at each corner'. • If your horse begins to step backwards during the halt, ride forwards immediately. Ride the halt again and ease your hand as you do so. Be positive with your legs and keep thinking forwards.

NOTES:

....

....

....

....

....

....

....

....

....

....

....

EXERCISE 32C

	INSTRUCTIONS	TIPS/DIRECTIVES
1.	[Start on the left rein] C Working trot. H/E Transition to medium walk for one horse's length then proceed in working trot. E Turn left. X Halt. Immobility 4 seconds. Proceed in working trot. B Track right. [Repeat the exercise on both reins]	• When riding the trot-walk-trot movement, the transitions must be obedient, balanced, and straight, and the horse must be reactive to your aids. • During the halt, the horse should remain still and relaxed but attentive whilst waiting for his rider's next instruction. • Use your half-halts to slightly collect the trot and prepare the horse for the transition to halt before you go over the first pole. Don't simple slam the handbrake on when you're on top of X!

NOTES:

....

....

....

....

....

....

....

....

....

....

....

....

....

....

....

EXERCISE 32D

	INSTRUCTIONS	TIPS/DIRECTIVES
1.	[Start on the left rein] C Collected canter left. E Turn left. X Simple change to collected canter right. B Track right. [Repeat the exercise on both reins]	• Collection should be thought of as a rebalancing of the weight carriage towards the haunches, and NOT as a shortening of the stride. • Look straight ahead of you and not down at the poles well before you ride the simple change. • The horse will need to bend his hocks as he negotiates the first pole. You can use this extra flexion to create more engagement and improve the balance of the downward transition.

NOTES:

....

....

....

....

....

....

....

....

....

....

....

....

....

....

....

....

EXERCISE 32E

	INSTRUCTIONS	TIPS/DIRECTIVES
1.	[Start on the left rein] C Working canter left. H/E Medium walk. E Turn left. X Full walk pirouette left Proceed in medium walk. B Track right. B/F Working canter right. [Repeat the exercise on both reins]	• Use the poles to prevent the horse from creeping forward in the pirouette. • In the pirouette, it's crucial that a clear 4-beat walk sequence is maintained, and the tempo of the walk should remain the same before and after the movement. • If the horse is lazy or becomes 'stuck' in the pirouette, use your legs throughout the turn in an alternating fashion, matching each of your legs to his hind legs, so that your left leg asks him to lift his left hind and vice versa.

NOTES:

....

....

....

....

....

....

....

....

....

....

....

....

....

....

....

EXERCISE 32F – Make Your Own

	INSTRUCTIONS
1. C H G M E ✕ B K D F A	- 517 -

NOTES:

....

....

....

....

....

....

....

....

....

....

....

....

....

....

EXERCISE 32G – Make Your Own

	INSTRUCTIONS
1. H G M E x B K D F A	

NOTES:

....

....

....

....

....

....

....

....

....

....

....

....

....

EXERCISE 32H – Make Your Own

	INSTRUCTIONS
1. H ··· C ··· M G E ··· X ··· B K ··· D ··· F A	

NOTES:

....
....
....
....
....
....
....
....
....
....
....
....
....
....

"It is the difficult horses that have the most to teach you."

FLOORPLAN #33

'Double Parallel Lines'

PRACTICE LOG – Note the dates when you last practiced this floorplan.

#33 'DOUBLE PARALLEL LINES' - 20X40 DIAGRAM

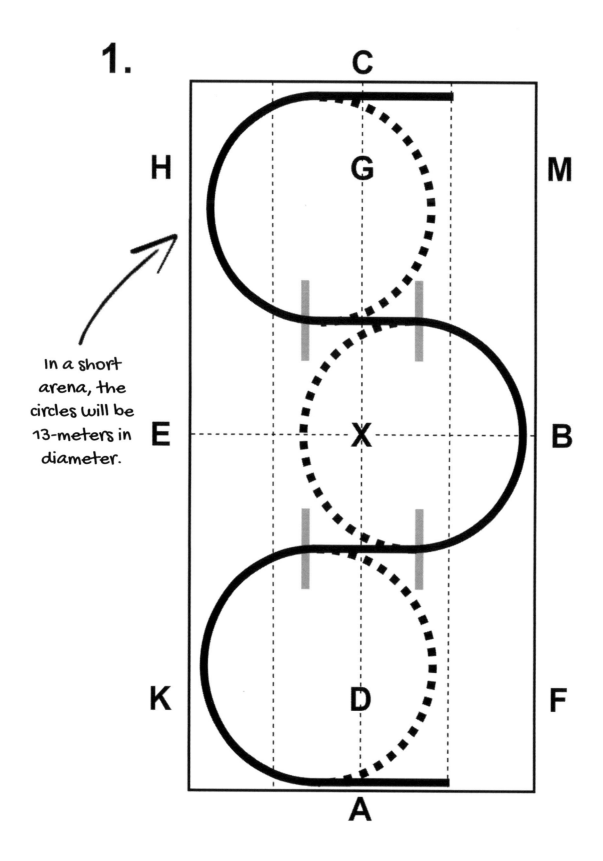

1.

C

H   G   M

In a short
arena, the
circles will be
13-meters in
diameter.

E   X   B

K   D   F

A

#33 'DOUBLE PARALLEL LINES' - 20X60 DIAGRAM

1.

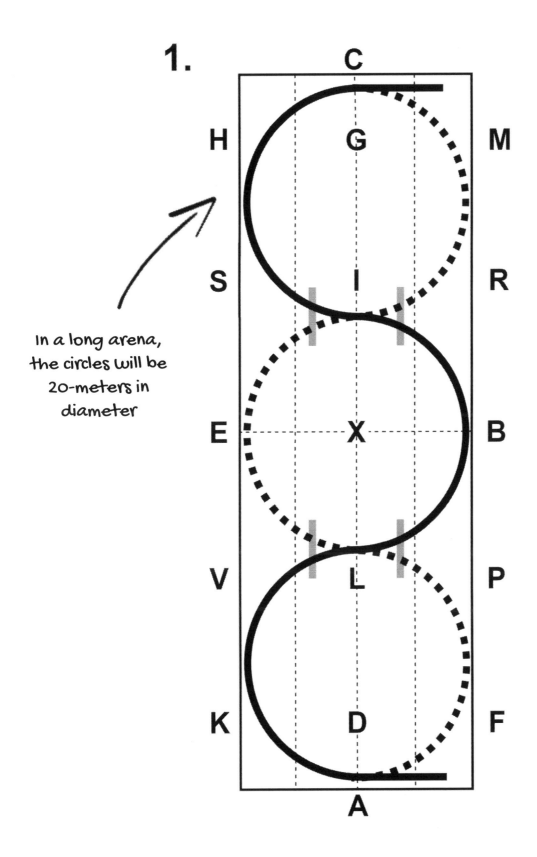

In a long arena, the circles will be 20-meters in diameter

EXERCISE 33A

	INSTRUCTIONS	TIPS/DIRECTIVES
1.	[Start at C on the left rein] Ride a 3-loop serpentine in working trot crossing through both sets of poles. When you reach B, transition to medium walk and ride a circle (13-meters diameter for a 20x40 arena, and 20-meters diameters for a 20x60 arena) Transition back into working trot and finish the rest of the serpentine to A [Repeat the exercise on both reins]	• During the serpentine, the horse should continue to work forward over his back to seek the contact, not drop behind the rider's leg, draw back from the hand or stiffen against the new bend of each loop. • Look up and over the poles. If you look down, you risk unbalancing your horse onto his forehand. • When transitioning to medium walk, ensure that the horse continues to work forwards and doesn't just collapse in a heap! • The transition back into trot should be obedient and reactive, whilst remaining fluent and calm.

NOTES:

....

....

....

....

....

....

....

....

....

....

....

....

....

....

EXERCISE 33B

	INSTRUCTIONS	TIPS/DIRECTIVES
1.	Start at C on the left rein Ride a 3-loop serpentine in working trot crossing through both sets of poles. On each loop, ride a circle (13-meters diameter for a 20x40 arena, and 20-meters diameter for a 20x60 arena) [Repeat the exercise on both reins]	• During this exercise the horse should use his inside hind leg to help maintain his balance, and he should show a clear change of bend through each change of direction. The horse should bend uniformly through his neck and body, traveling clearly on one track only around the loops and circles. • Keep the activity and rhythm in the trot steps. Be prepared for a slightly more elevated, bouncy step as the horse crosses each pole. • Look up and around your circles to maintain accuracy and ensure that all circles and loops are of equal size.

NOTES:

....

....

....

....

....

....

....

....

....

....

....

....

....

....

EXERCISE 33C

	INSTRUCTIONS	TIPS/DIRECTIVES
1.	Start at C on the left rein Ride a 3-loop serpentine in working trot crossing through both sets of poles. When you're approaching B, transition to working canter left and ride a circle (13-meters diameter for a 20x40 arena, and 20-meters diameter for a 20x60 arena) Transition back to working trot and finish the rest of the serpentine to A [Repeat the exercise on both reins]	• To ride the 13-meter circle (20x40 arena), you'll need to slightly collect the canter. That doesn't mean that the pace needs less energy, it needs more! • Your goal during the canter is to develop regularity and lightness of the strides, an uphill tendency, and the natural ability of the horse to carry himself whilst maintaining active well-placed hind legs. • Encourage the horse to step through into the working trot, rather than 'fall' out of the canter.

NOTES:

....

....

....

....

....

....

....

....

....

....

....

....

....

....

....

EXERCISE 33D

	INSTRUCTIONS	TIPS/DIRECTIVES
1.	Start at C on the left rein Ride a 3-loop serpentine. On the first loop, ride a circle in working canter left. (13-meters diameter for a 20x40 arena, and 20-meters diameter for a 20x60 arena) Transition to working trot and go over the first set of poles ready to ride the second loop of the serpentine. Transition to working canter right before B and ride another circle. (13-meters diameter for a 20x40 arena, and 20-meters diameter for a 20x60 arena) Transition to working trot and go over the second set of poles ready to ride the third loop of the serpentine. Transition to working canter left before K and ride another circle. (13-meters diameter for a 20x40 arena, and 20-meters diameter for a 20x60 arena) Proceed in working canter left and finish the rest of the serpentine to A [Repeat the exercise on both reins]	• This exercise is simpler to ride than it reads! • Be sure to should sit straight. Don't lean to one side or twist through the upper body. Instead, keep your hips and shoulders parallel with your horse's shoulders, keep your body upright, and look ahead of you around the circle. • During this exercise the horse should continue to work forward over his back to seek the contact, not drop behind the rider's leg, draw back from the hand or stiffen against the new bend of each loop or circle. • The canter transition should be reactive, uphill, and balanced. The horse should maintain his round frame. • The trot transitions should be fluent with the horse stepping through and under with his hind legs. • Try not to micro-manage the horse's strides when approaching a pole. Instead, maintain the rhythm in an appropriate temp and allow the horse a little freedom to adjust his own strides accordingly.

NOTES:

....

....

....

....

....

EXERCISE 33E

	INSTRUCTIONS	TIPS/DIRECTIVES
1.	Start at C on the left rein Ride a 3-loop serpentine in working canter left crossing through both sets of poles. On the middle loop, ride counter-canter. [Repeat the exercise on both reins]	• Ideally, this exercise should be ridden in a 20x60 arena where the middle loop is a half 20-meter circle (and not a half 13-meter circle in a 20x40 arena!). However, if you are in short arena, make the first and last loop of the serpentine smaller and ride over the outer edges of the poles. This will give you a large middle loop for you to ride counter canter. • In counter-canter, be sure to keep the flexion to the leading leg. If you lose the correct flexion, the horse will become unbalanced and possibly change lead.

NOTES:

....

....

....

....

....

....

....

....

....

....

....

....

....

....

....

....

EXERCISE 33F – Make Your Own

	INSTRUCTIONS
1. C H · G · M E · X · B K · D · F A	

NOTES:

....

....

....

....

....

....

....

....

....

....

....

....

....

....

EXERCISE 33G – Make Your Own

	INSTRUCTIONS
1. H C M G E X B K D F A	

NOTES:

....

....

....

....

....

....

....

....

....

....

....

....

....

EXERCISE 33H – Make Your Own

	INSTRUCTIONS
1.	

NOTES:

....
....
....
....
....
....
....
....
....
....
....
....
....
....

"Success is not final.
Failure is not fatal.
It is the courage to
continue that counts."

FLOORPLAN #34

'The Hourglass'

PRACTICE LOG – Note the dates when you last practiced this floorplan.

....

....

....

....

....

....

....

....

....

....

....

....

....

....

....

....

....

....

....

....

#34 'THE HOURGLASS' - 20X40 DIAGRAM

1.

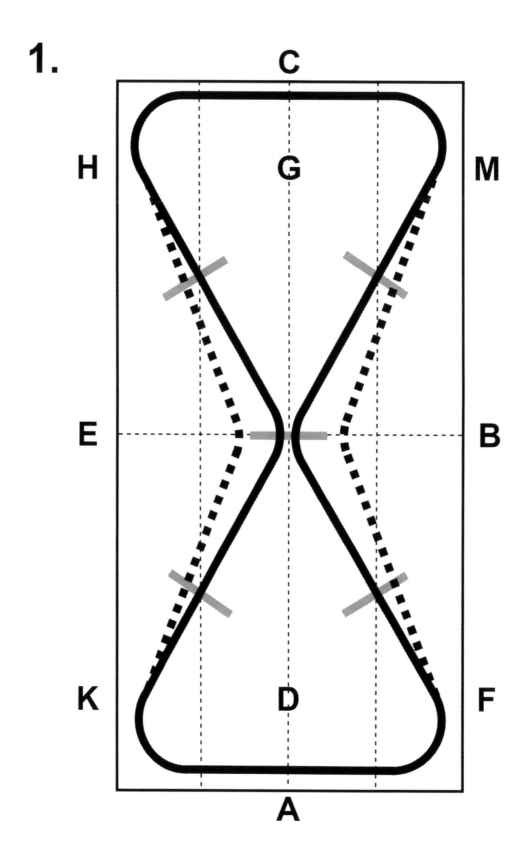

#34 'THE HOURGLASS' - 20X60 DIAGRAM

1.

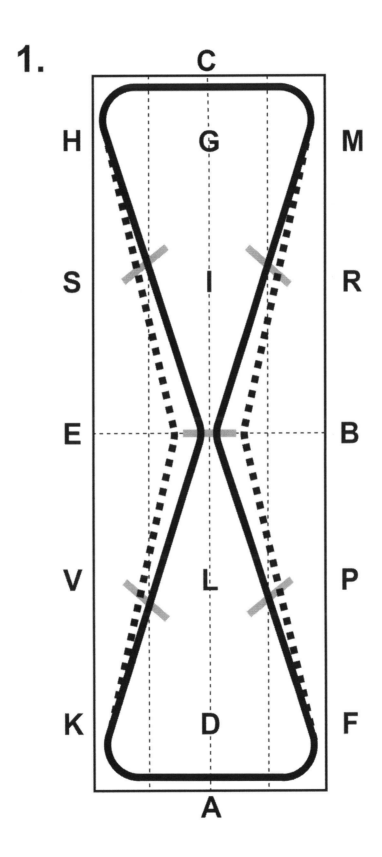

EXERCISE 34A

	INSTRUCTIONS	TIPS/DIRECTIVES
1.	[Start on the right rein] C Medium walk. M 10-meter loop to finish at F. A Halt. Immobility 4 seconds. Proceed in working trot. K 10-meter loop to finish at H. C Medium walk. [Repeat the exercise on both reins]	• A 10-meter loop must touch X at the widest point. • The loop should be a series of gradual curves and changes of bend, not a straight line to a sharp turn. • It's important 'think forward' when riding into halt, otherwise the horse will lose engagement as he halts. The halt will become unbalanced and the horse may come against the contact.

NOTES:

....

....

....

....

....

....

....

....

....

....

....

....

....

....

....

....

....

EXERCISE 34B

	INSTRUCTIONS	TIPS/DIRECTIVES
1. *(arena diagram with markers C, H, G, M, E, B, K, D, F, A)*	[Start on the right rein] C Working trot. M 10-meter loop to finish at F. A Halt. Immobility 4 seconds. Proceed in working trot. K 10-meter loop to finish at H. [Repeat the exercise on both reins]	• When riding the loops, do not allow your horse to cling to the track and drift past the marker; you should be leaving the track by the time your own body passes M and K. • More advanced horses should be able to step smoothly into and out of the halt directly without losing balance and frame. If your horse is less experienced, allow him a step or two of walk to help him remain in balance and prevent him coming against the hand.

NOTES:

....

....

....

....

....

....

....

....

....

....

....

....

....

....

....

....

....

EXERCISE 34C

	INSTRUCTIONS	TIPS/DIRECTIVES

1.	[Start on the right rein]
	
	C Working canter right.
	
	M 7-meter loop (don't go over the pole at X) to finish at F.
	
	        Proceed in working canter right.
	
	K 7-meter loop (don't go over the pole at X) to finish at H.
	
	        Proceed in working canter right.
	
	[Repeat the exercise on both reins]
		• The second half of the loops is ridden in counter canter. Don't go over the middle pole as it may encourage the horse to change canter lead.
		
		• Look where you're going! If you focus on the middle pole, so will your horse.
		
		• When returning to the track to complete your loop, take care not to arrive more than one stride before the marker. This helps ensure that your inward and return lines are symmetrical in shape and length.

NOTES:

....

....

....

....

....

....

....

....

....

....

....

....

....

....

....

EXERCISE 34D – Make Your Own

	INSTRUCTIONS
1. C H G M E B K D F A	

NOTES:

....

....

....

....

....

....

....

....

....

....

....

....

....

....

EXERCISE 34E – Make Your Own

	INSTRUCTIONS
1. C H G M E B K D F A	

NOTES:

....

....

....

....

....

....

....

....

....

....

....

....

....

EXERCISE 34F – Make Your Own

	INSTRUCTIONS
1.	

NOTES:

....

....

....

....

....

....

....

....

....

....

....

....

....

....

"A good rider rides from transition to transition. A great rider rides from half-halt to half-halt."

FLOORPLAN #35

'The Pyramid'

PRACTICE LOG – Note the dates when you last practiced this floorplan.

#35 'THE PYRAMID' - 20X40 DIAGRAMS

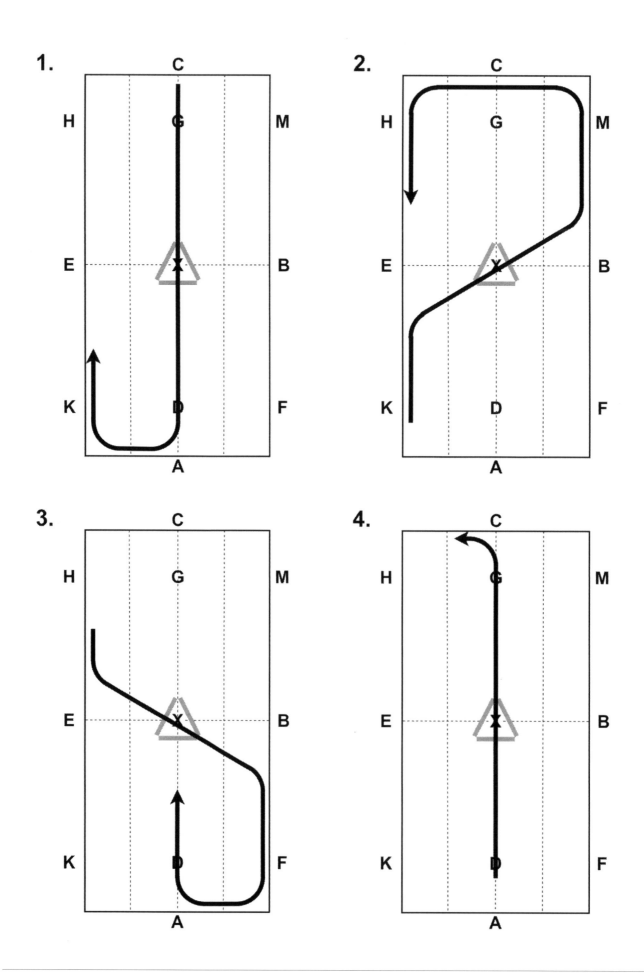

5.

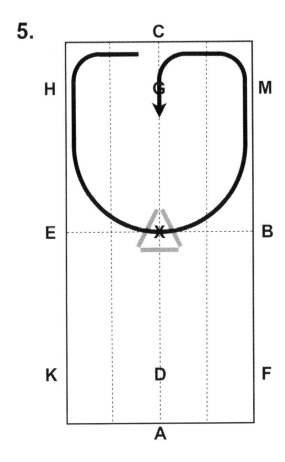

#35 'THE PYRAMID' - 20X60 DIAGRAMS

1.
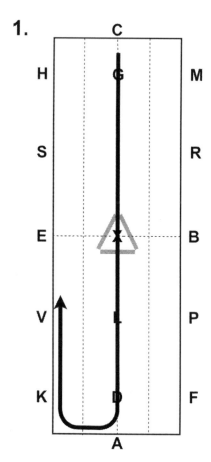

2.
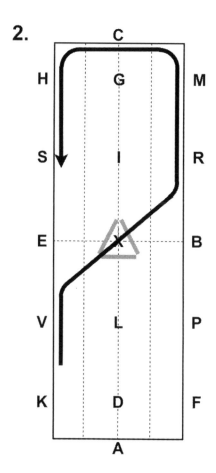

3.
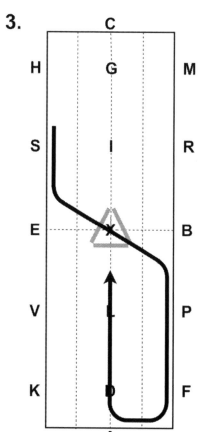

4.
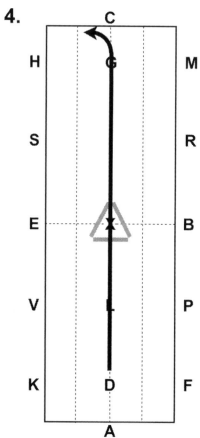

5.

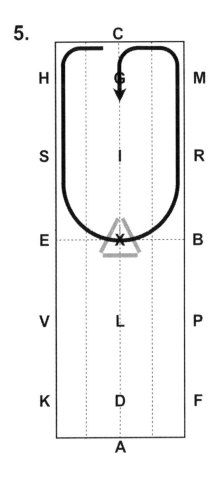

EXERCISE 35A

	INSTRUCTIONS	TIPS/DIRECTIVES
1.	[Proceed down the center line] C Medium walk. G Working trot. A Track right.	• Your goal is to develop a good, rhythmical and active working trot. • Your horse will stay straighter if he is working nicely forward; horses that are dawdling behind their riders' leg are far more likely to wander up the center line or drift to one side of it.
2.	K/E Change the rein via a diagonal through the poles. M Medium walk. C Halt. Immobility 4 seconds. Proceed in medium walk. H Working trot.	• Ride forward through the poles, keeping the tempo and rhythm the same. • A square halt will only happen if the horse was straight and engaged. If the horse is moving crooked, it's virtually impossible to arrive at a square halt.
3.	H/E Change the rein via a diagonal through the poles. A Turn right onto center line	• Look up and across the poles, rather than down at them. If you look down, you'll encourage the horse to drop onto his shoulders.
4.	C Track left.	• When riding the center line, make sure that your horse is working from both your legs into both reins equally. It can be helpful to envisage that your horse is working along a tunnel created by your leg and rein.

5. 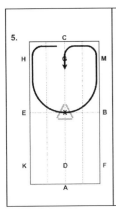	**H/E** Half 20-meter circle left to cross through X. **M** Medium walk. **C** Turn left onto the center line. [Repeat the exercise on both reins]	• Allow the horse to adjust his stride length to negotiate the poles. Don't try to "pick a stride" for him. • When transitioning to medium walk, ensure that the horse continues to work forwards and doesn't just collapse in a heap!

NOTES:

....

....

....

....

....

....

....

....

....

....

....

....

....

....

....

....

....

....

....

....

....

....

EXERCISE 35B

	INSTRUCTIONS	TIPS/DIRECTIVES
1.	[Proceed down the center line] C Working trot. D Halt. Immobility 4 seconds. Proceed in working trot. A Track right.	• It's important 'think forward' when riding into halt, otherwise the horse will lose engagement as he halts. The halt will become unbalanced and the horse may come against the contact.
2.	K/E Change the rein via a diagonal through the poles. M/C Working canter left.	• When riding the trot-canter transition, emphasis should be on the horse pushing from the hind legs that are placed under the body rather than launching off the shoulders. • The canter transition should be reactive, uphill, and balanced. The horse should maintain his round frame.
3.	H/E Change the rein via a diagonal through the poles. Transition working trot before reaching the outside track. A Turn right onto the center line.	• Keep the horse into your outside rein (right rein) whilst cantering across the diagonal and through the poles. Change the bend and establish a new outside rein after the transition to working trot.
4.	C Track left.	• On the center line the horse's poll should be the highest point, and the contact should be quiet, elastic and steady, without any tilting or swinging of the horse's head. • Ride your horse forward (not faster) to help keep him straight.

5. 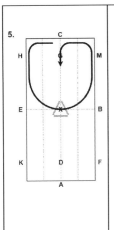	C/H	Working canter left.	• Keep the tempo and rhythm of the canter the same as you pass over the poles.
	H/E	Half 20-meter circle left to cross through X.	
	M	Working trot.	• During the half circle, your horse should continue to work forwards, in a good rhythm, and show a clear uniform bend along his body around the circle.
	C	Turn left onto the center line.	
		[Repeat the exercise on both reins]	

NOTES:

....

....

....

....

....

....

....

....

....

....

....

....

....

....

....

....

....

....

....

....

....

....

....

EXERCISE 35C

	INSTRUCTIONS	TIPS/DIRECTIVES
1.	[Proceed down the center line] C Working canter right. A Track right.	• Your goal during the canter is to develop regularity and lightness of the strides, an uphill tendency, and the natural ability of the horse to carry himself whilst maintaining active well-placed hind legs. • The rhythm should remain the same throughout the center line execution, and the horse should not slow down or anticipate halting.
2.	K/E Change the rein via a diagonal through the poles. Transition to working trot before reaching the outside track. M/C Working canter left.	• Ride forward and allow the horse to adjust his stride length as he passes over the poles. Don't try to influence the horse's stride, as that will upset his balance and rhythm.
3.	H/E Change the rein via a diagonal through the poles. Transition to working trot before reaching the outside track. A Turn right onto the center line.	• Keep the horse into your outside rein (right rein) whilst cantering across the diagonal and through the poles. Change the bend and establish a new outside rein after the transition to working trot.
4.	G Halt. Immobility 4 seconds. Rein-back one horse's length and proceed in working trot. C Track left.	• The rein-back is defined as a rearward movement of diagonal pairs. It has a two-beat rhythm and no moment of suspension. Each pair of legs is raised and returned to the ground alternately, while the horse stays straight and moves on one track.

5. 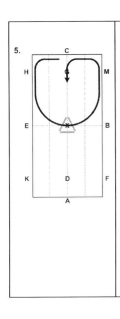	H/E Half 20-meter circle left through X and allow the horse to stretch. M/C Working canter left. C Turn left down the center line. [Repeat the exercise on both reins]	• When allowing the horse to stretch, don't give away the contact. Instead maintain and elastic contact (but on a longer rein) and keep your leg on and ride forward. The steps should be more elevated and the horse's back should lift underneath you. • Always ride the stretch exercise in rising trot so that the horse can use his back.

NOTES:

....
....
....
....
....
....
....
....
....
....
....
....
....
....
....
....
....
....
....
....
....
....

EXERCISE 35D

	INSTRUCTIONS	TIPS/DIRECTIVES
1.	[Proceed down the center line] C Working trot. D Medium walk. A Track right.	• During the trot, the horse's hind feet should step clearly into the prints left by the fore feet. • On the center line the horse should travel forward and straight, as though he is on railway tracks.
2.	K/E Change the rein in extended walk via a diagonal through the poles. M Medium walk. C Working canter left.	• During the extended walk, allow the horse to lengthen his frame and have complete freedom of his shoulder, but don't allow the reins to get too long as he may drop his poll too low and the movement may morph into a stretch exercise. • Keep your body relaxed in the medium walk so that the horse doesn't anticipate the canter transition. Any tension during the walk may disrupt the rhythm and regularity of the steps, so you should prioritize relaxation in the walk.
3.	H/E Change the rein via a diagonal through the poles. When reaching the outside track, simple change to working canter right. A Turn right onto the center line.	• Keep the horse moving forward in the simple change to avoid the horse staying too upright. Instead, you want to encourage the weight-bearing capacity (in the canter-walk) and the pushing power (in the walk-canter) of the hind legs. • Maintain an elastic outside rein contact and ride a smooth turn onto the center line – not a handbrake right-angled turn!

4.		G	Working trot.	• Ride forward (not faster!) down the center line and don't look down at the poles. The horse will adjust his stride accordingly. • Encourage the horse to step through into the working trot, rather than 'fall' out of the canter.
5.		H H/E M C	Medium walk. Half 20-meter circle left in free walk on a long rein. Working trot. Turn left onto the center line. [Repeat the exercise on both reins]	• To start the free walk, let the reins slide through your fingers gradually to allow the horse to take the rein forwards, round and down. It can be helpful to allow the inside rein to lengthen slightly before the outside rein. This can prevent the horse from hollowing and coming off the aids as you begin to ride the free walk, and will encourage him to remain into the contact.

NOTES:

....

....

....

....

....

....

....

....

....

....

....

....

....

....

EXERCISE 35E

	INSTRUCTIONS	TIPS/DIRECTIVES
1.	[Proceed down the center line] C Medium walk. D Half walk pirouette left. Walk straight for 3-4 strides, then half walk pirouette right. Walk straight for 3-4 strides, then proceed in working trot. A Track right.	• In the pirouettes it's crucial that a clear 4-beat walk sequence is maintained, and the tempo of the walk should remain the same before and after the movement. • If the horse is lazy or becomes 'stuck' in the pirouettes, use your legs throughout the turn in an alternating fashion, matching each of your legs to his hind legs, so that your left leg asks him to lift his left hind and vice versa.
2.	K Working canter right. K/E Change the rein via a diagonal through the poles. When reaching the outside track, continue in counter canter to M. M Working trot. C Working canter left.	• The canter transitions should be reactive, uphill, and balanced. The horse should maintain his round frame. • Diligent riding of transitions from trot to canter will build the 'pushing and propulsion' capacity of the horse, enabling him to develop incremental levels of engagement of the hind legs. • During the counter-canter, maintain a little flexion over the leading leg, but no more than what is asked in true canter.
3.	H/E Change the rein via a diagonal through the poles. When reaching the outside track, continue in counter canter to F. F Working trot. A Turn right onto the center line.	• You must take care to maintain a good riding position during the counter canter and keep your weight in the inside (left) seat bone on the side of the leading foreleg. • The value of the counter canter lies in its suppling, engaging, and collecting effects.

4.	C	Track left.	• Focus on the C marker and ride straight toward it, keeping the tempo and rhythm of the trot consistent. • Allow the horse a little more freedom of his neck so that he can judge the distance between the poles.
5.	H H/E M C G	Working canter left. Half 20-meter circle through X and allow the horse to stretch. Working canter. Turn left onto the center line. Medium walk. [Repeat the exercise on both reins]	• When allowing the horse to stretch, keep your leg on and ride forward. You should begin to feel the horse's back really swinging underneath you as he rounds over his topline and pushes himself along from behind. • Use your back, core, and seat to hold the horse in a good balance during the downward transition from canter to walk.

NOTES:

....

....

....

....

....

....

....

....

....

....

....

....

....

....

EXERCISE 35F – Make Your Own

	INSTRUCTIONS
1. 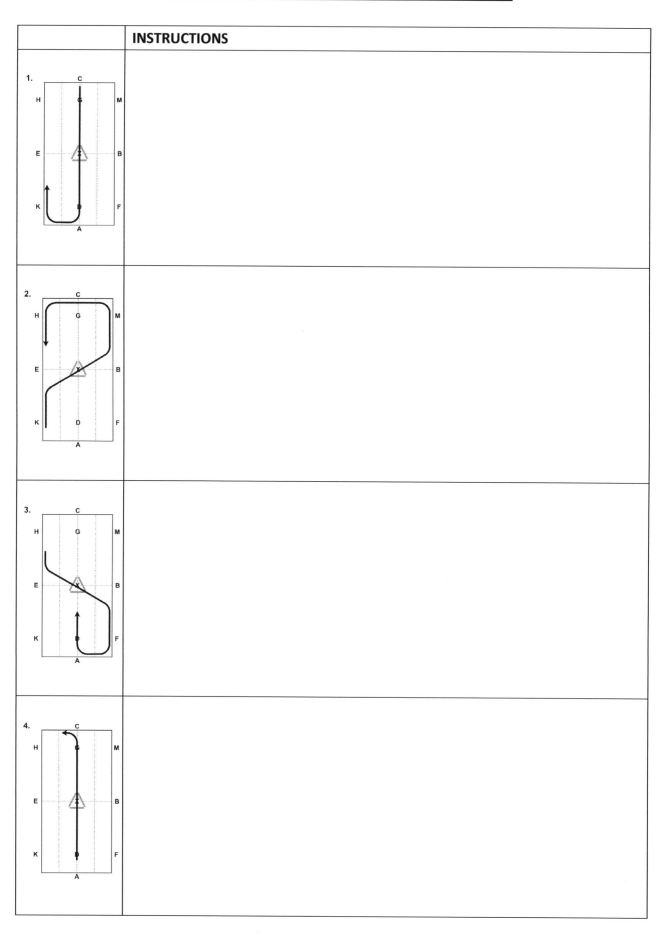	
2.	
3.	
4.	

5.

NOTES:

....

....

....

....

....

....

....

....

....

....

....

....

....

....

....

....

....

....

....

....

....

....

....

EXERCISE 35G – Make Your Own

	INSTRUCTIONS
1.	
2.	
3.	
4.	

5.

NOTES:

....
....
....
....
....
....
....
....
....
....
....
....
....
....
....
....
....
....
....
....
....
....
....
....
....
....
....
....

EXERCISE 35H – Make Your Own

	INSTRUCTIONS
1.	
2.	
3.	
4.	

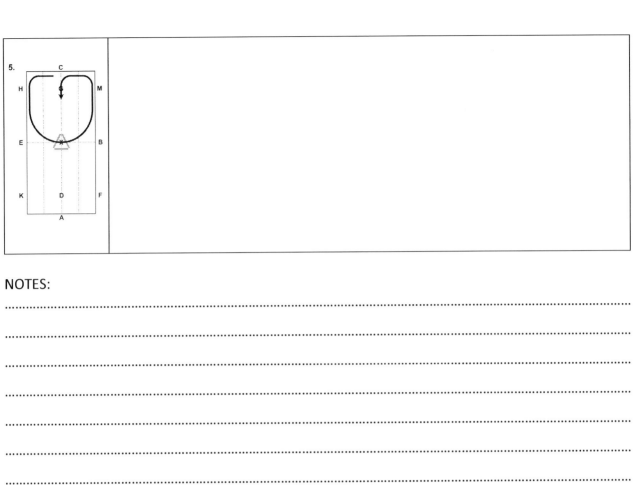

5.

NOTES:

....
....
....
....
....
....
....
....
....
....
....
....
....
....
....
....
....
....
....
....
....
....
....
....
....
....

"The primary avenue of communication between you and your horse is your horse's back."

FLOORPLAN #36

'Target Practice'

PRACTICE LOG – Note the dates when you last practiced this floorplan.

#36 'TARGET PRACTICE' - 20X40 DIAGRAM

1.

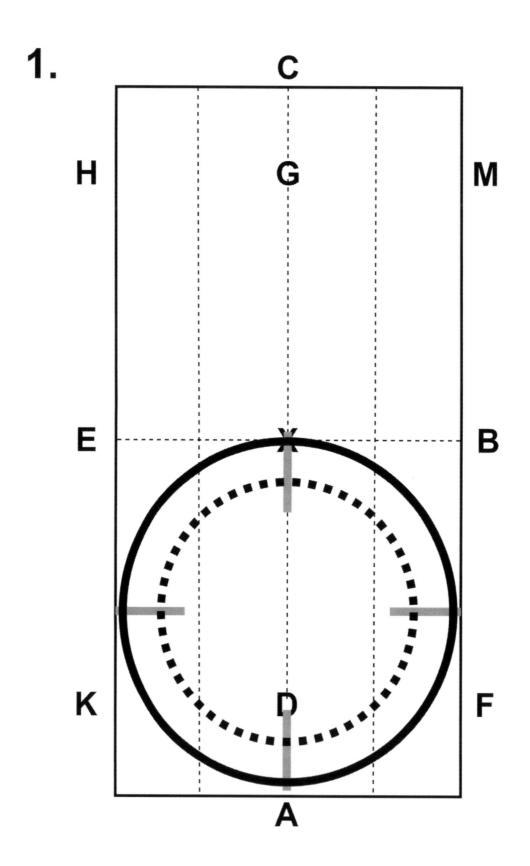

#36 'TARGET PRACTICE' - 20X60 DIAGRAM

1.

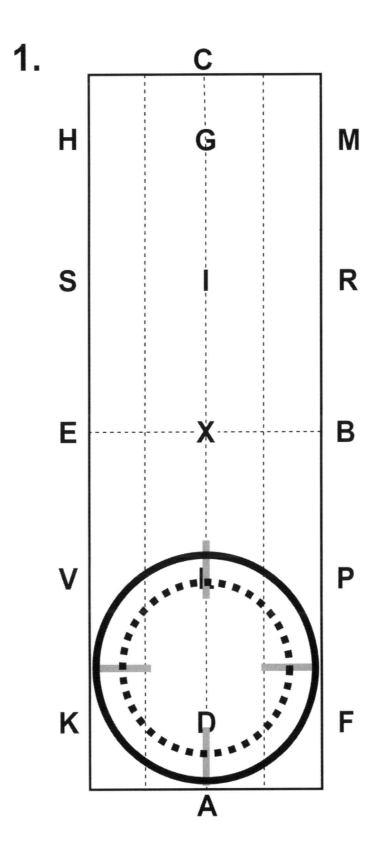

EXERCISE 36A

	INSTRUCTIONS	TIPS/DIRECTIVES
1.	Complete the circle in medium walk. Ride at the outside of the poles for a more extended walk, and ride at the inside of the poles for a more collected walk. [Repeat the exercise on both reins]	• The horse's walk is a four-beat gait without any suspension. • Any tension during the walk may disrupt the rhythm and regularity of the steps, so you should prioritize relaxation in the walk. • For a little variation, allow the horse to stretch and work long and low or bring him up into a more compact competition frame.

NOTES:

....

....

....

....

....

....

....

....

....

....

....

....

....

....

....

....

....

....

EXERCISE 36B

	INSTRUCTIONS	TIPS/DIRECTIVES
1.	Complete the circle in working trot. Ride at the outside of the poles for a more open trot with longer strides, and ride at the inside of the poles for a shortened, more collected trot. [Repeat the exercise on both reins]	• The trot has a two-beat rhythm during which the horse's legs move in diagonal pairs. There should be a clear moment of suspension when all the horse's feet are off the floor. It's this moment of suspension that gives the trot its expression and lift. • The trot tempo and rhythm should stay the same whichever size circle you're riding. Only the length of stride should change. • For a little variation, allow the horse to stretch and work long and low or bring him up into a more compact competition frame.

NOTES:

....

....

....

....

....

....

....

....

....

....

....

....

....

....

EXERCISE 36C

	INSTRUCTIONS	TIPS/DIRECTIVES
1.	Complete the circle in working canter. Ride at the outside of the poles for a more extended canter, and ride at the inside of the poles for a more collected canter. [Repeat the exercise on both reins]	• The canter is a pace of 3-beat. It should have 'uphill' cadenced strides, followed by a moment of suspension. • For a little variation, allow the horse to stretch and work long and low, or bring him up into a more compact competition frame. • Keep the canter balanced and don't try to "pick a stride." The horse will do that for himself. • The canter tempo and rhythm should stay the same whichever size circle you're riding. Only the length of stride should change.

NOTES:

....

....

....

....

....

....

....

....

....

....

....

....

....

....

EXERCISE 36D – Make Your Own

	INSTRUCTIONS
1.	

NOTES:

....

....

....

....

....

....

....

....

....

....

....

....

....

....

EXERCISE 36E – Make Your Own

	INSTRUCTIONS
1. C H G M E B K D F A	

NOTES:

....

....

....

....

....

....

....

....

....

....

....

....

....

EXERCISE 36F – Make Your Own

	INSTRUCTIONS
1.	

NOTES:

....
....
....
....
....
....
....
....
....
....
....
....
....

"Treat every mistake as a training opportunity."

FLOORPLAN #37

'The Half-Pipe'

PRACTICE LOG – Note the dates when you last practiced this floorplan.

....

....

....

....

....

....

....

....

....

....

....

....

....

....

....

....

....

....

....

....

....

#37 'THE HALF-PIPE' - 20X40 DIAGRAM

1.

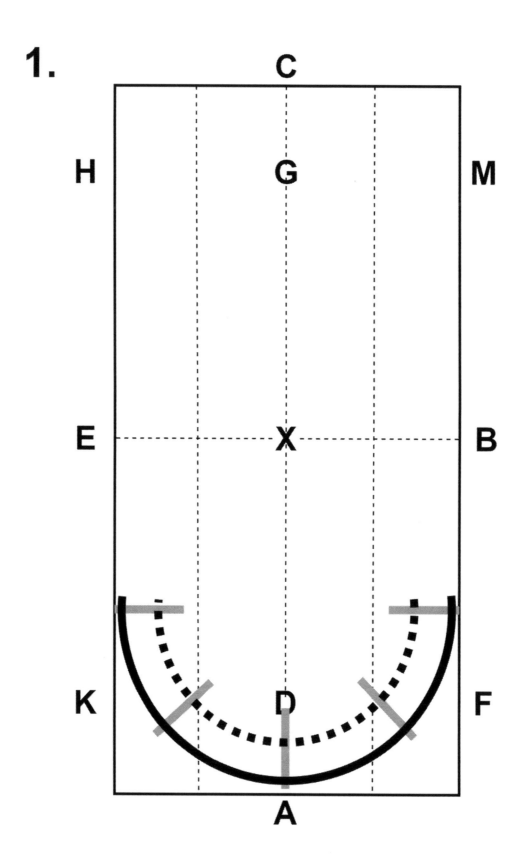

#37 'THE HALF-PIPE' - 20X60 DIAGRAM

1.

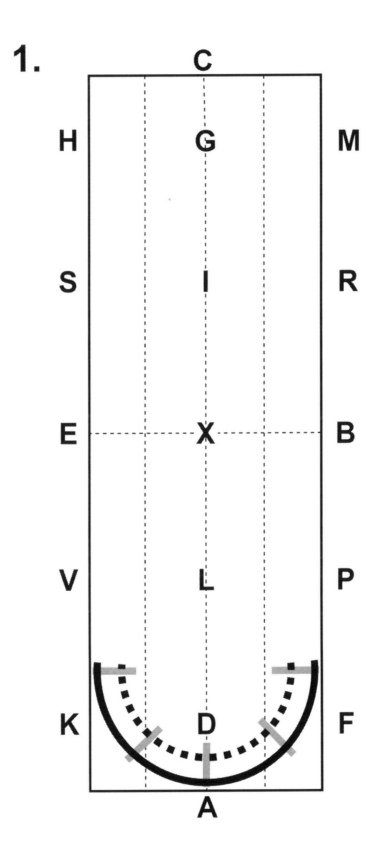

EXERCISE 37A

	INSTRUCTIONS	TIPS/DIRECTIVES
1.	Complete the half-circle in medium walk. Ride at the outside of the poles for a more extended walk, and ride at the inside of the poles for a more collected walk. [Repeat the exercise on both reins]	• The horse's walk is a four-beat gait without any suspension. • Any tension during the walk may disrupt the rhythm and regularity of the steps, so you should prioritize relaxation in the walk. • For a little variation, allow the horse to stretch and work long and low or bring him up into a more compact competition frame.

NOTES:

....

....

....

....

....

....

....

....

....

....

....

....

....

....

....

....

....

....

EXERCISE 37B

	INSTRUCTIONS	TIPS/DIRECTIVES
1. *(arena diagram with points C, H, G, M, E, X, B, K, D, F, A and a half-circle)*	Complete the half-circle in working trot. Ride at the outside of the poles for a more extended trot, and ride at the inside of the poles for a more collected trot. [Repeat the exercise on both reins]	• The trot has a two-beat rhythm during which the horse's legs move in diagonal pairs. There should be a clear moment of suspension when all the horse's feet are off the floor. It's this moment of suspension that gives the trot its expression and lift. • The trot tempo and rhythm should stay the same whichever size circle you're riding. Only the length of stride should change. • For a little variation, allow the horse to stretch and work long and low or bring him up into a more compact competition frame.

NOTES:

....

....

....

....

....

....

....

....

....

....

....

....

....

....

EXERCISE 37C

	INSTRUCTIONS	TIPS/DIRECTIVES
1.	Complete the circle in working canter. Ride at the outside of the poles for a more extended canter, and ride at the inside of the poles for a more collected canter. [Repeat the exercise on both reins]	• The canter is a pace of 3-beat. It should have 'uphill' cadenced strides, followed by a moment of suspension. • For a little variation, allow the horse to stretch and work long and low, or bring him up into a more compact competition frame. • Keep the canter balanced and don't try to "pick a stride." The horse will do that for himself. • The canter tempo and rhythm should stay the same whichever size circle you're riding. Only the length of stride should change.

NOTES:

....

....

....

....

....

....

....

....

....

....

....

....

....

....

EXERCISE 37D – Make Your Own

	INSTRUCTIONS
1.	

NOTES:

....

....

....

....

....

....

....

....

....

....

....

....

....

....

EXERCISE 37E – Make Your Own

	INSTRUCTIONS
1.	

NOTES:

....

....

....

....

....

....

....

....

....

....

....

....

....

EXERCISE 37F – Make Your Own

	INSTRUCTIONS
1. C H G M E X B K D F A	

NOTES:

....

....

....

....

....

....

....

....

....

....

....

....

....

....

"Champions do not become champions when they win an event, but in the hours, weeks, months, and years they spent preparing for it. The victorious performance is merely a demonstration of their champion character."

FLOORPLAN #38

'Single, Single, Double'

PRACTICE LOG – Note the dates when you last practiced this floorplan.

#38 'SINGLE, SINGLE, DOUBLE' - 20X40 DIAGRAMS

1.

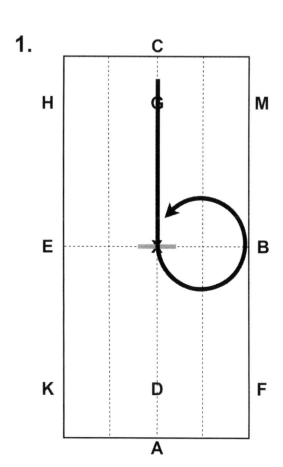

2.

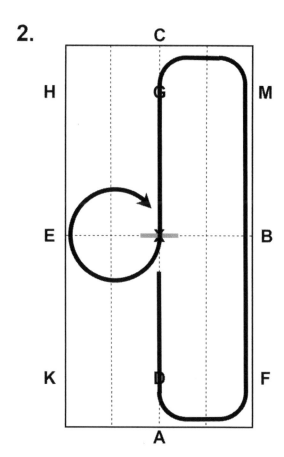

3.

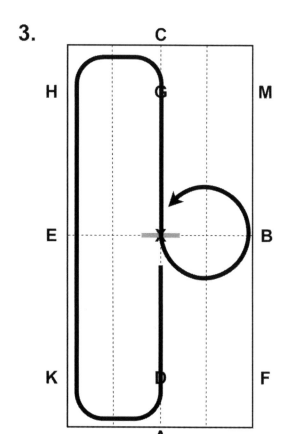

4.

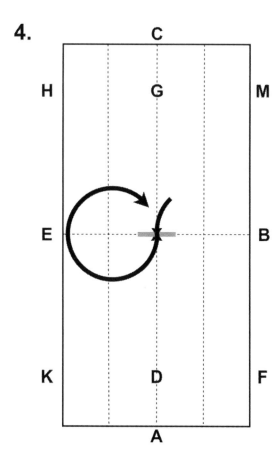

5.

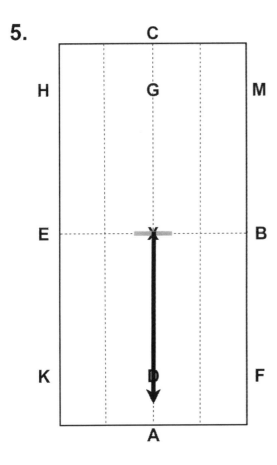

Okay, so we admit that the diagrams for this floorplan look a little complicated!

...but it's not really, let us explain.

STEP 1: You come down the center line and ride a single 10-meter circle left.

STEP 2: Go around the arena and come down the center line again, but this time ride a single 10-meter circle right.

STEP 3: Go around the arena again, come down this center line again, but this time ride two (double) 10-meter circles.

#38 'SINGLE, SINGLE, DOUBLE' - 20X60 DIAGRAMS

1.
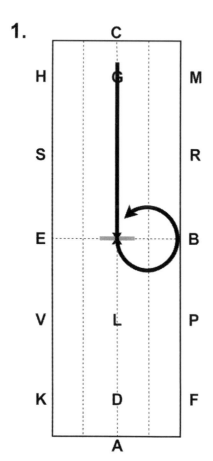

2.
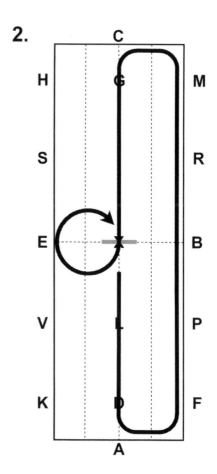

3.
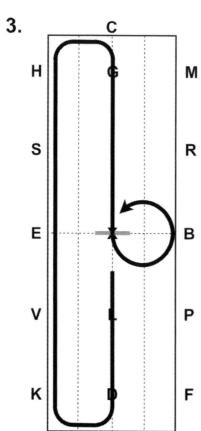

4.
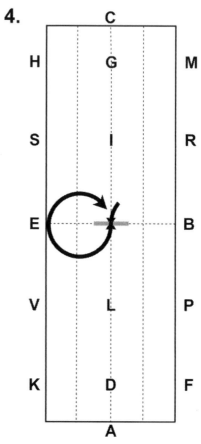

5.

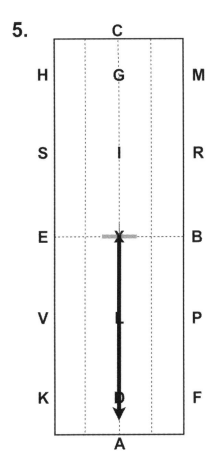

EXERCISE 38A

	INSTRUCTIONS	TIPS/DIRECTIVES
1.	[Proceed down the center line] C Working trot. G Medium walk. X 10-meter circle left.	• A 10-meter circle is quite a small diameter, so it is the rider's job to choose exactly the right tempo (speed of the rhythm), to enable the horse to manage the rhythm ad bend without any disturbances or unevenness to the stride length.
2.	X Proceed down the center line in medium walk. D Working trot. A Track left. B Halt. Immobility 4 seconds. Proceed in working trot. C Turn left onto the center line. G Medium walk. X 10-meter circle right.	• More advanced horses should be able to step smoothly into and out of the halt directly without losing balance and frame. If your horse is less experienced, allow him a step or two of walk to help him remain in balance and prevent him coming against the hand. • During the circle, your horse should continue to work forwards, in a good rhythm, and show a clear uniform bend along his body around the circle.
3.	X Proceed down the center line in medium walk. A Track right. K Free walk on a long rein. H Medium walk. C Turn right onto the center line. X 10-meter circle left.	• The rhythm during the free walk should remain in a clear four beat, correct sequence, and the horse should clearly over-track, covering maximum ground, and demonstrating complete freedom of his shoulder. • Allow the horse to take the rein gradually as you ride the free walk. Don't throw the contact at the horse! That will cause him to come off your aids and hollow, rather than following the bit round and down.

4.	X	10-meter circle right.	• Ride straight over the pole before changing the bend. • Keep the activity and rhythm in medium walk. Don't allow your horse to drop behind your leg. • Both circles should be of equal shape and size.
5.	X D	Proceed down the center line in medium walk. Working trot. [Repeat the exercise on both reins]	• Make the horse straight before you reach the pole so that he doesn't trip over it! • On the center line the horse should travel forward and straight, as though he is on railway tracks.

NOTES:

....
....
....
....
....
....
....
....
....
....
....
....
....
....
....
....
....

EXERCISE 38B

	INSTRUCTIONS	TIPS/DIRECTIVES
1.	[Proceed down the center line] C Working trot. X 10-meter circle left.	• If you have a young or 'green' horse, always ride rising trot so that he can use his back • When riding the circle, keep your hips and shoulders parallel with your horse's shoulders, keep your body upright, and look ahead of you around the circle.
2.	X Proceed down the center line in working trot. A Track left. A/F Working canter left. M Working trot. C Turn left onto the center line. X 10-meter circle right.	• When riding the trot-canter transition, emphasis should be on the horse pushing from the hind legs that are placed under the body rather than launching off the shoulders. • The circle must be accurate in order to demonstrate that the horse is supple and connected enough to negotiate the movement without losing his balance and rhythm.
3.	X Proceed down the center line in working trot. D Medium walk. A Track right. E Working trot. C Turn right onto the center line. X 10-meter circle left.	• When transitioning to medium walk, ensure that the horse continues to work forwards and doesn't just collapse in a heap! • The transition back into trot should be obedient and reactive, whilst remaining fluent and calm. • When completing the circle there should be no tilting of the horse's head.

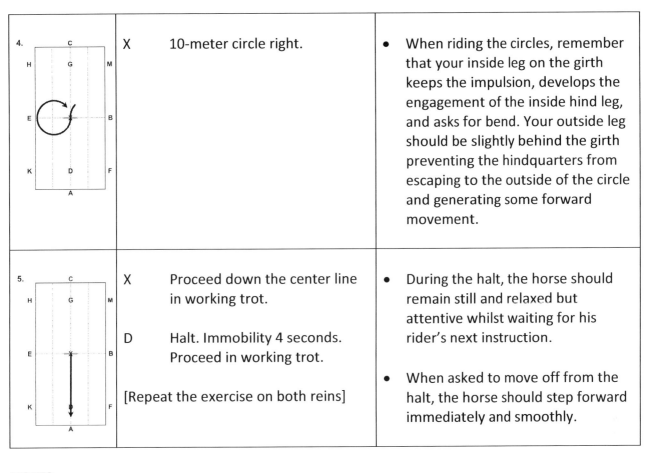

4.	X	10-meter circle right.	• When riding the circles, remember that your inside leg on the girth keeps the impulsion, develops the engagement of the inside hind leg, and asks for bend. Your outside leg should be slightly behind the girth preventing the hindquarters from escaping to the outside of the circle and generating some forward movement.
5.	X	Proceed down the center line in working trot.	• During the halt, the horse should remain still and relaxed but attentive whilst waiting for his rider's next instruction.
	D	Halt. Immobility 4 seconds. Proceed in working trot. [Repeat the exercise on both reins]	• When asked to move off from the halt, the horse should step forward immediately and smoothly.

NOTES:

....
....
....
....
....
....
....
....
....
....
....
....
....
....
....

EXERCISE 38C

	INSTRUCTIONS	TIPS/DIRECTIVES
1.	[Proceed down the center line] C Working trot. X 10-meter circle left.	• Your goal is to develop a good, rhythmical and active working trot. • Guard the outside of the horse with your rein and leg to prevent him from falling out through his shoulder or swinging his quarters out.
2.	D Halt. Immobility 4 seconds. Rein-back one horse's length. Proceed in working trot. A Track left. F Medium trot. M Working trot. C Turn left onto the center line. X 10-meter circle right.	• Make sure the halt is square and straight before commencing rein-back. • Use your seat, back, weight, and leg aids to ride rein-back. Keep your hand quiet and your contact elastic. • Although your horse should be working with good impulsion during the medium trot, he should not hurry or lose rhythm and must remain in a good uphill balance.
3.	X Proceed down the center line in working trot. A Track right. A/K Working canter right. K Medium canter. H Working canter. C Turn right onto the center line. G Working trot. X 10-meter circle left.	• Diligent riding of transitions from trot to canter will build the 'pushing and propulsion' capacity of the horse, enabling him to develop incremental levels of engagement of the hind legs. • The medium canter is a longer version of the working canter. It covers more ground because the horse's frame and strides lengthen. • When riding the medium canter, maintain the regularity and lightness of the canter strides

4.	X	10-meter circle right.	• A 10-meter circle is quite a small diameter, so it is your job to choose exactly the right tempo (speed of the rhythm), to enable the horse to manage the rhythm and bend without any disturbances or unevenness to the stride length.
5.	X	Proceed down the center line in working trot. [Repeat the exercise on both reins]	• Ride the horse forward (not faster) to help keep him straight.

NOTES:

....
....
....
....
....
....
....
....
....
....
....
....
....
....
....
....
....
....

EXERCISE 38D

	INSTRUCTIONS	TIPS/DIRECTIVES
1.	[Proceed down the center line] C Working canter left. X Collected canter. 10-meter circle left.	• The collected canter should have shorter and higher steps due to the horse carrying more of the weight towards its haunches, not because you've kept the handbrake on. • Remember that the degree of collection required in the canter is only so much as to be able to perform the 10-meter circle with ease.
2.	X Proceed down the center line in working canter. A Track left. F Medium canter. M Working canter. C Turn left onto the center line. G Working trot. X 10-meter circle right.	• The medium canter is a longer version of the working canter. It covers more ground because the horse's frame and strides lengthen. • During the medium canter, the horse's hind legs must come further under the body and appear to 'push' the horse forwards, whilst you remain in full control through light and supple seat and rein aids. • Encourage the horse to step through into the working trot, rather than 'fall' out of the canter.
3.	X Procced down the center line in working trot. A Track right. K Medium walk. K/H Show some extended walk steps. H Working trot. C Turn right onto the center line. X 10-meter circle left.	• The horse's walk is a four-beat gait without any suspension. • Any tension during the walk may disrupt the rhythm and regularity of the steps, so you should prioritize relaxation in the walk. • In extended walk, allow the horse freedom to stretch his neck and open his shoulders. Don't allow your rein to get too long, as that will allow the horse's poll to come too low.

4.	X	10-meter circle right.	• Both circles should be of equal shape and size and the horse must maintain the same rhythm, regularity of steps, and equal bend on both reins.
5.	X	Proceed down the center line in working trot. [Repeat the exercise on both reins]	• Your horse will stay straighter if he is working nicely forward; horses that are dawdling behind their riders' leg are far more likely to wander on the center line.

NOTES:

....

....

....

....

....

....

....

....

....

....

....

....

....

....

....

....

....

....

EXERCISE 38E

	INSTRUCTIONS	TIPS/DIRECTIVES
1.	[Proceed down the center line] C Collected canter left. X 10-meter circle left in collected canter.	• Collected canter needs just as much impulsion as working canter! Be sure to keep plenty of energy in the canter so that you don't lose the 3-beat rhythm and moment of suspension. • When riding the circle, remember that your inside leg on the girth keeps the impulsion, develops the engagement of the inside hind leg, and asks for bend. Your outside leg should be slightly behind the girth preventing the hindquarters from escaping to the outside of the circle and generating some forward movement.
2.	X Proceed down the center line in collected canter. A Track left. F Working canter. B Travers left. M Working canter. C Turn left onto the center line. G Simple change to collected canter right. X 10-meter circle right.	• In travers, the horse's inside forefoot and outside hindfoot are on the same track, and the angle of the horse's body should be maintained at 35 degrees. The bend should be uniform from the poll to the tail, and the horse should look in the direction in which he is moving. • If your horse is inclined to bring his quarters in during the canter, ride shoulder-in rather than travers. • During the simple change, try to avoid the horse staying too upright in the walk to canter and hence not really covering enough ground forward. • The shorter, higher steps of collection are the result of the horse carrying more of the weight towards its haunches.

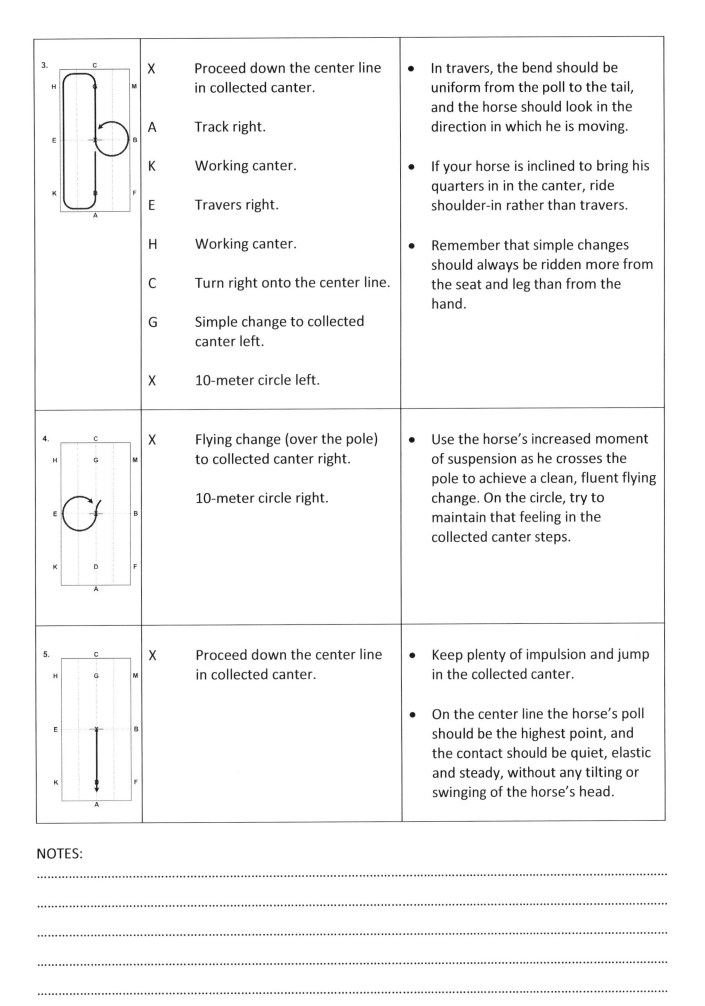

3.	X	Proceed down the center line in collected canter.	• In travers, the bend should be uniform from the poll to the tail, and the horse should look in the direction in which he is moving.
	A	Track right.	
	K	Working canter.	• If your horse is inclined to bring his quarters in in the canter, ride shoulder-in rather than travers.
	E	Travers right.	
	H	Working canter.	• Remember that simple changes should always be ridden more from the seat and leg than from the hand.
	C	Turn right onto the center line.	
	G	Simple change to collected canter left.	
	X	10-meter circle left.	
4.	X	Flying change (over the pole) to collected canter right. 10-meter circle right.	• Use the horse's increased moment of suspension as he crosses the pole to achieve a clean, fluent flying change. On the circle, try to maintain that feeling in the collected canter steps.
5.	X	Proceed down the center line in collected canter.	• Keep plenty of impulsion and jump in the collected canter. • On the center line the horse's poll should be the highest point, and the contact should be quiet, elastic and steady, without any tilting or swinging of the horse's head.

NOTES:

....

....

....

....

....

EXERCISE 38F – Make Your Own

	INSTRUCTIONS
1.	
2.	
3.	
4.	

5.

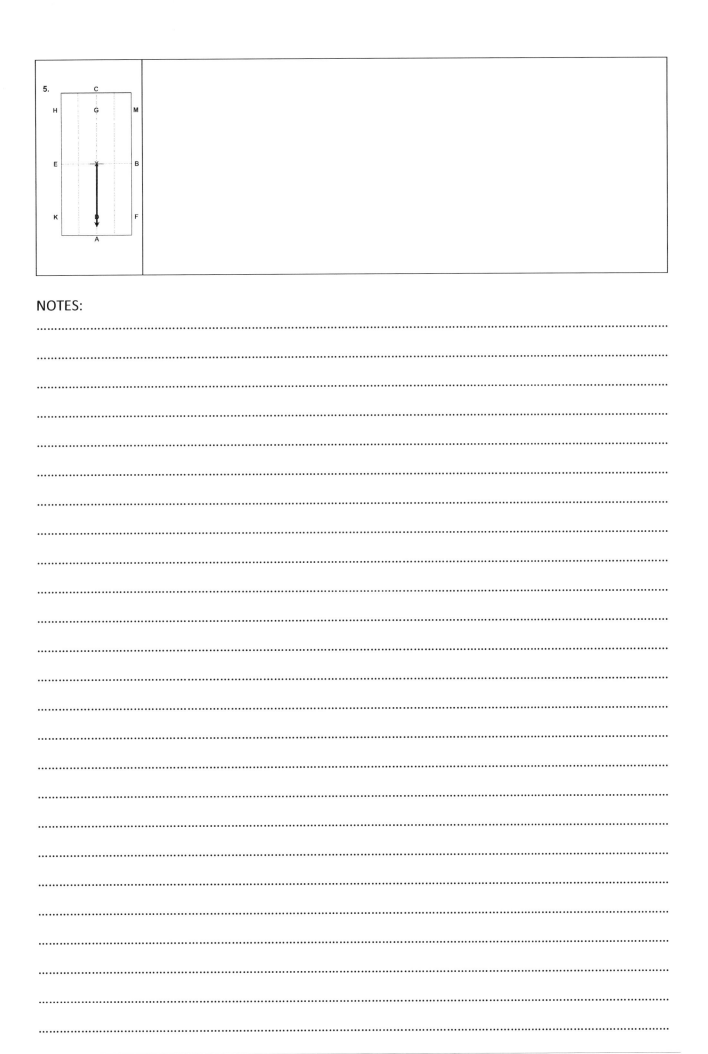

NOTES:

....

....

....

....

....

....

....

....

....

....

....

....

....

....

....

....

....

....

....

....

....

....

....

....

....

....

EXERCISE 38G – Make Your Own

	INSTRUCTIONS
1.	
2.	
3.	
4.	

5.

NOTES:

....
....
....
....
....
....
....
....
....
....
....
....
....
....
....
....
....
....
....
....
....
....
....
....
....
....
....
....
....

EXERCISE 38H – Make Your Own

	INSTRUCTIONS
1.	
2.	
3.	
4.	

5.

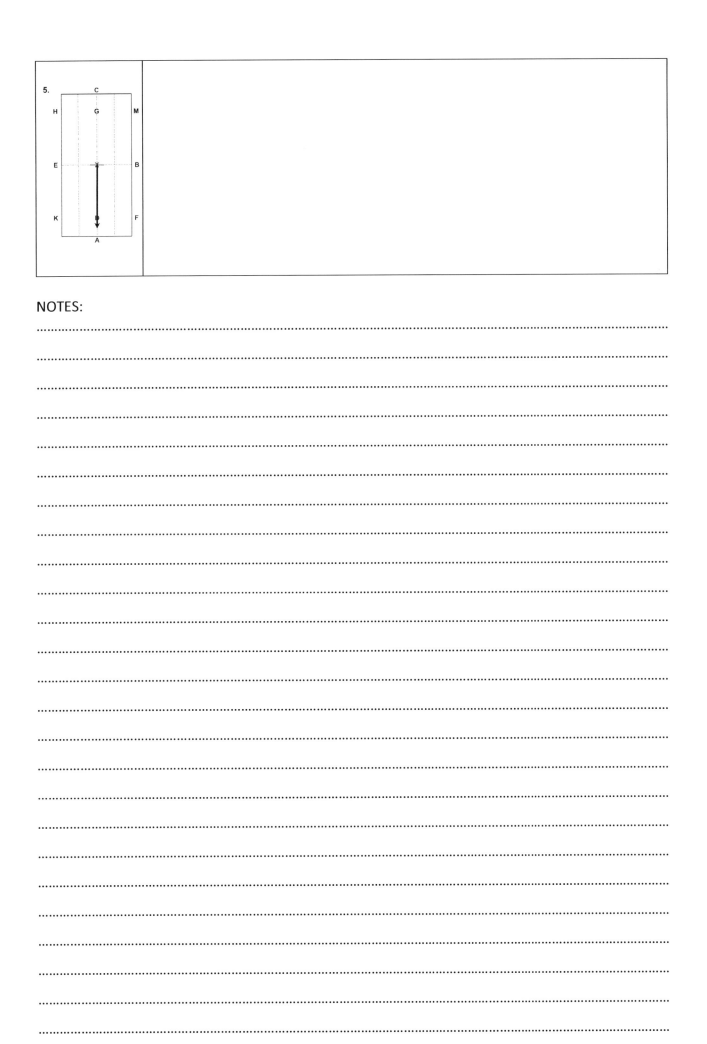

NOTES:

....
....
....
....
....
....
....
....
....
....
....
....
....
....
....
....
....
....
....
....
....
....
....
....
....

"People rarely succeed unless they have fun in what they are doing."

FLOORPLAN #39

'Snakes & Ladders'

PRACTICE LOG – Note the dates when you last practiced this floorplan.

....

....

....

....

....

....

....

....

....

....

....

....

....

....

....

....

....

....

....

....

....

#39 'SNAKES & LADDERS' - 20X40 DIAGRAMS

1.

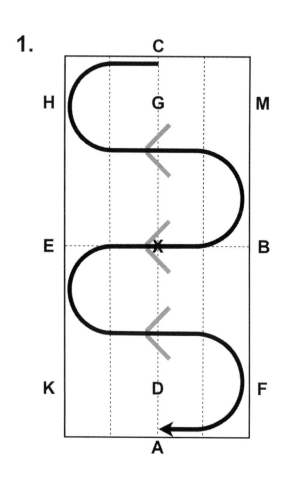

2.

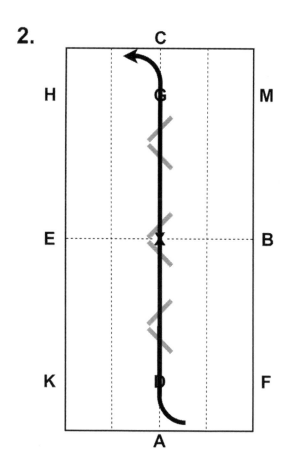

3.

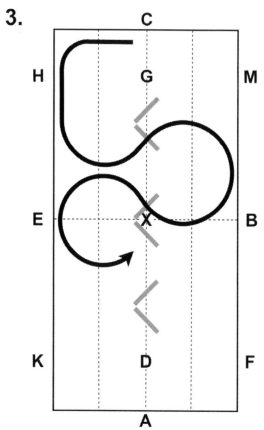

4.

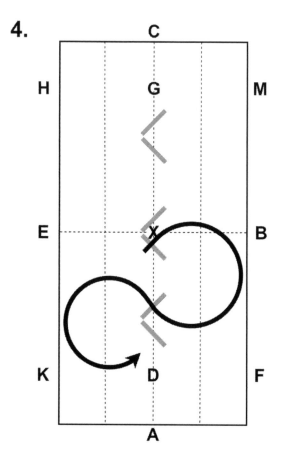

5.

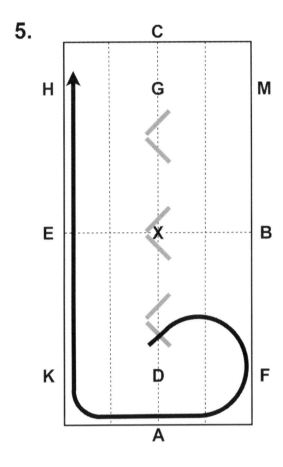

#39 'SNAKES & LADDERS' - 20X60 DIAGRAMS

1.

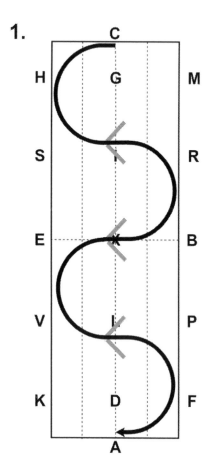

2.

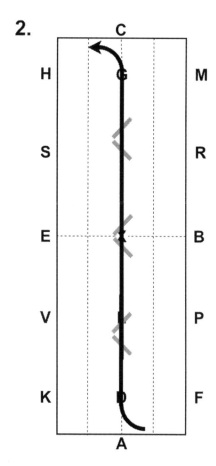

3.

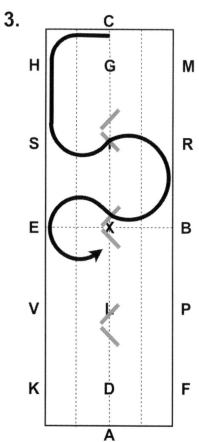

4.

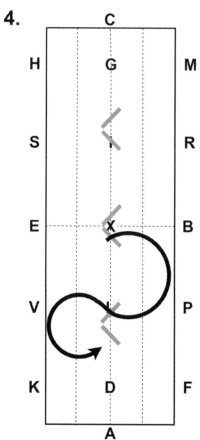

5.

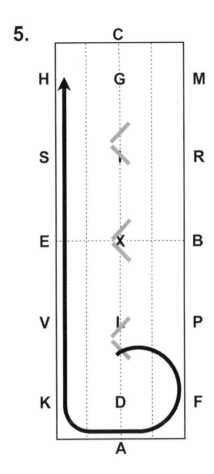

...just a little word of encouragement from us to let you
know that we think you're doing great!

EXERCISE 39A

	INSTRUCTIONS	TIPS/DIRECTIVES
1.	[Start on the left rein] C Medium walk. 4-loop serpentine crossing through all of the poles.	• The horse's walk is a four-beat gait without any suspension. • Any tension during the walk may disrupt the rhythm and regularity of the steps, so you should prioritize relaxation in the walk. • Look where you're going, and make sure that the horse is straight when you reach the poles.
2.	A Turn right onto the center line. D Working trot through all poles. C Track left.	• The trot has a two-beat rhythm during which the horse's legs move in diagonal pairs. • Keep the activity and rhythm in the trot, allowing the horse to lengthen or shorten his stride accordingly as he negotiates the poles.

3.	H Medium walk.
	
	H/E Turn left to go over the second pole.
	
	       10-meter circle right to go over the third pole.
	
	       10-meter circle left to go over the fourth pole.
		• Use half-halts to balance your horse and keep his attention through this exercise.
		
		• Look up to where you want to go, not down at the poles!
		
		• These circles are designed to test the horse's balance, suppleness to the bend, and straightness.

4.	10-meter circle right to go over the fifth pole. 10-meter circle left to go over the sixth pole.	• Keep the activity and rhythm in the walk steps. Even if the horse lengthens or shortens his stride to go over a pole, the rhythm should remain the same.

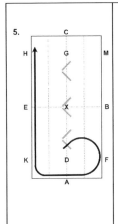

5.

Turn right to re-join the track at F.

A   Continue in medium walk.

K   Free walk on a long rein.

H   Medium walk.

[Repeat the exercise on both reins]

- During the free walk, the horse should follow the contact round and down, stretching his neck and head to show relaxation and suppleness over his back.

- To ride a good transition from free walk back to medium walk, shorten your reins gradually. Keep your leg on to maintain the impulsion and engagement and to encourage the horse's hind leg to remain active.

NOTES:

....

....

....

....

....

....

....

....

....

....

....

....

....

....

....

....

....

....

....

....

EXERCISE 39B

	INSTRUCTIONS	TIPS/DIRECTIVES

1.	[Start on the left rein]
	
	C Working trot.
	      4-loop serpentine crossing
	      through all of the poles.
		• Look where you're going, and make sure that the horse is straight when you reach the poles.
		
		• The rhythm of the pace should remain consistent throughout the serpentine, and the horse should not speed up or slow down as he negotiates each loop.

2.	A Turn right onto the center line. D Working trot through all poles. C Track left.	• Your goal is to develop a good, rhythmical and active working trot. • Keep the horse straight by riding him forwards (not faster!)

3.	C Continue in working trot.
	
	H/E Turn left to go over the second pole.
	
	      10-meter circle right to go over the third pole.
	
	      10-meter circle left to go over the fourth pole.
		• When riding the circles, the horse should be supple enough to be able to negotiate the circles accurately, whilst maintaining his rhythm and balance. He should show an adequate degree of bend without losing his quarters to the outside of the circle.
		
		• Use half-halts to balance your horse and keep his attention through this exercise.

4.	10-meter circle right to go over the fifth pole. 10-meter circle left to go over the sixth pole.	• Keep riding forward and into a steady rhythm. • When completing the circles there should be no tilting of the horse's head.

5. 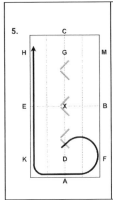	Turn right to re-join the track at F. F/A Working canter right. H Working trot. [Repeat the exercise on both reins]	• The canter transition should be reactive, uphill, and balanced. The horse should maintain his round frame. • Encourage the horse to step through into the working trot, rather than 'fall' out of the canter.

NOTES:

....

....

....

....

....

....

....

....

....

....

....

....

....

....

....

....

....

....

....

....

....

....

EXERCISE 39C

	INSTRUCTIONS	TIPS/DIRECTIVES

1.	[Start on the left rein]
	
	C Working canter left.
	        4-loop serpentine crossing through all of the poles.
	
	        After the poles, ride a simple change ready for the next loop OR ride counter canter.
	
	F Working trot.
		• Ride forward but don't allow the horse to 'jump' over the poles. He should take them in his stride without breaking rhythm.
		
		• If riding the simple change, maintain the relaxation and the clarity of the walk steps.
		
		• If riding counter-canter, maintain a little flexion over the leading leg, but no more than what would be asked for in true canter.

2.	A Turn right onto the center line. D Working trot through all poles. C Track left.	• Encourage the horse to step through into the working trot, rather than 'fall' out of the canter.

3.	H Collected canter left.
	
	H/E Turn left to go over the second pole.
	       Flying change over the pole.
	
	       10-meter circle right to go over the third pole.
	       Flying change over the pole.
	
	       10-meter circle left to go over the fourth pole.
	       Flying change over the pole.
		• The degree of collection required in the canter is only so much as to be able to perform the required movement with ease.
		
		• The quality of your flying changes will be determined by the suppleness and elasticity of the horse's canter. If the canter is flat, lacking impulsion, or on the forehand, the flying changes will most likely be incorrect.

4.	10-meter circle right to go over the fifth pole. Flying change over the pole. 10-meter circle left to go over the sixth pole. Flying change over the pole.	• Throughout the flying change and during the approach to it, the horse should remain calm and relaxed. • When riding a flying change the tempo of the canter and the rhythm should remain unchanged.
5.	Turn right to re-join the track at F. A Medium walk. K Free walk on a long rein. H Medium walk. [Repeat the exercise on both reins]	• In the free walk, although the horse is relaxed, he should march purposefully forward and look as though he is 'going somewhere'. • The transition from free walk back to medium walk should be smooth, with no loss of rhythm or signs of tension.

NOTES:

....

....

....

....

....

....

....

....

....

....

....

....

....

....

....

....

EXERCISE 39D – Make Your Own

	INSTRUCTIONS
1.	
2.	
3.	
4.	

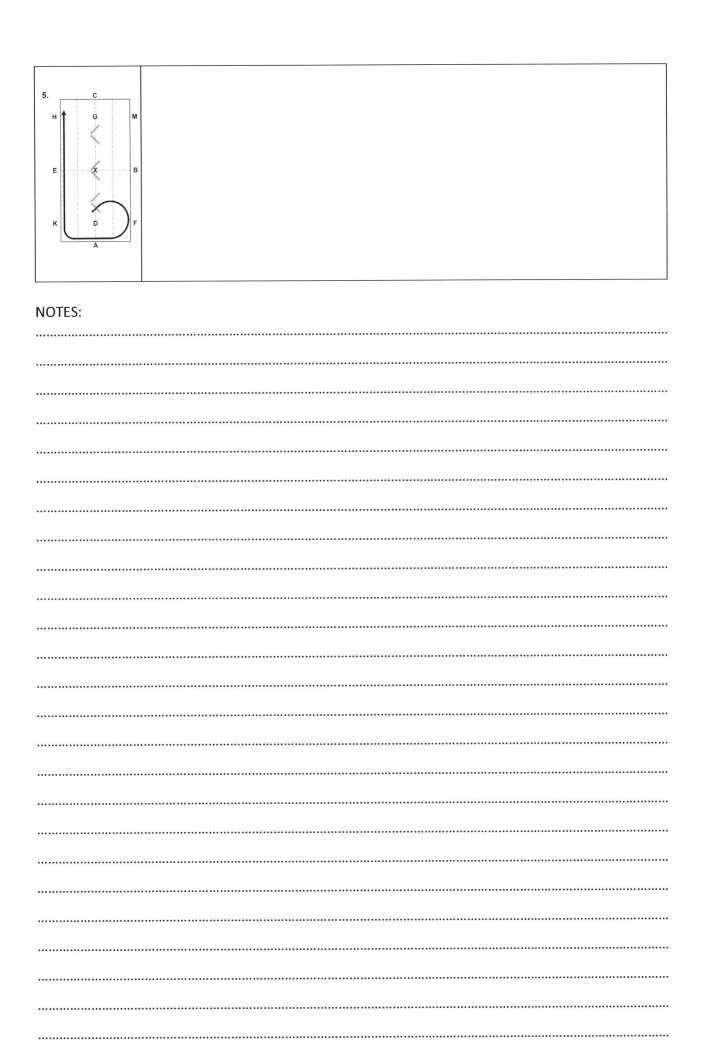

5.

```
        C
  H     G     M
        ↑
        <
  E  ───X───  B
        <
  K     D     F
        A
```

NOTES:

....

....

....

....

....

....

....

....

....

....

....

....

....

....

....

....

....

....

....

....

....

....

....

....

EXERCISE 39E – Make Your Own

	INSTRUCTIONS
1.	
2.	
3.	
4.	

5.

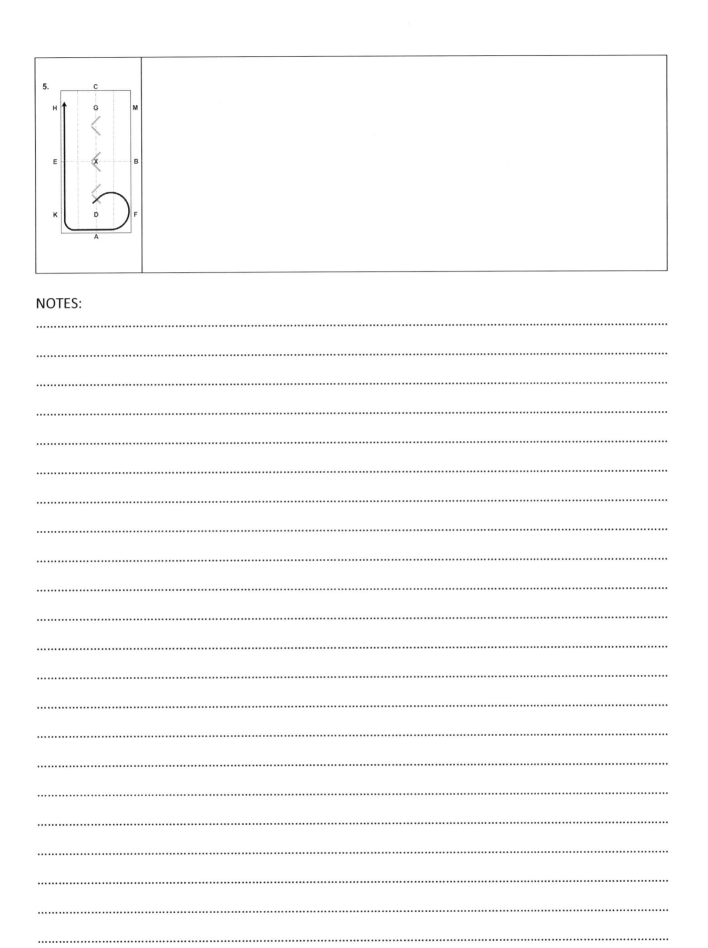

NOTES:

....

....

....

....

....

....

....

....

....

....

....

....

....

....

....

....

....

....

....

....

....

....

....

....

....

....

....

EXERCISE 39F – Make Your Own

	INSTRUCTIONS
1.	
2.	
3.	
4.	

5.

NOTES:

....
....
....
....
....
....
....
....
....
....
....
....
....
....
....
....
....
....
....
....
....
....
....
....
....

"Every horse has something to teach. Every person has something to learn."

FLOORPLAN #40

'Think Outside the Box'

PRACTICE LOG – Note the dates when you last practiced this floorplan.

#40 'THINK OUTSIDE THE BOX' - 20X40 DIAGRAMS

1.

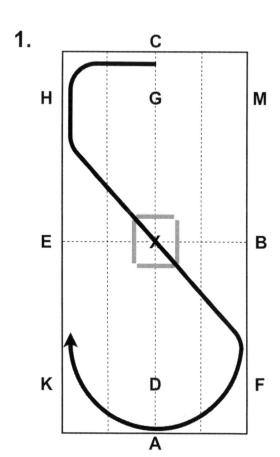

2.

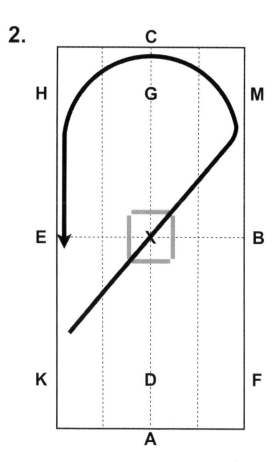

3.

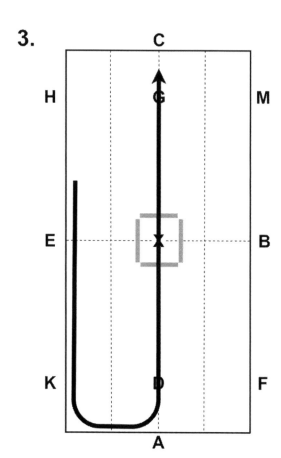

#40 'THINK OUTSIDE THE BOX' - 20X60 DIAGRAMS

1.

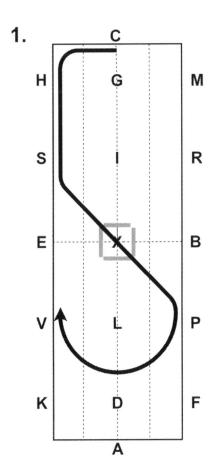

2.

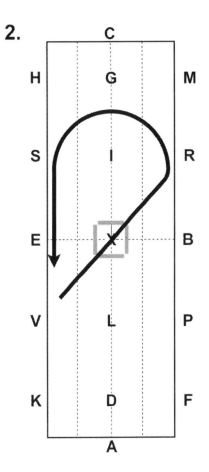

3.

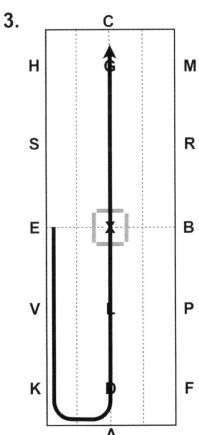

EXERCISE 40A

	INSTRUCTIONS	TIPS/DIRECTIVES
1.	[Start on the left rein] C Medium walk. H/E Change the rein via a diagonal through the corners of the poles in free walk on a long rein. Transition to medium walk before reaching the outside track. Then half 20-meter circle left, and transition to working trot as you pass A.	• The rhythm during the free walk should remain in a clear four beat, correct sequence, and the horse should clearly over-track, covering maximum ground, and demonstrating complete freedom of his shoulder. • Look straight through the corners of the poles and to the arena fence line. Don't look down the poles. • The transition into working trot should be obedient and reactive, whilst remaining fluent and calm.
2.	K/E Change the rein via a diagonal through the corners of the poles in working trot. When reaching the outside track, half 20-meter circle right	• Look up as you change the rein. Keep the horse moving forward from both legs into both reins to keep him straight so that he doesn't drift and collide with the poles. • Change your horse's bend and diagonal either before or after the poles. Don't try to change them as X as this can upset your horse's balance whilst he tries to negotiate the poles.
3.	E Transition to medium walk for one horse's length and then proceed in working trot. A Turn right down the center line. [Repeat the exercise on both reins]	• The horse should remain in the same outline throughout the whole trot-walk-trot movement, and the trot rhythm and energy following the transition should be the same as it was prior to the walk steps. • As you ride toward the poles, allow the horse a little freedom to stretch his neck so that he can see the poles and adjust his stride length accordingly.

NOTES:

EXERCISE 40B

	INSTRUCTIONS	TIPS/DIRECTIVES
1.	[Start on the left rein] C Working trot. H/E Change the rein via a diagonal through the corners of the poles. Transition to medium walk before reaching the outside track. Then half 20-meter circle left in free walk on a long rein.	• Keep the horse moving forward from both legs into both reins to keep him straight so that he doesn't drift and collide with the poles. • To start the free walk, let the reins slide through your fingers gradually to allow the horse to take the rein forwards, round and down. It can be helpful to allow the inside rein to lengthen slightly before the outside rein. This can prevent the horse from hollowing and coming off the aids as you begin to ride the free walk, and will encourage him to remain into the contact.
2.	K/E Medium walk. Change the rein via a diagonal through the corners of the poles in medium walk. When reaching the outside track, transition to working trot and ride a half 20-meter circle right. C/H Working canter left.	• Medium walk should be a marching pace. Keep your horse active and encourage the horse to walk purposefully. • The transition into trot should be obedient and reactive, whilst remaining fluent and calm. • When riding the trot-canter transition, emphasis should be on the horse pushing from the hind legs that are placed under the body rather than launching off the shoulders.
3.	A Turn right onto the center line. [Repeat the exercise on both reins]	• As you ride down the center line toward the poles, allow the horse a little freedom to stretch his neck so that he can see the poles and adjust his stride length accordingly.

NOTES:

EXERCISE 40C

	INSTRUCTIONS	TIPS/DIRECTIVES
1.	[Start on the left rein] C Working canter left. H/F Change the rein via a diagonal through the corners of the poles. Transition to working trot before reaching the outside track. Then half 20-meter circle left, transition to working canter right as you pass A.	• You will need to use a half-halt to engage and balance your horse as you reach the poles. Look up and forward, not down at the poles. Allow your horse a little more freedom so that he can see where he's putting his feet and adjust his stride if necessary. • Encourage the horse to step through into the working trot, rather than 'fall' out of the canter.
2.	K/M Change the rein via a diagonal through the corners of the poles. Transition to working trot before reaching the outside track, then half 20-meter circle right. H Medium trot	• When going over the poles, ride forward, straight, and maintain the rhythm. Try not to micro-manage the strides going into the poles and this often causes more problems. • Medium trot is a pace of moderate lengthening. Whilst maintaining a round frame and working over his back to the contact, the horse should clearly lengthen his stride to cover more ground.
3.	K Working trot. A Turn right down the center line. [Repeat the exercise on both reins]	• The transition back to working trot from medium trot should be balanced and smooth, and the rhythm should not change – only the stride length. • When riding the center line, make sure that your horse is working from both your legs into both reins equally. It can be helpful to envisage that your horse is working along a tunnel created by your leg and rein.

NOTES:

EXERCISE 40D – Make Your Own

	INSTRUCTIONS
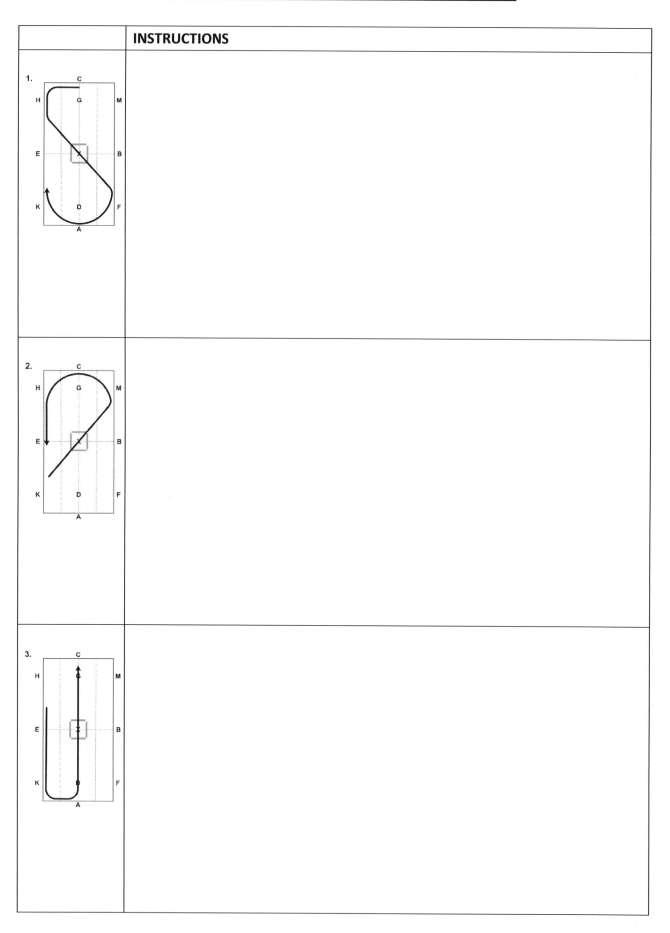	

NOTES:

EXERCISE 40E – Make Your Own

	INSTRUCTIONS
1. 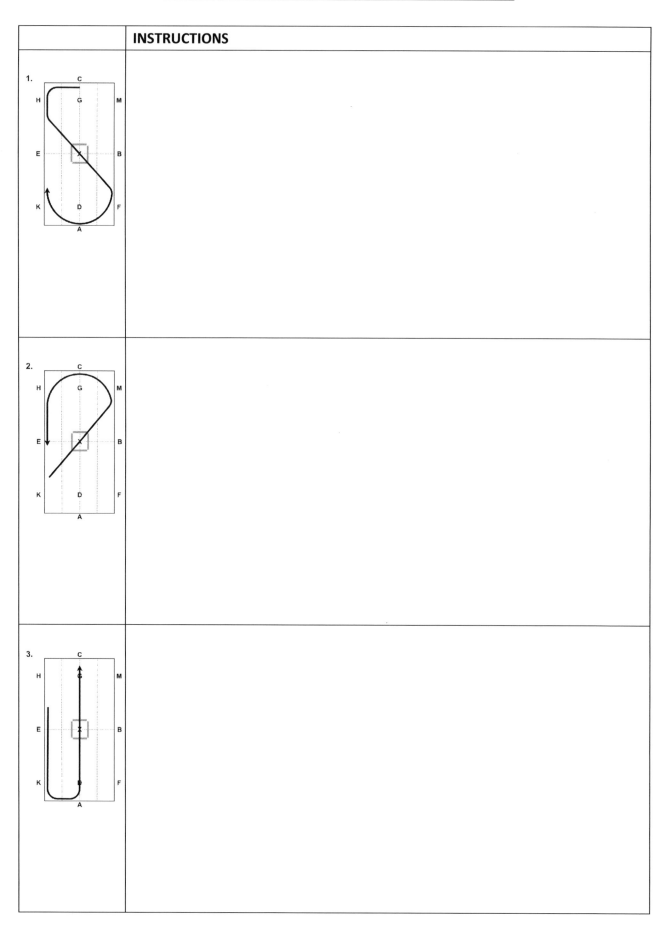	
2.	
3.	

NOTES:

EXERCISE 40F – Make Your Own

	INSTRUCTIONS
1.	
2.	
3.	

NOTES:

"The riders at the top
didn't just fall there."

FLOORPLAN #41
'Keep Thinking Outside the Box'

PRACTICE LOG – Note the dates when you last practiced this floorplan.

....
....
....
....
....
....
....
....
....
....
....
....
....
....
....
....
....
....
....
....
....
....

#41 'KEEP THINKING OUTSIDE THE BOX' - 20X40
DIAGRAMS

1.

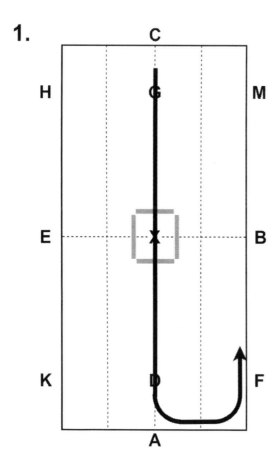

2.

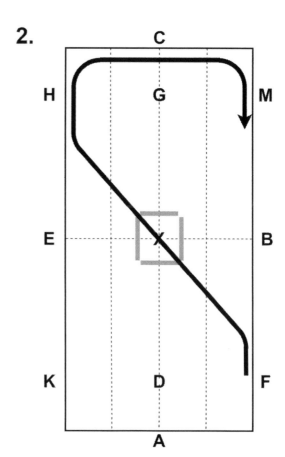

3.

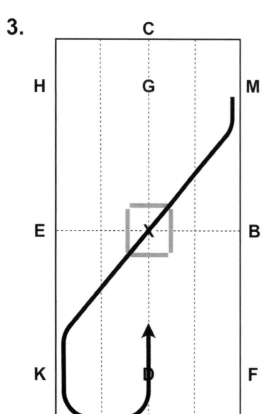

4.

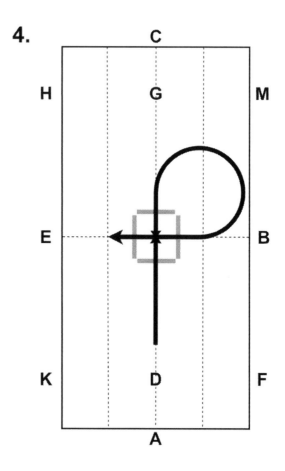

5.

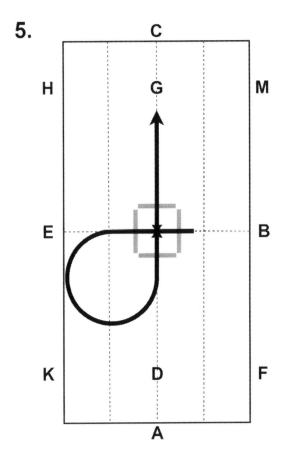

#41 'KEEP THINKING OUTSIDE THE BOX' - 20X60
DIAGRAMS

1.

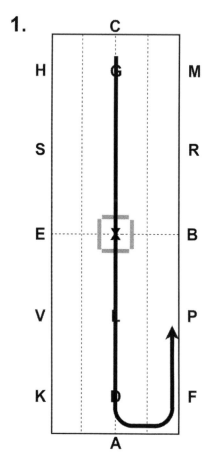

2.

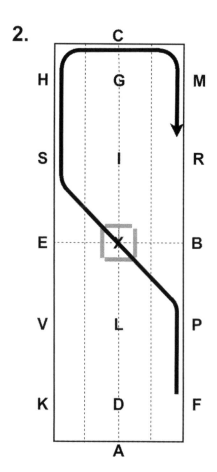

3.

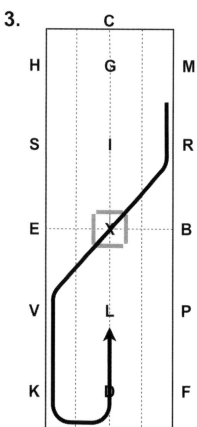

4.

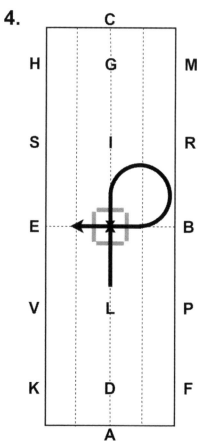

5.

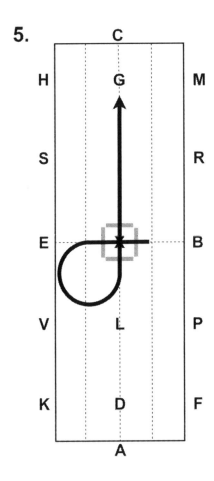

EXERCISE 41A

	INSTRUCTIONS		TIPS/DIRECTIVES
1.	C	Proceed down the center line in medium walk.	• As you ride down the center line toward the poles, allow the horse a little freedom to stretch his neck so that he can see the poles and adjust his stride length accordingly.
	X	Halt. Immobility 4 seconds. Proceed in medium walk.	
	D	Working trot.	• Use the poles to help keep the horse straight in halt.
	A	Track left.	
2.	F/B	Change the rein via a diagonal through the corners of the poles.	• Look up and ahead as you change the rein. Keep the horse moving forward from both legs into both reins to keep him straight so that he doesn't drift and collide with the poles.
	H	Medium walk.	
	C	Working trot.	• Keep the medium walk purposeful around the corner to help achieve a positive transition to working trot.
3.	M/B	Change the rein via a diagonal through the corners of the poles.	• When approaching M, look towards your poles and pick a line that runs straight through the corners of the poles. Then continue to ride straight to the track.
	A	Turn left onto the center line.	
	D	Medium walk.	• When transitioning to medium walk, keep the horse working forwards and ride straight.
4.	X	Ride straight out of the box and then ride a 10-meter circle right, making sure you're straight before going back over the poles.	• Look up and around your circle so you can get your horse straight and centered before going back over the poles.
			• Maintain a uniform bend around the circle, guarding the quarters with your outside aids to prevent them from swinging out.

5. 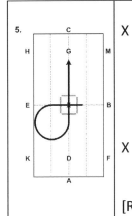	X	Ride straight out of the box and then ride a 10-meter circle left, making sure you're straight before going back over the poles.	•	When riding the circle, keep your hips and shoulders parallel with your horse's shoulders, keep your body upright, and look ahead of you around the circle.
	X	Proceed down the center line in medium walk	•	Keep the medium walk marching forward with purpose.
		[Repeat the exercise on both reins]	•	Remember to look where you are going and not down at the poles.

NOTES:

....

....

....

....

....

....

....

....

....

....

....

....

....

....

....

....

....

....

....

....

EXERCISE 41B

	INSTRUCTIONS		TIPS/DIRECTIVES
1.	C	Proceed down the center line working trot.	• When riding the center line, make sure that your horse is working from both your legs into both reins equally. It can be helpful to envisage that your horse is working along a tunnel created by your leg and rein.
	A	Track left.	
	A/F	Working canter left.	• Allow the horse a little freedom to stretch his neck so that he can see the poles and adjust his stride length accordingly.
2.	F/H	Change the rein via a diagonal through the corners of the poles. Transition to working trot before reaching the outside track.	• Keep the canter engaged and straight. • Maintain the weight through your left seat bone and a slight bit of left flexion so that your horse doesn't feel tempted to change canter leads when going over the poles. • The horse may need to extend his canter strides to get over the poles. Allow him to do this but maintain the same rhythm. • Encourage the horse to step through into the working trot, rather than 'fall' out of the canter.
	H/C	Working canter right.	
3.	M/K	Change the rein via a diagonal through the corners of the poles. Transition to working trot before reaching the outside track.	• Your goal during the canter is to develop regularity and lightness of the strides, an uphill tendency, and the natural ability of the horse to carry himself whilst maintaining active well-placed hind legs.
	A	Turn left onto the center line	

4.		X	Ride straight out of the box and then ride a 10-meter circle right, making sure you're straight before going back over the poles.	• If you have a young or 'green' horse, always ride rising trot so that he can use his back
				• Maintain a uniform bend around the circle, guarding the quarters with your outside aids to prevent them from swinging out.
5.		X	Ride straight out of the box and then ride a 10-meter circle left making sure you're straight before going back over the poles	• Keep the trot working forward and encourage the horse to step under with his inside hind legs. Smaller circles do not mean a slower trot.
		X	Proceed down the center line in working trot	• Your goal is to develop a good, rhythmical and active working trot and to ride two circles of equal size and shape.
			[Repeat the exercise on both reins]	

NOTES:

....
....
....
....
....
....
....
....
....
....
....
....
....
....
....
....

EXERCISE 41C

	INSTRUCTIONS		TIPS/DIRECTIVES
1.	C	Proceed down the center line working canter left.	• The canter is a pace of 3-beat. It should have 'uphill' cadenced strides, followed by a moment of suspension.
	A	Track left.	• On the center line the horse should travel forward and straight, as though he is on railway tracks.
			• The horse may need to extend his canter strides slightly to get over the poles. Allow him to do this but maintain the same rhythm.
			• Half-halt before the turn at A to keep the horse's balance.
2.	F/H	Change the rein on the diagonal line through the corners of the poles.	• Maintain the weight through your left seat bone and a slight bit of left flexion so that your horse doesn't feel tempted to change canter leads when going over the poles or when re-joining the track.
		Re-join the track and counter canter until H.	
	H	Simple change to working canter right	• Prepare for the simple change by using half-halts to balance the canter. Keep the horse straight and moving forward through the change.
3.	M/K	Change the rein via a diagonal through the corners of the poles.	• The transition to working canter at D is tricky because you are on the center line and you are asking for right canter after coming off the left rein. Therefore, you need to make your aids very clear in order to get a correct strike off. If you need to make it easier for your horse, ride a 10-meter circle right at D and then ask for the canter transition.
		Transition to working trot before reaching the outside track.	
	A	Turn left onto the center line.	
	D	Working canter right.	

4.	X	Ride straight out of the box and then ride a 10-meter circle right, making sure you're straight before going back over the poles. Ride a flying change over the first or second pole.	• This exercise requires total control and the ability to collect your horse. • The quality of your flying changes will be determined by the suppleness and elasticity of the horse's canter.
5.	X X	Ride straight out of the box and then ride a 10-meter circle left making sure you're straight before going back over the poles Proceed down the center line in working canter left [Repeat the exercise on both reins]	• Because you previously changed lead going over the poles, be careful that your horse doesn't anticipate a change of lead again. Be very clear with your seat, weight, leg, and rein aids that you want to maintain left canter.

NOTES:

....

....

....

....

....

....

....

....

....

....

....

....

....

....

....

EXERCISE 41D – Make Your Own

	INSTRUCTIONS
1.	652 -
2.	
3.	
4.	

- 652 -

5.

NOTES:

....
....
....
....
....
....
....
....
....
....
....
....
....
....
....
....
....
....
....
....
....
....
....
....
....

EXERCISE 41E – Make Your Own

	INSTRUCTIONS
1.	
2.	
3.	
4.	

5.

NOTES:

....
....
....
....
....
....
....
....
....
....
....
....
....
....
....
....
....
....
....
....
....
....
....
....

EXERCISE 41F – Make Your Own

	INSTRUCTIONS
1.	
2.	
3.	
4.	

5.

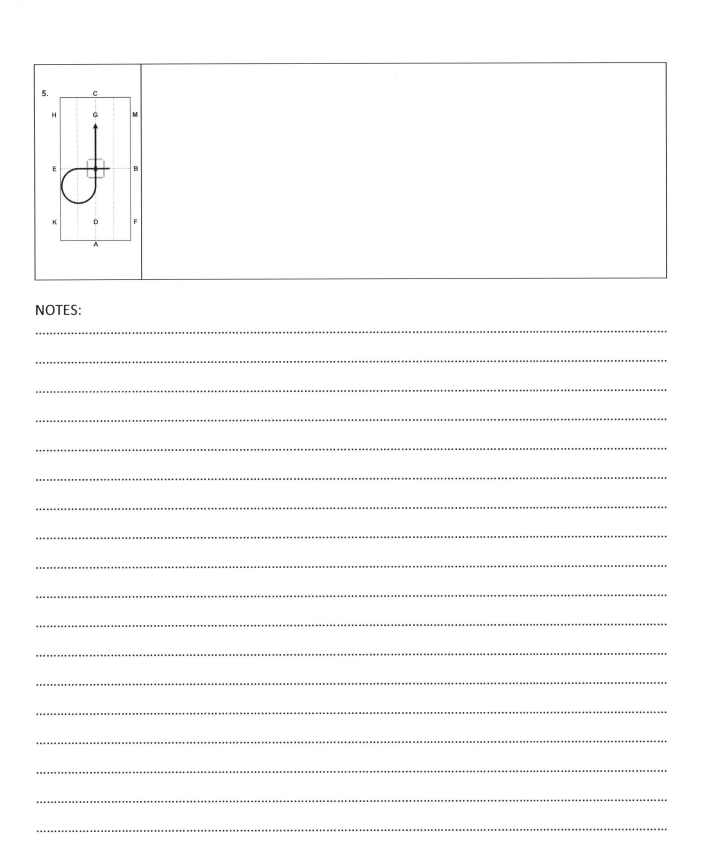

NOTES:

....

....

....

....

....

....

....

....

....

....

....

....

....

....

....

....

....

....

....

....

....

....

....

....

"Others can stop you temporarily. Only you can do it permanently."

MAKE YOUR OWN
FLOORPLANS
(20x40)

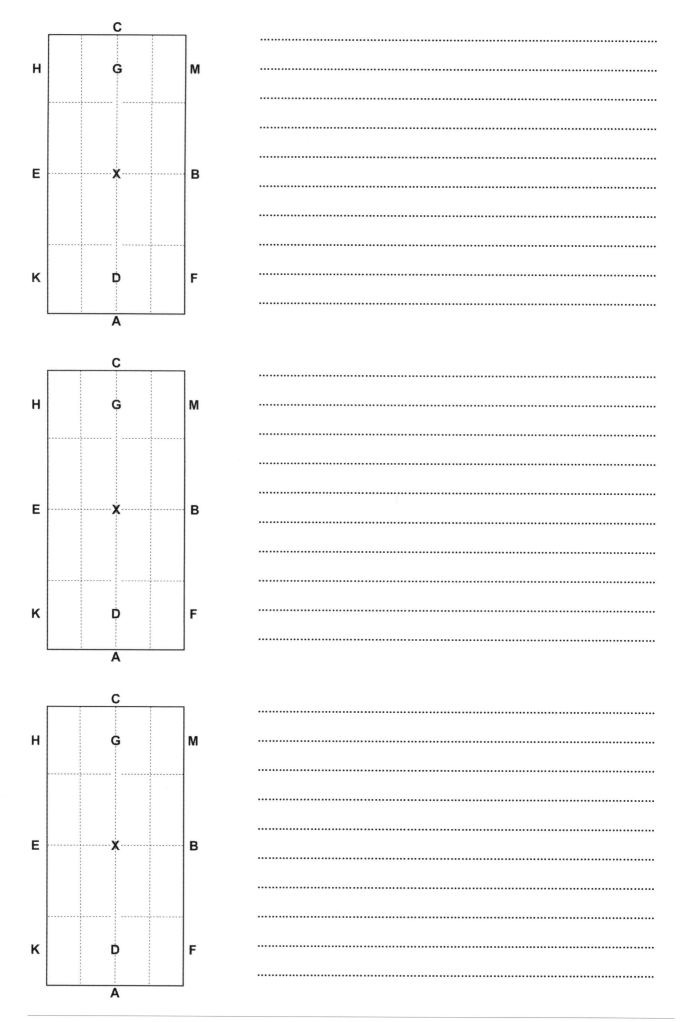

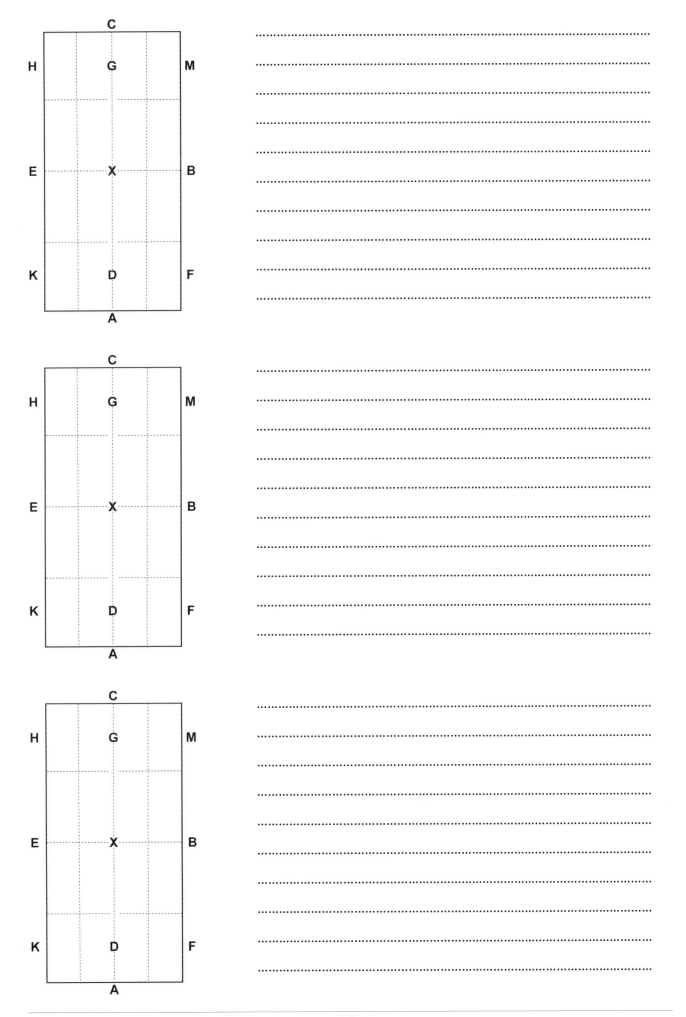

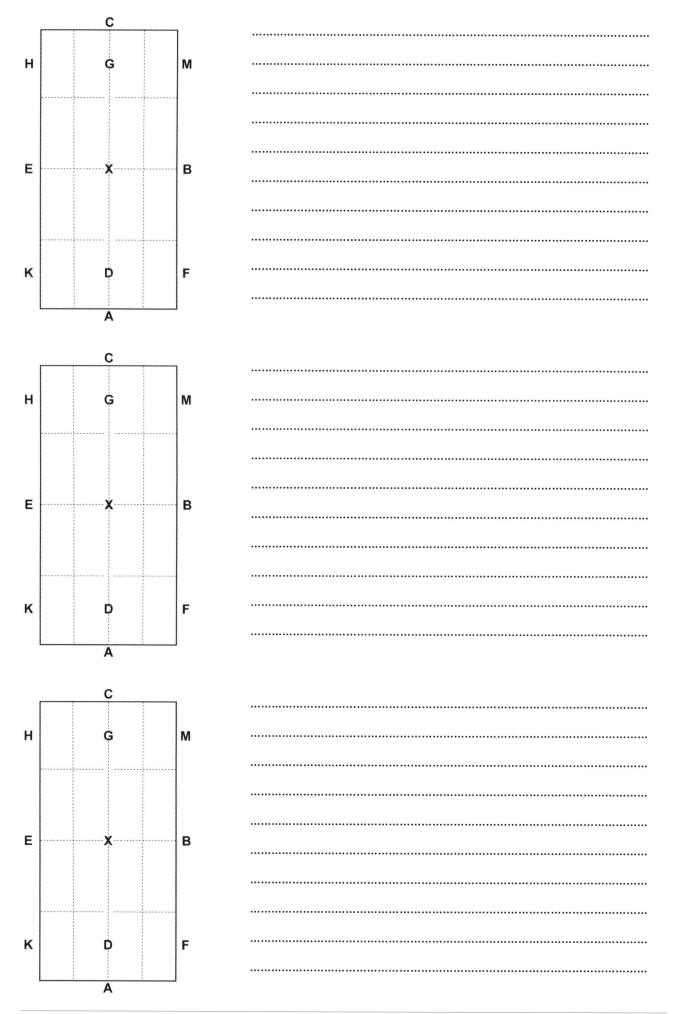

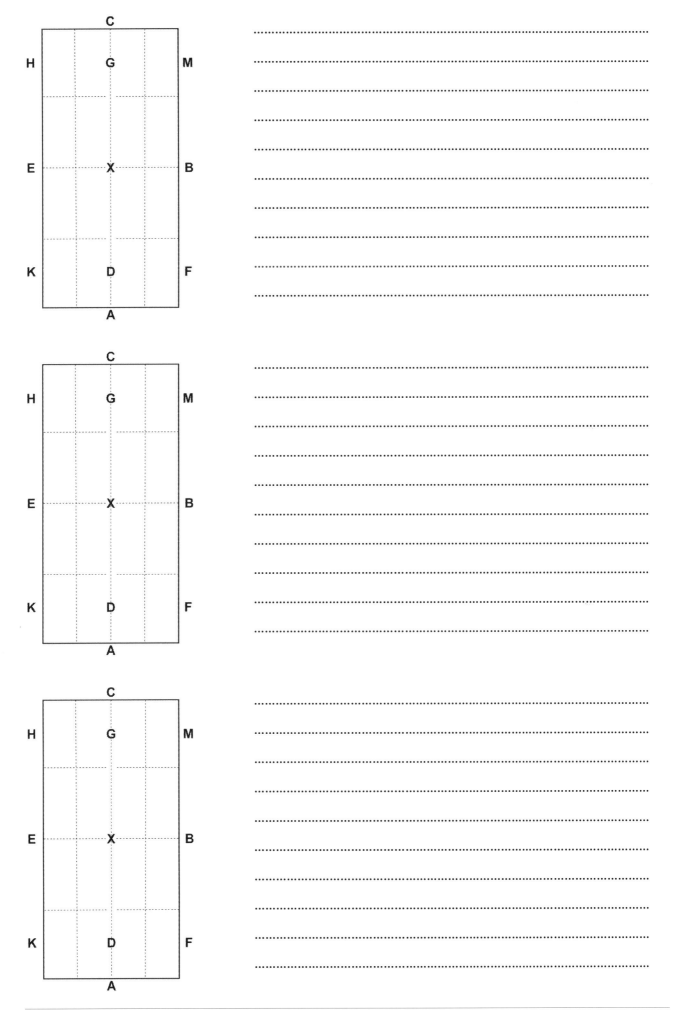

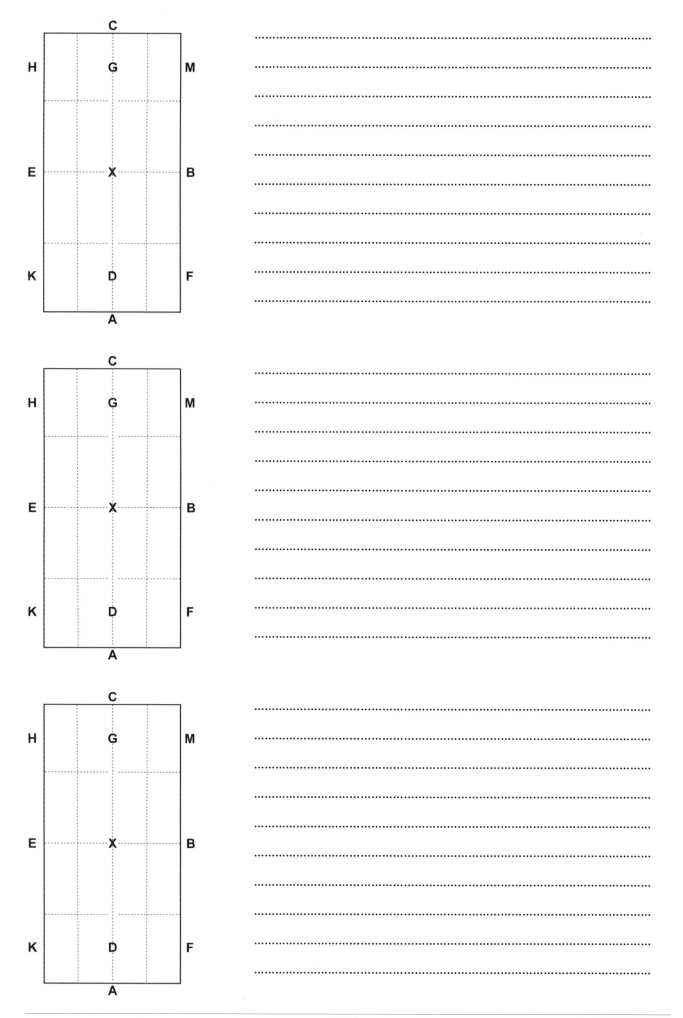

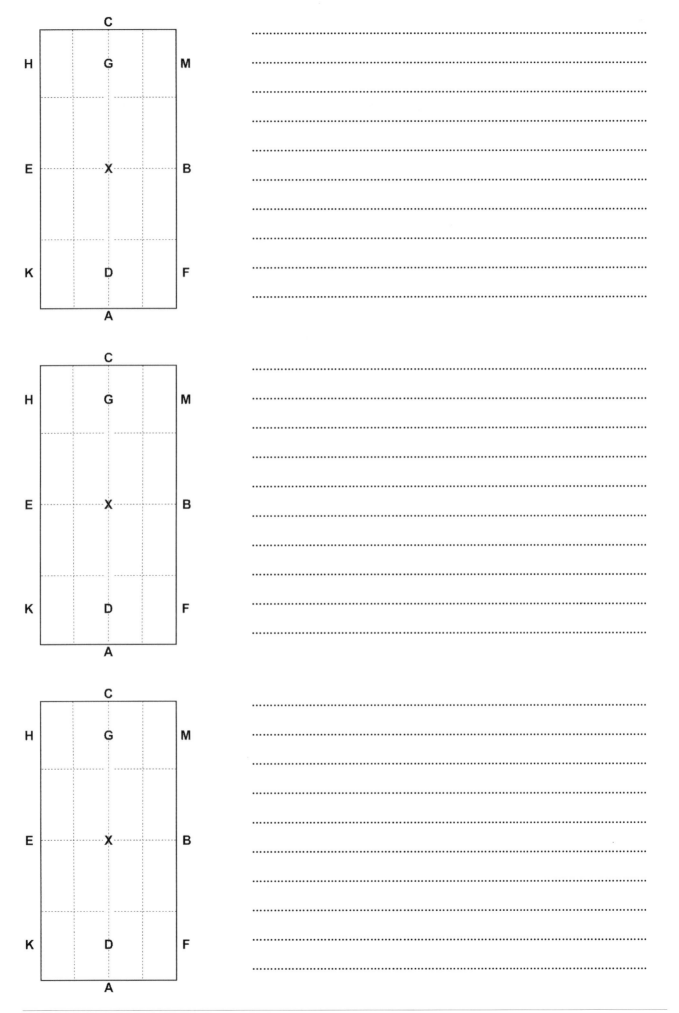

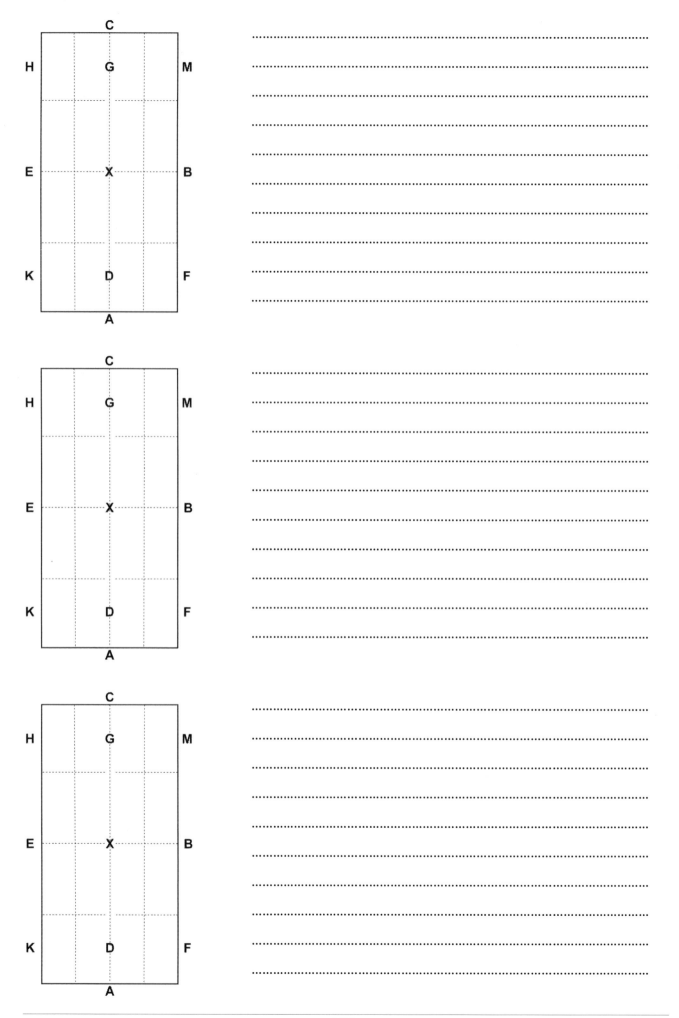

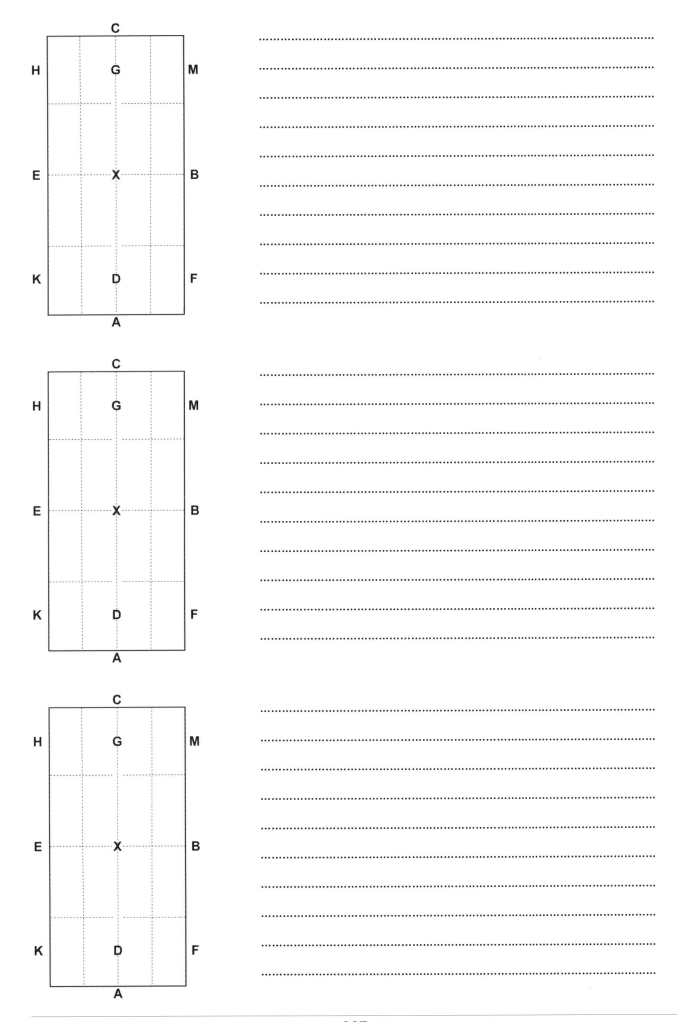

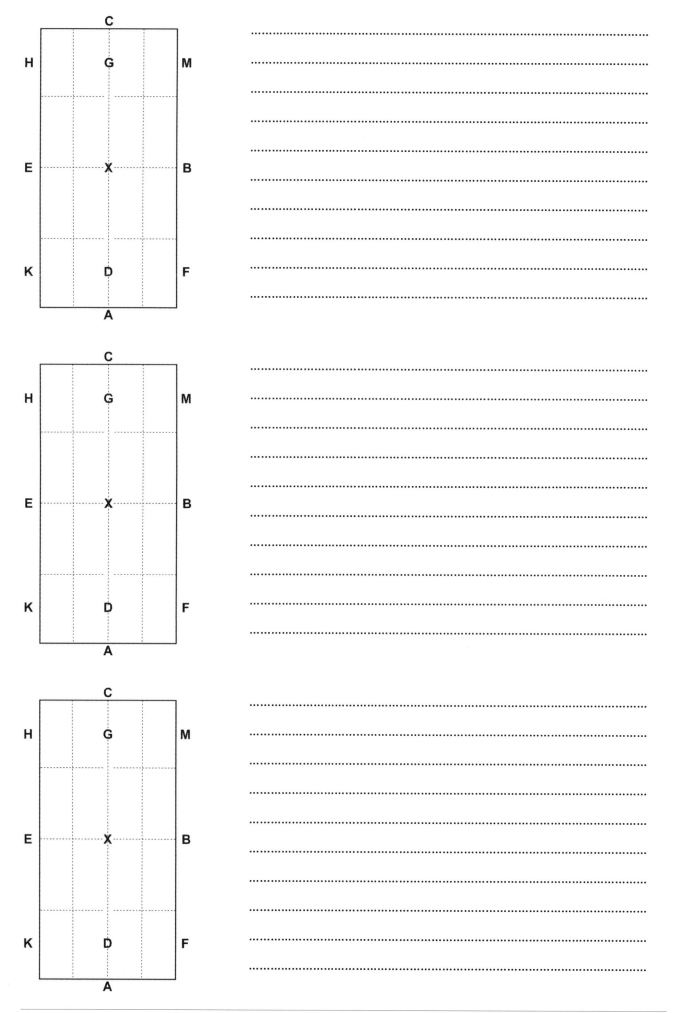

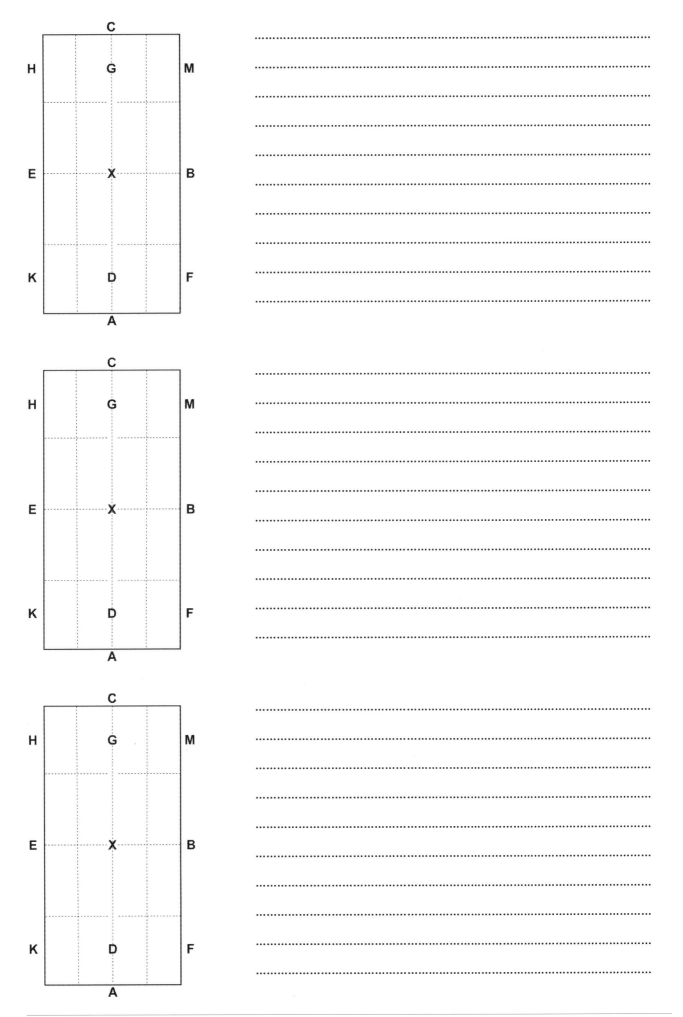

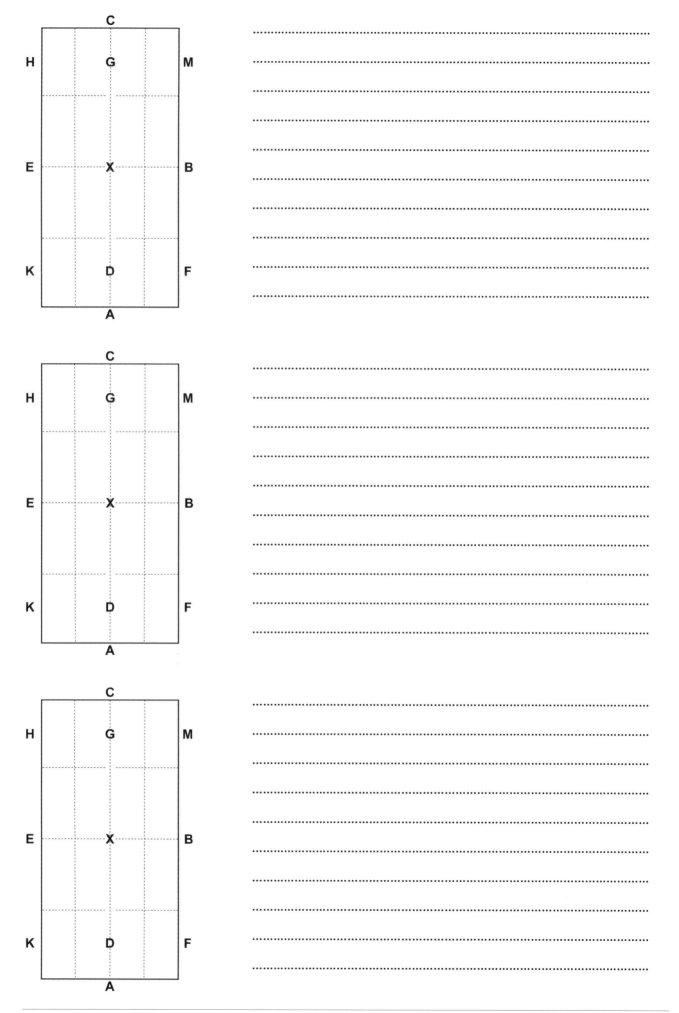

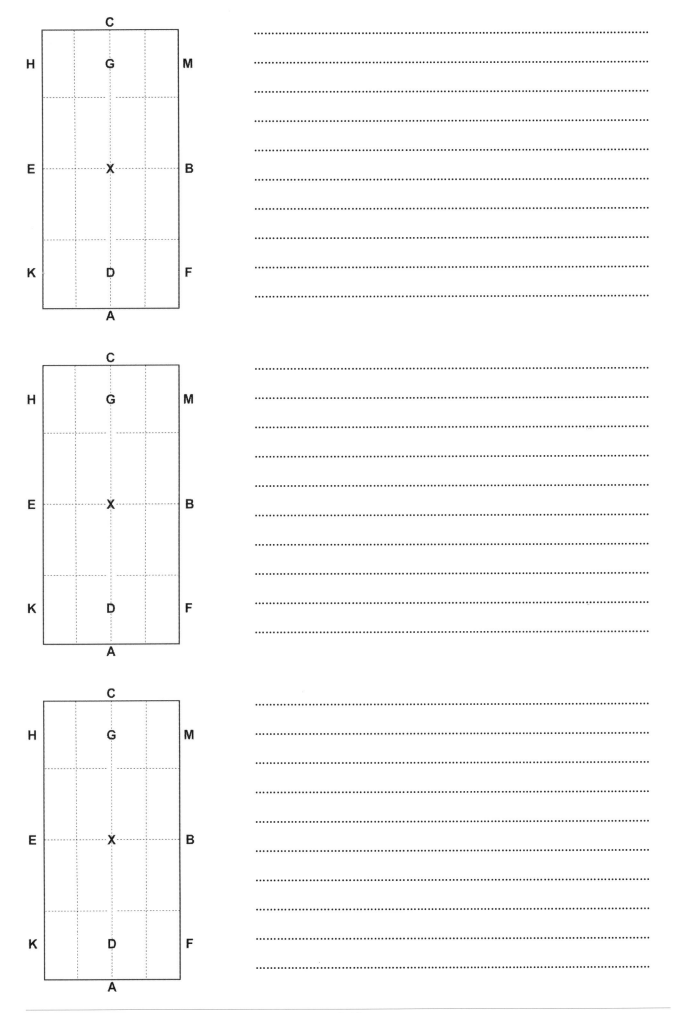

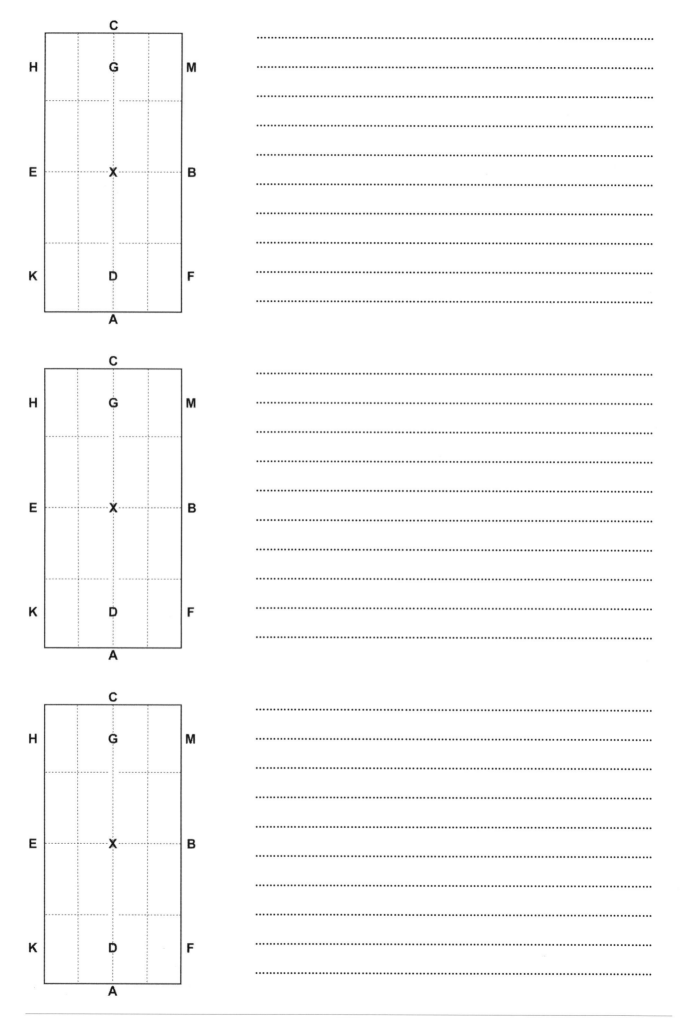

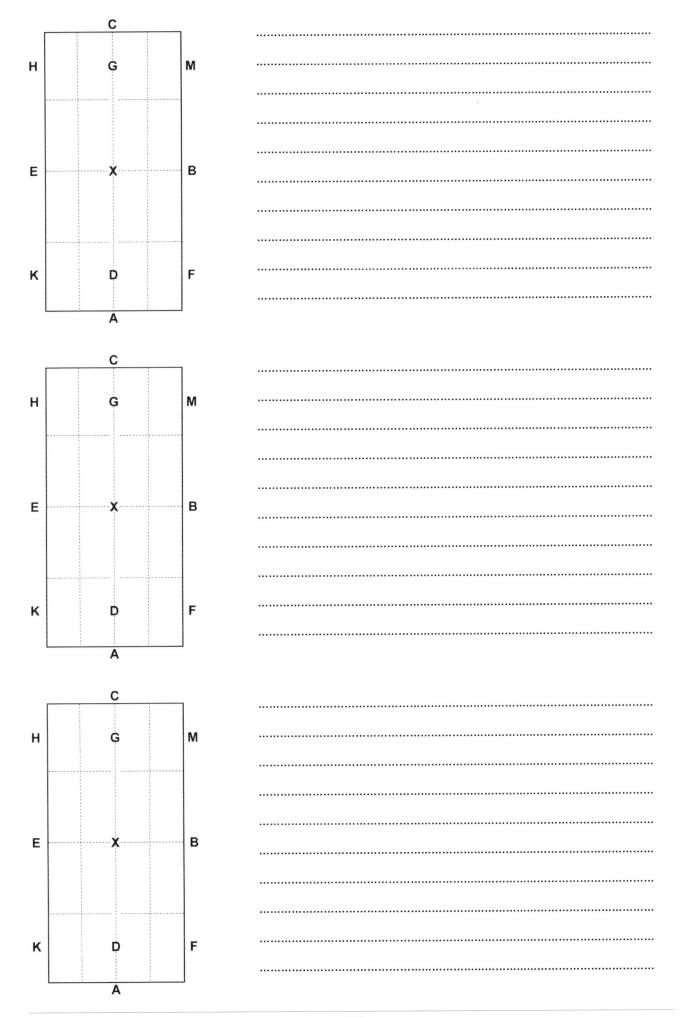

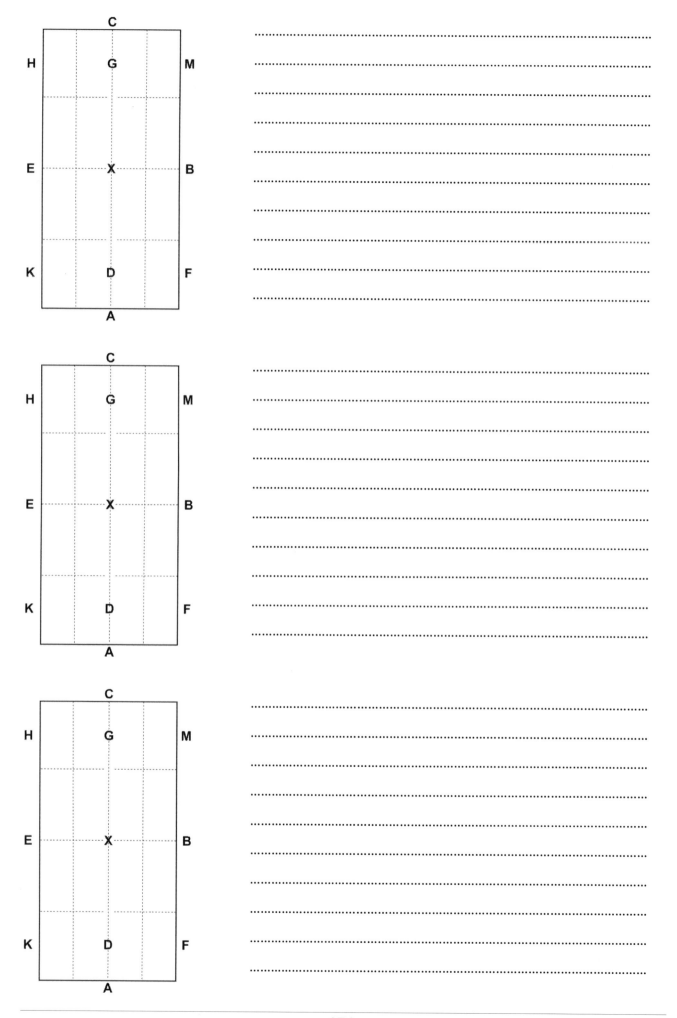

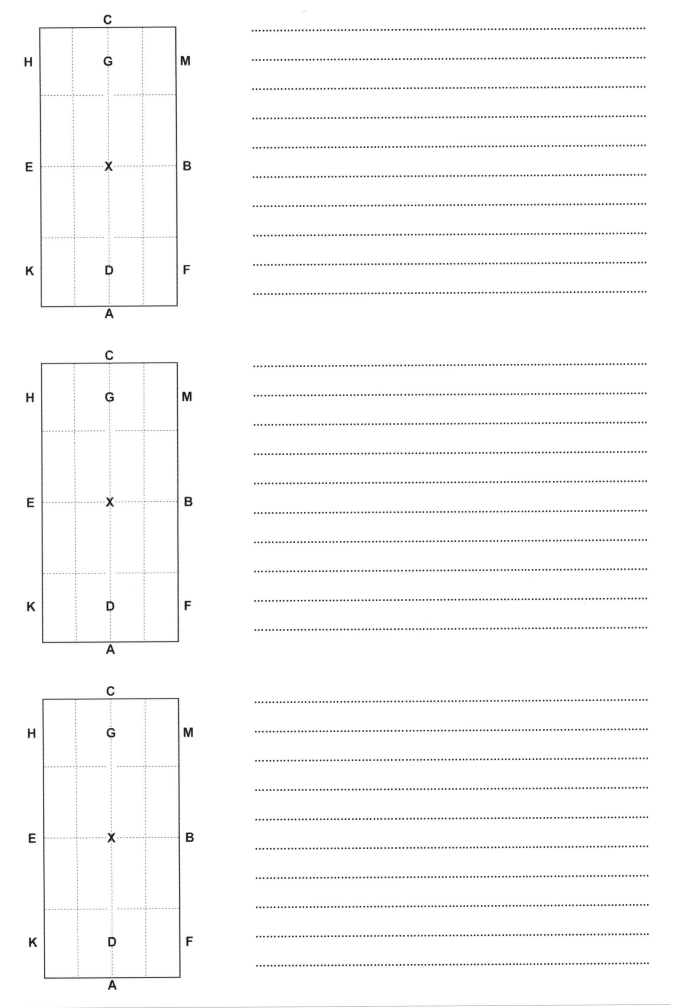

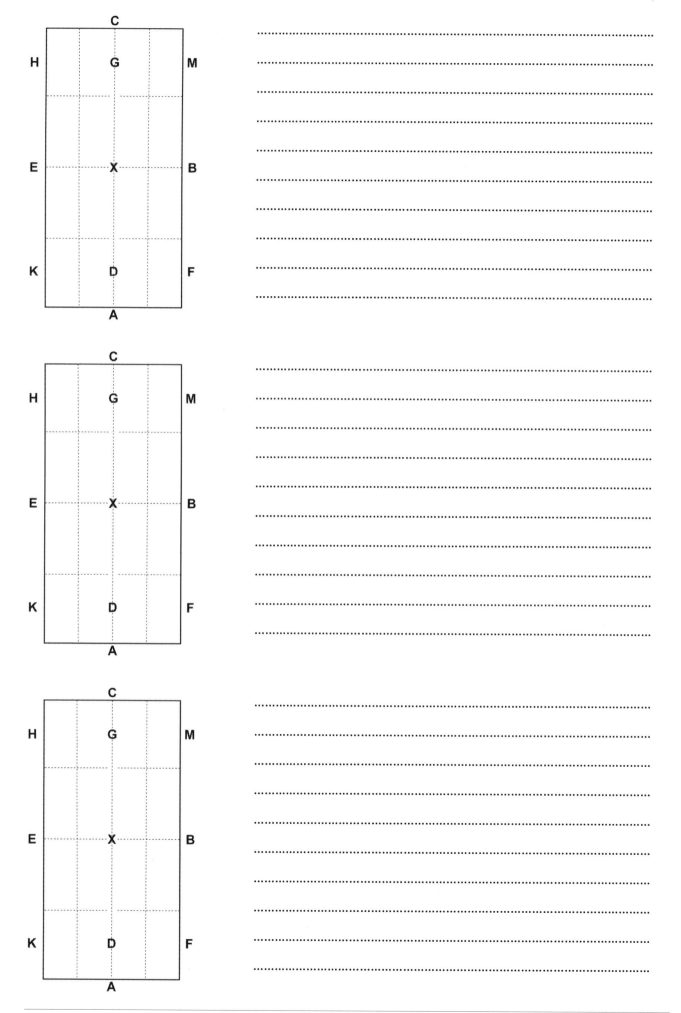

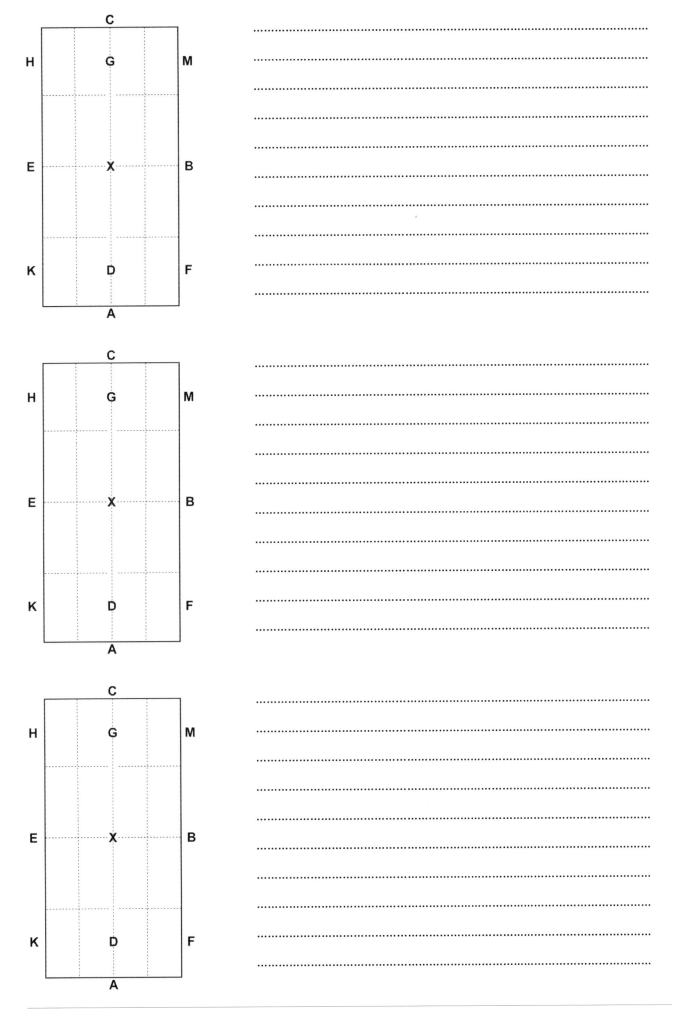

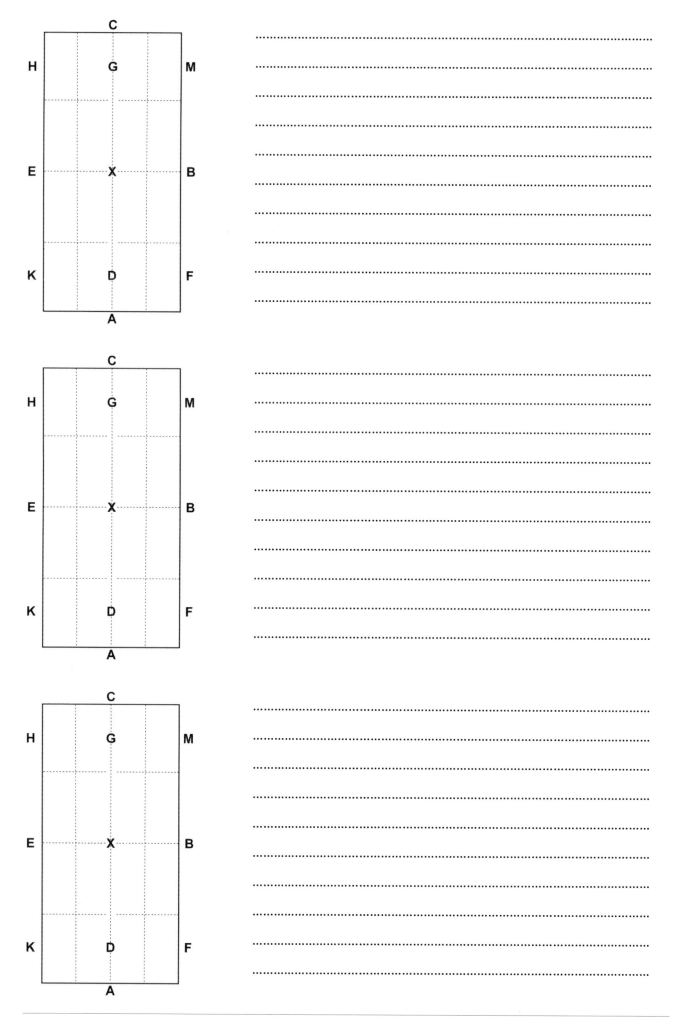

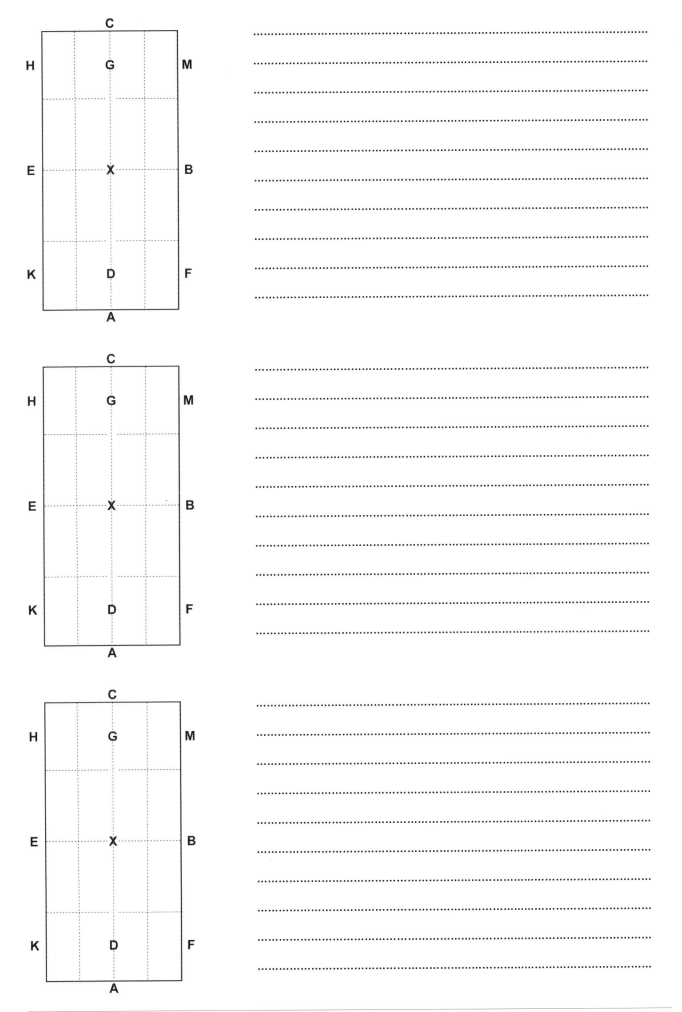

For more 20x40 'make your own floorplans' check out our Dressage Test Planners on Amazon

20x40
DRESSAGE
TEST PLANNER

☑ Create Your Own Dressage Exercises

☑ Choreograph Dressage to Music Floorplans

☑ Memorize and Learn Your Dressage Tests

CREATED BY HOW TO DRESSAGE

MAKE YOUR OWN FLOORPLANS (20x60)

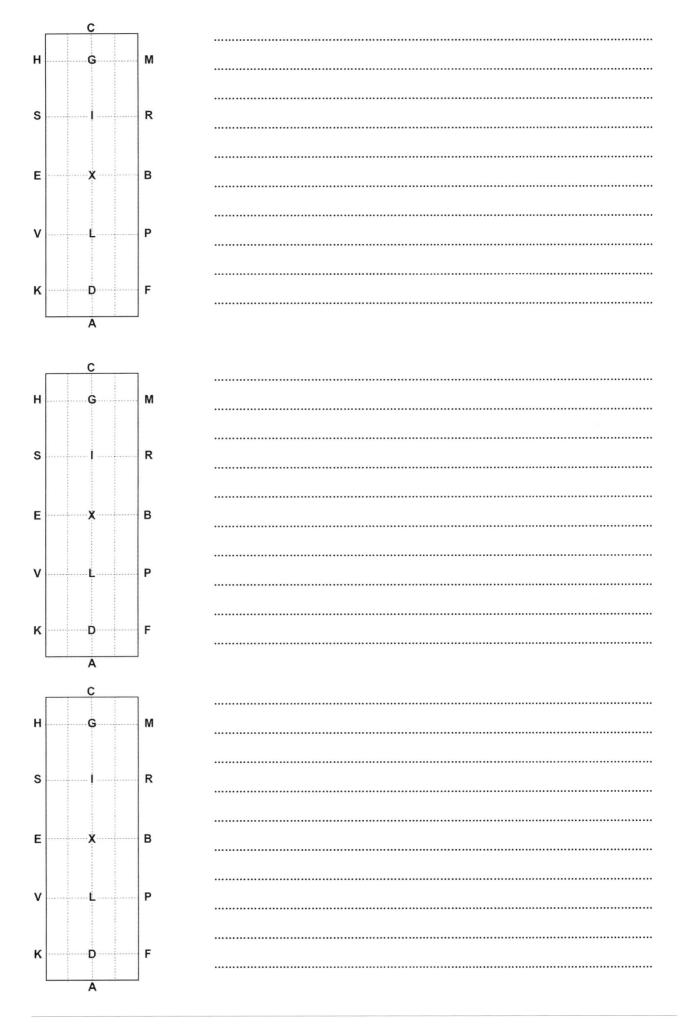

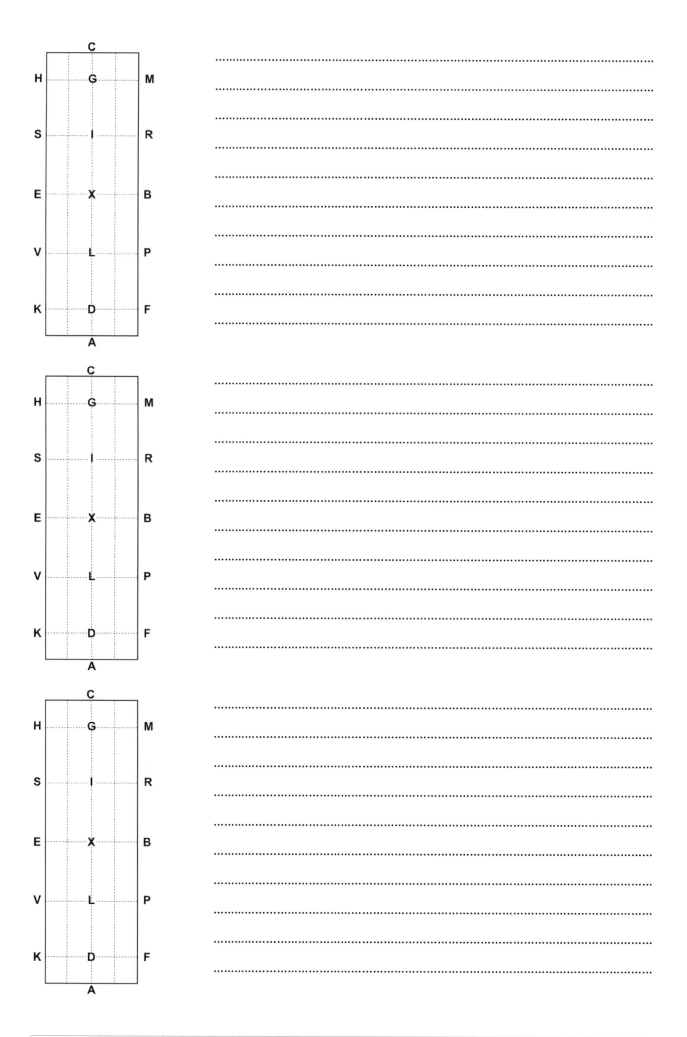

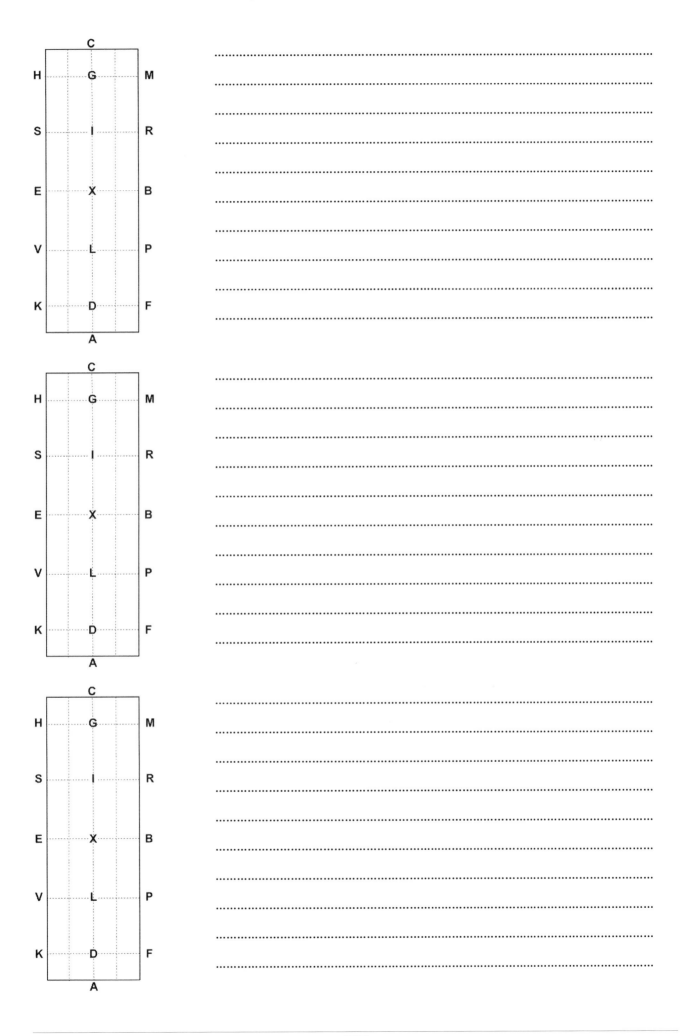

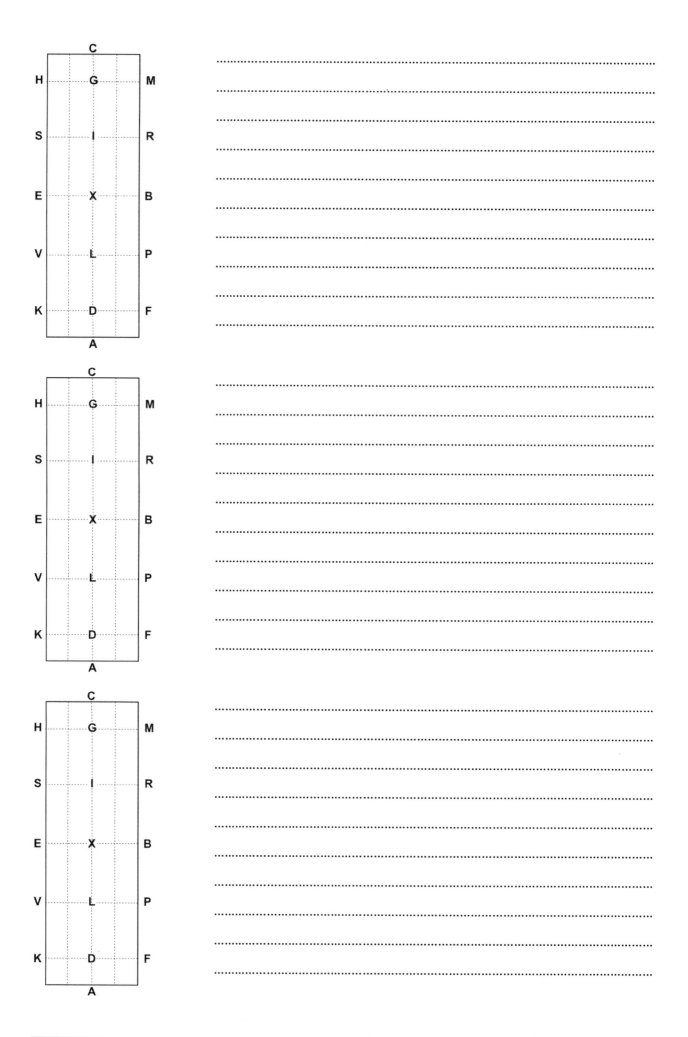

For more 20x60 'make your own floorplans' check out our Dressage Test Planners on Amazon

20x60
DRESSAGE
TEST PLANNER

☑ Create Your Own
Dressage Exercises

☑ Choreograph Dressage
to Music Floorplans

☑ Memorize and Learn
Your Dressage Tests

CREATED BY HOW TO DRESSAGE

FREE STUFF!

FREE - DRESSAGE NEWBIE EMAIL COURSE

A free 6-part email course specifically designed for those that are new to dressage.

To find out more, visit the website below.

HowToDressage.com/NewbieCourse

FREE - DRESSAGE COMPETITION EMAIL COURSE

A free 6-part email course specifically designed for those that are new to the competition arena.

To find out more, visit the website below.

HowToDressage.com/CompetitionCourse

FREE - 7 SIMPLE STEPS TO BOOST YOUR DRESSAGE SCORES DOWNLOAD

A free document where we share with you 7 simple ways any horse and rider can boost their dressage scores.

To download the PDF, visit the website below.

HowToDressage.com/7Steps

FINAL WORD

If things don't go to plan...

We all know that some days it's just not going to happen.

This sport didn't get the nickname of 'stressage' for nothing!

But on those days when things don't click into place, once you have put your horse away, you can come to this section and be reminded of the bigger picture...

...because truth be told, your horse doesn't really care how good or bad that last medium trot was.

Riders can sometimes feel as though they are 'letting their horse down', but let's face it, your horse isn't going to sleep every night wishing he was a top Grand Prix horse covered in rosettes and flowers. His requirements from life are a lot simpler.

Sometimes you need to take the pressure off yourself, take a deep breath, smile, and hug your horse. We know that you're doing your best, so cut yourself some slack!

It's always good to remember that everyone started somewhere. World-class riders were once where you are now. We're all trying to climb the same ladder.

Use your 'bad days' as a training experience. If every ride was foot perfect, not only would that get very boring very quickly, you and your horse would never learn anything.

So, make yourself a cup of tea, maintain a positive attitude, think about what you have learned from today's session and how it will help you be a better rider in the future.

This is all part of the journey, and as the saying goes, 'if it was easy, everyone would be doing it'.

How To Dressage
xx

Printed in Great Britain
by Amazon

15001187R00402